The NOLO *News*—

Our free magazine devoted to everyday legal & consumer issues

To thank you for sending in the postage-paid feedback card in the back of this book, you'll receive a free two-year subscription to the **NOLO** *News*—our quarterly magazine of legal, small business and consumer information. With each issue you get updates on important legal changes that affect you, helpful articles on everyday law, answers to your legal questions in Auntie Nolo's advice column, a complete Nolo catalog and, of course, our famous lawyer jokes.

Legal information online–24 hours a day

Get instant access to the legal information you need 24 hours a day.

Visit a Nolo online self-help law center and you'll find:

- hundreds of helpful articles on a wide variety of topics
- selected chapters from Nolo books
- online seminars with our lawyer authors and other experts
- downloadable demos of Nolo software
- frequently asked questons about key legal issues
- our complete catalog and online ordering info
- our ever popular lawyer jokes and more.

Here's how to find us:

America Online Just use the key word Nolo.

On the **Internet** our World Wide Web address (URL) is: http://www.nolo.com.

Prodigy/CompuServe Use the Web Browsers on CompuServe or Prodigy to access Nolo's Web site on the Internet.

NOLO PRESS
25 YEARS
LAW FOR ALL

CREDIT REPAIR

by Attorney Robin Leonard

edited by Attorney Shae Irving

NOLO PRESS   BERKELEY

Your Responsibility When Using a Self-Help Law Book

We've done our best to give you useful and accurate information in this book. But laws and procedures change frequently and are subject to differing interpretations. If you want legal advice backed by a guarantee, see a lawyer. If you use this book, it's your responsibility to make sure that the facts and general advice contained in it are applicable to your situation.

Keeping Up to Date

To keep its books up to date, Nolo Press issues new printings and new editions periodically. New printings reflect minor legal changes and technical corrections. New editions contain major legal changes, major text additions or major reorganizations. To find out if a later printing or edition of any Nolo book is available, call Nolo Press at 510-549-1976 or check the catalog in the Nolo News, our quarterly publication.

To stay current, follow the "Update" service in the Nolo News. You can get a free two-year subscription by sending us the registration card in the back of the book. In another effort to help you use Nolo's latest materials, we offer a 25% discount off the purchase of the new edition of your Nolo book if you turn in the cover of an earlier edition. (See the "Recycle Offer" in the back of this book.) This book was last revised in November 1996.

First Edition	NOVEMBER 1996
Cover Design	TONI IHARA
Book Design	TERRI HEARSH
Index	JANE MEYERHOFER
Proofreading	KRISTIN BARENDSEN
Printing	CONSOLIDATED PRINTING, INC.

Leonard, Robin.
    Credit repair / by Robin Leonard. -- 1st ed.
            p.   cm.
    Includes bibliographical references.
    ISBN 0-87337-354-5
    1. Consumer credit--United States--Handbooks, manuals, etc.
    2. Credit control--United States--Handbooks, manuals, etc.
    3. Finance, Personal--United States--Handbooks, manuals, etc.
    4. Consumer credit--Law and legislation--United States.   I. Title.
    HG3756.U54L46   1996
    332.7'43--dc21
                                            96-39230
                                            CIP

For information on bulk purchases or corporate premium sales, please contact the Special Sales Department. For academic sales or textbook adoptions, ask for Academic Sales. Call 800-955-4775 or write to Nolo Press, Inc., 950 Parker Street, Berkeley, CA 94710.

Acknowledgments

Thank you to my editor, Shae Irving, who brought great ideas and energy to this project.

Table of Contents

3 Handling Existing Debts

4 Cleaning Up Your Credit File

5 Establishing and Keeping a Good Credit Record

Appendices

1   Resources

2a   Federal and State Credit Reporting Laws
Effective Until September 29, 1997

2b Federal and State Credit Reporting Laws
Effective September 30, 1997

3 Tear-Out Forms

Index

Introduction to Credit Repair

Whether you've fallen behind on your bills, been sued or even declared bankruptcy, this book can help you take simple and effective steps to repair your credit. As you read, keep in mind these four important points:

You're not alone. All over the country, disposable incomes are down and savings are evaporating. Millions of honest, hard-working people—the same ones who received credit offers almost daily in better economic times—are having problems paying their bills. And approximately one million people file for bankruptcy each year.

You have legal rights. By knowing and asserting your rights, you can do much to get bill collectors off your back and give yourself a fresh financial start. Debtors who assert themselves often get more time to pay, have late fees dropped, settle debts for less than the full amount and get negative marks removed from credit files.

You can do it yourself. The information and forms in this book are good in all 50 states and the District of Columbia. You can follow the instructions on your own, without paying high fees to a lawyer or credit repair clinic. (See Chapter 5, Section H, for information on why to avoid using a credit repair clinic.)

Nobody's credit is too "bad" to repair. If you've been through devastating financial times, you may think you'll never get credit again. That's simply not true. In a short time, you'll probably qualify for limited types of credit. Within about two years, you should be able to repair your credit so that you can obtain a major credit card or loan. Most creditors are willing to extend credit to people who have turned their financial situations around, even if their credit records are less than stellar.

This book contains in-depth information on all aspects of credit repair. Easy-to-use forms in Appendix 3 help you with the sometimes daunting tasks of assessing your debt situation, planning a budget, contacting your creditors or bill collectors, and dealing with credit bureaus—all necessary steps in repairing your credit.

⚠ **Credit Laws Are Changing September 30, 1997.**

The Consumer Credit Reporting Reform Act of 1996 takes effect September 30, 1997. Throughout this book, we provide you with both the law as it is before September 30, 1997, and the law as it will be after that date. Read carefully to avoid confusion.

A. Credit Repair Fast Facts

Here are some quick answers to many common questions people have about repairing their credit. All of these topics are explored in more detail later in the book.

What's the first step in repairing credit?

To turn your financial problems around, you must understand your flow of income and expenses. Some people call this making a budget. Others find the term budget too restrictive and use the term "spending plan." Whatever you call it, spend at least two months writing down every cash or cash equivalent (such as check or debit) expenditure. At each month's end, compare your total expenses with your income. If you're overspending, you have to cut back or find more income. As best you can, plan how you'll spend your money each month. If you have trouble putting together your own budget, consider getting help from a nonprofit group such as Consumer Credit Counseling Service, which provides budgeting help for free or at a low cost. (The steps for creating a budget are detailed in Chapter 2.)

Okay, I've made my budget. What do I do next?

Now it's time to clean up your credit report. Credit reports are compiled by credit bureaus—private, for-profit companies that gather information about your credit history and sell it to banks, mortgage lenders, credit unions, credit card companies, department stores, insurance companies, landlords and even a few employers.

Credit bureaus get most of their data from creditors and collection agencies. They also search court records for lawsuits, judgments and bankruptcy filings. And they go through county records to find recorded liens (legal claims) against property.

Non-credit data made part of a credit report usually includes names you previously used, past and present addresses, Social Security number, employment history, and current and previous spouses' names. Your credit history includes the names of your creditors, type and number of each account, when each account was opened, your payment history for the previous 24–36 months, your credit limit or the original amount of a loan, and your current balance. The report will show if an account has been turned over to a collection agency or is in dispute. (See Chapter 4, Section A, for more information on the contents of a credit report.)

How can I get a copy of my credit report?

There are three major credit bureaus—Equifax, Trans Union and Experian (formerly known as TRW). The federal Fair Credit Reporting Act (FCRA) entitles you to a copy of your credit report, and you can get one for free if:

- you've been denied credit because of information in your credit report and you request a copy within 60 days of being denied credit, or
- you haven't requested a copy in the previous 12 months—Experian gives every consumer one free copy per year.

If you weren't denied credit, you may have to pay a small fee to obtain a report from Equifax or Trans Union, or to obtain a second copy from Experian. (See Chapter 4, Section B, for information on obtaining a credit report.)

Beginning September 30, 1997, you will be entitled to a free copy of your credit report for the following additional reasons:

- you are unemployed and intend to apply for a job within the 60 days following your request for your credit file
- you receive public assistance, or
- you believe your credit report contains errors due to fraud.

What should I do if I find mistakes in my report?

As you read through your report, make a list of everything out-of-date:

- Lawsuits, paid tax liens, accounts sent out for collection, criminal records, late payments and any other adverse information older than seven years.
- Bankruptcies older than ten years from the discharge or dismissal. (Credit bureaus usually list completed Chapter 13 bankruptcies for only seven years, but they can stay for as many as ten.)
- Credit inquiries (requests by companies for a copy of your report) older than two years.

Next, look for incorrect or misleading information, such as:

- incorrect or incomplete name, address, phone number, Social Security number or employment information
- bankruptcies not identified by their specific chapter number
- accounts not yours or lawsuits in which you were not involved
- incorrect account histories—such as late payments when you paid on time
- closed accounts listed as open—it may look as if you have too much open credit
- accounts listed more than once, and
- any account you closed that doesn't say "closed by consumer."

After reviewing your report, complete the "request for reinvestigation" form the credit bureau sent you or send a letter listing each incorrect item and explain exactly what is wrong. Once the credit bureau receives your request, it must investigate the items you dispute and contact you within 30 days.

If you don't hear back within 30 days, send a follow-up letter. If you let them know that you're trying to obtain a mortgage or car loan, they can do a "rush" investigation. (See Chapter 4, Sections C and D, for more information on reviewing and correcting your credit report.)

Will the credit bureau automatically remove the incorrect information from my report?

The credit bureau will review your letter or "request for reinvestigation" form. If you are right, or if the creditor who provided the information can no longer verify it, the credit bureau must remove the information from your report. Often credit bureaus will remove an item on request without an investigation if rechecking the item is more bother than it's worth.

If the credit bureau insists that the information is correct, you will want to call the bureau to discuss the problem.

If you don't get anywhere with the credit bureau, contact the creditor directly and ask that the information be removed. Write to the customer service department, vice president of marketing and president or CEO. If the information was reported by a collection agency, send the agency a copy of your letter, too.

If a credit bureau is including the wrong information in your report, or you want to explain a particular entry, you have the right to put a 100-word statement in your report. The credit bureau must give a copy of your statement—or a summary—to anyone who requests your report. (See Chapter 4, Sections D and E, for additional information on correcting your credit report.)

What else can I do to repair my credit?

After you've cleaned up your credit report, the key to rebuilding credit is to get positive information into your record. For example:

- If your credit report is missing accounts you pay on time, send the credit bureaus a recent account statement and copies of canceled checks showing your payment history. Ask that these be added to your report. The credit bureau doesn't have to add anything, but often it will.

- Creditors like to see evidence of stability, so if any of the following information is not in your report, send it to the bureaus and ask that it be added: your current employment, your previous employment (especially if you've been at your current job fewer than two years), your current residence, your telephone number (especially if it's unlisted), your date of birth and your checking account number. Again, the credit bureau doesn't have to add these, but often it will.

(See Chapter 4, Sections F and G, for more information on adding positive data to your credit report.)

I've been told that I need to use credit to repair my credit. Is this true?

Yes. The one type of positive information creditors like to see in credit reports is credit payment history. If you have a credit card, use it every month. (Make small purchases and pay them off to avoid interest charges.) If you don't have a credit card, apply for one. If your application is rejected, try to find a cosigner or apply for a secured card—where you deposit some money into a savings account and then get a credit card with a line of credit around the amount you deposited. (See Chapter 5, Section D, for more information about using credit.)

How long will it take to repair my credit?

If you follow the steps outlined in this book, it will take about two years to repair your credit so that you won't be turned down for a major credit card or loan. After around four years, you may be able to qualify for a mortgage.

B. When to Get Help Beyond This Book

This book can help you assess your financial situation and repair your credit. In some circumstances, however, you may need to take immediate action—or more drastic action—which may be beyond the scope of this book. Nolo Press publishes several detailed books on debtors' rights and bankruptcy, which may provide the answers you need. In some situations, it may make sense to see a lawyer right away.

C. Icons to Help You Along

Throughout this book, you'll encounter the following icons:

 When you see the "fast track" icon, you'll be alerted to a chance to skip some material you may not need to read.

 This icon cautions you about potential problems.

Suggested references for additional information follow this icon.

When to Get Help Beyond This Book

Seek additional help if...	Explanation	Where to get help
You're behind on your house payments.	Your lender has the option of foreclosing—declaring the entire balance due, selling the house at an auction and kicking you out.	General information on foreclosures is in Chapter 1. For more detailed information, see *The Homeowner's Guide to Foreclosure: How to Protect Your Home and Your Rights*, by James I. Wiedemer (Dearborn Financial Publishing). In California, see *Stop Foreclosure Now*, by Lloyd Segal (Nolo Press). You can get more specific help from your lender or a lawyer.
You owe child support or alimony.	If you can't afford to pay your child support or alimony, you need a court order reducing your obligation. Don't hesitate; child support and alimony are virtually never modified retroactively.	In California, see *How to Raise or Lower Child Support*, by Roderic Duncan and Warren Siegel (Nolo Press). Or see a lawyer.
You're behind on a student loan.	Congress has enacted several laws to change the way student loans are collected and repaid, and has limited the defenses former students can raise when sued on outstanding loans.	See *Money Troubles: Legal Strategies to Cope With Your Debts*, by Robin Leonard (Nolo Press) or *Take Control of Your Student Loans*, by Robin Leonard and Shae Irving (Nolo Press, available Spring 1997).
You owe income taxes.	The IRS has the right to seize virtually all of your assets of value and close to 100% of your wages without first suing you. Fortunately, you have several options in dealing with the IRS. You may be able to negotiate an installment agreement for repayment or drastically reduce what you have to pay.	See *Stand Up to the IRS*, by Frederick W. Daily (Nolo Press). Or see a tax attorney.
You face eviction.	In some states, an eviction can take place in just three days. Rather than risk being homeless, take steps to get immediate help.	In California, see *Tenants' Rights*, by Myron Moscovitz and Ralph Warner (Nolo Press). Or contact a local tenants' rights group or a tenant's rights lawyer. Outside of California, you can get an overview of eviction and eviction defense issues in *Every Tenant's Legal Guide*, by Janet Portman and Marcia Stewart (Nolo Press, available Spring 1997).
You've been sued.	If you just received court papers, you need to file a response with the court. If the creditor already has a judgment, he can attach your wages, take money from bank accounts and place a lien on your real estate (and in some states, personal property). You may be able to prevent certain collection tactics, particularly if you don't own much.	See *Money Troubles: Legal Strategies to Cope With Your Debts*, by Robin Leonard (Nolo Press). Or see a lawyer.
You are considering filing for bankruptcy.	Many people overwhelmed by their debts conclude that bankruptcy is the best option. There are several types, called "Chapters," of bankruptcy. In Chapter 7, you ask for an out-and-out erasure of your debts. In Chapter 13, you set up a repayment plan whereby your creditors receive some—or all—of what you owe. Chapter 12 is like Chapter 13 but it's for family farmers. Chapter 11 is for individuals with enormous debts or for businesses that want to reorganize.	For information on Chapter 7 bankruptcy, see *How to File for Bankruptcy*, by Stephen Elias, Albin Renauer and Robin Leonard (a detailed bankruptcy guide) or *Law Form Kit: Personal Bankruptcy*, by Stephen Elias, Albin Renauer and Robin Leonard and Lisa Goldoftas (a streamlined bankruptcy guide). For information on Chapter 13 bankruptcy, see *Chapter 13 Bankruptcy: Repay Your Debts*, by Robin Leonard. (All are published by Nolo Press).

CHAPTER

1

Assessing Your Debt Situation

➡ *If your debt problems are behind you and you're only concerned with cleaning up your credit report, skip ahead to Chapter 4,* Cleaning Up Your Credit File. *Also read Chapter 2,* Avoiding Overspending.

Before you jump into rebuilding your credit, you'll need to take care of any financial emergencies. Then you'll need to tally up your debt burden and assess your options for handling what you owe.

A. Take Care of Financial Emergencies

A financial emergency is any situation that can leave you homeless or without some very important property or service. A pending eviction, a letter threatening foreclosure, an IRS seizure of your house, a utility cut-off and possibly a car repossession are financial emergencies. A nasty letter or threatening phone call from a bill collector is not. If you are being hassled by a collection agency, see Chapter 3, Section D.

If you face an emergency, act on it at once. Begin by contacting the creditor. You may be able to work out a temporary solution that will keep you off the street or on your wheels. If that doesn't work, you'll probably need to get in touch with a lawyer. One of your options is to file for bankruptcy, assuming your overall debt burden justifies it. A bankruptcy filing immediately stops all your creditors in their tracks and can buy you some valuable time. (See Sections C.4 and C.5, below, for more information on bankruptcy.)

B. Face Your Debt Problems

Some people with debt problems believe that the less they know, the less it hurts. They think, "I'm having trouble paying a lot of my bills. I can't stand the thought of knowing just how much I can't pay." But you must come to terms with your total debt burden. You cannot take steps to rebuild your credit without knowing exactly where your money goes—or is obligated to go.

Figuring out what you owe may result in a pleasant surprise. Most debt counselors find that people tend to overestimate—not underestimate—their debt burden. This may bring little comfort to those of you who find out that you owe more than you thought, but there is always a benefit: knowing what you really owe will help you make wise choices about how you spend your money.

Use *Form F-1: Outstanding Debts* (in Appendix 3) to tally up your total debt burden. Look at the most recent bills you've received. If you've thrown out your bills without opening them, you can probably find out the balance by calling the customer service department of the creditor. If you've been long avoiding your creditors and fear they'll hassle you when you call, ask for balance information only. If the customer service representative turns into a bill collector, explain that you are exploring your options and need to know how much you owe before you proceed. Let the representative know that you will contact the company as soon as possible, but for now you need only to know how much you owe. If the representative still hassles you, hang up and use your best guess as to how much you owe that creditor.

Total up both your past due installment bills (such as credit cards and loans) and any regular monthly obligations that are overdue (such as your utility bill).

C. Understand Your Options for Dealing With Your Debts

You normally have about a half dozen options for dealing with your debts—probably more possibilities than you imagined. Read this entire section before taking action.

ASSESSING YOUR DEBT SITUATION **1/3**

1. Do Nothing

Surprisingly, the best approach for some people deeply in debt is to take no action at all. If you live simply, with little income and property, and look forward to a similar life in the future, you may be what's known as "judgment proof." This means that anyone who sues you and obtains a court judgment won't be able to collect simply because you don't have anything they can legally take. You can't be thrown in jail for not paying your debts. And state and federal laws prohibit a creditor—even the IRS—from taking away such essentials as basic clothing, ordinary household furnishings, personal effects, food, Social Security, disability benefits, unemployment or public assistance.

So, if you don't anticipate having a steady income or property a creditor could grab, sit back. Your creditors may decide not to sue you because they know they can't collect. Many will simply write off your debt and treat it as a deductible business loss on their income tax returns. In several years, the debt will become legally uncollectible under state law.

A complete list of property you get to keep even if your creditors sue you or you file for bankruptcy, called exempt property, is found in Money Troubles: Legal Strategies to Cope With Your Debts, *by Robin Leonard (Nolo Press).*

2. Negotiate With Your Creditors

If you can get some money, consider negotiating with your creditors. Negotiation can buy you time to get your finances in order. You can also negotiate to get your creditors to agree to accept considerably less than you owe as a complete settlement of your debts.

Suggestions and forms for negotiating with your creditors are in Chapter 3. What follows are some ideas on how to raise cash that will allow you to negotiate.

Beware of the IRS if you settle any debts for less than you owe. IRS regulations state that if a bank (including a bank that issues credit cards), savings and loan, credit union or other financial institution forgives (or even writes off as uncollectible) a debt or part of a debt for $600 or more, the financial institution must send you and the IRS a Form 1099-C at the end of the tax year. A Form 1099-C is a report of income, which means that when you file your tax return for the tax year in which the debt was forgiven, the IRS will make sure that you report the amount on the Form 1099 as income. The only exceptions to this rule arise when:

- *you discharge (eliminate) the debt in bankruptcy*
- *you are no longer obligated to pay the debt because the time limit to collect (called the statute of limitations) has expired, or*
- *the amount forgiven or written off is for late fees, interest and other amounts that don't include the principal of the debt.*

If your debts are enormous and your bank or other financial institution is willing to settle for less than you owe, it could cost you a lot in the end. Before taking the deal, have a tax preparer calculate your tax liability, including your likely Form 1099-C income. If your tax bill will be too high, you may be better off filing for bankruptcy.

a. Sell a Major Asset

One of the best ways you can raise cash and keep associated costs to a minimum is to sell a major asset, such as a house or car. With the proceeds of the sale, you'll have to pay off anything still owed on the asset and any secured creditor to whom you pledged the asset as collateral. Then you'll have to pay off any liens placed on the property by your creditors. You can use what's left to help pay your other debts.

b. Cut Your Expenses

Another excellent way to raise cash is to cut your expenses. It will also help you in negotiating with your creditors, who will want to know why you can't pay your bills and what steps you've taken to live more frugally. Here are some suggestions:

- Shrink food costs by clipping coupons, buying on sale, purchasing generic brands, buying in bulk and shopping at discount outlets.
- Improve your gas mileage by tuning up your car, checking the air in the tires and driving less—carpool, work at home (telecommute), ride your bicycle, take the bus or train, and combine trips.
- Conserve gas, water and electricity.
- Discontinue cable (or at least the premium channels) and subscriptions to magazines and papers.
- Instead of buying books and CDs, borrow them from the public library. Read magazines and newspapers there, too.
- Make long distance calls only when necessary and at off-peak hours. Also, compare programs offered by the various long distance carriers to make sure you are getting the best deal.
- Carry your lunch to work; eat dinner at home, not at restaurants.
- Buy secondhand clothing, furniture and appliances.
- Spend less on gifts and vacations.

c. Withdraw Money From a Tax-Deferred Account

If you have an IRA or other tax-deferred account into which you've deposited money, consider cashing it in, especially if you have other retirement funds. You'll have to pay the IRS a penalty—10% of the money you withdraw—and you'll owe income taxes on the money you take out. But paying these penalties to the IRS, especially if you have been laid off or face a major medical emergency, is probably better than losing your house.

You may also be able to tap your 401(k) plan. Again, you'll owe taxes on the money withdrawn and a 10% penalty if you're under age 59½. But there is a bit of good news: Not only can you withdraw money to cover your emergency expenses, but you can also withdraw enough to cover the taxes and penalty.

d. Obtain a Home Equity Loan or Credit Line

Many banks, savings and loans, credit unions and other lenders offer home equity loans, also called second mortgages, and home equity lines of credit. Lenders who make these loans establish how much you can borrow by starting with a percentage of the market value of your house—usually between 50% and 80%. Then, they deduct what you still owe on it.

Obtaining a home equity loan has both advantages and disadvantages. Be sure you understand all the terms before you sign up for one.

Advantages of Home Equity Loans and Credit Lines

- You can borrow a fixed amount of money and repay it in equal monthly installments for a set period (home equity loan). Or you can borrow as you need the money, drawing against the amount granted when you opened the account; you'll pay off this type of loan as you would a credit card bill (home equity line of credit).
- The interest you pay may be fully deductible on your income tax return.
- You can look for a home equity loan with fixed or adjustable rate interest. If you take out a loan with an adjustable interest rate, federal law requires that the lender cap the rate. This means that the rate will never be allowed to go above a certain percentage.

Disadvantages of Home Equity Loans

- You are obligating yourself to make another monthly or periodic payment. If you are unable to pay, you may have to sell your house, or even worse, face the possibility of foreclosure (the lender forcing a sale of your house to pay off what you owe). *Before you take out a home equity loan, be sure you can afford the monthly payment.*
- While interest is deductible and capped for adjustable rate loans, it's often high—up to 19% per year.
- You may have to pay an assortment of up-front fees for an appraisal, credit report, title insurance and points. These fees can run close to $1,000. In addition, for giving you an equity line of credit, many lenders charge a yearly fee of $25 to $50.

e. Use the Equity in Your Home if You Are Elderly

A variety of plans help older homeowners make use of the accumulated value (equity) in their homes without requiring them to move, give up title to the property or make payments on a loan. The most common types of plans are reverse mortgages.

Reverse mortgages are loans against the equity in the home that provide cash advances to a homeowner and require no repayment until the end of the loan term or when the home is sold. The borrower can receive the cash in several ways—a lump sum, regular monthly payments, a line of credit or a combination.

To qualify, you must be at least 62 years old and own your home free and clear or have a very small mortgage that can be paid off with an initial lump sum payment from the reverse mortgage. All reverse mortgages cost money—closing costs (title insurance, escrow fees and appraisal fees), loan origination fees, accrued interest, and in most cases, an additional charge to offset the lender's risk that you won't repay. All states except Alaska, South Dakota and Texas allow lenders to offer reverse mortgages.

The most widely available reverse mortgage plan is the Government-Insured Home Equity Conversion Mortgage Program, administered through the Federal Housing Administration. It provides a maximum of a little over $150,000. People with more valuable property can look into the Federal National Mortgage Association (Fannie Mae) program, which grants reverse mortgages for up to $203,000.

Additional Resources

The following brochures are free:

- *Reverse Mortgages*, Federal Trade Commission, Office of Consumer Education, 6th and Pennsylvania Avenue, NW, Washington, DC 20580, 202-326-2222.
- *Homemade Money*, American Association of Retired Persons (AARP), Home Equity Information Center, Consumer Affairs Division, 601 E Street, NW, Washington, DC 20049, 202-434-2277.
- *Money From Home: A Consumer's Guide to Home Equity Conversion Mortgages*, Fannie Mae, Consumer Education Group, 3900 Wisconsin Avenue NW, Washington, DC 20016-2899, 800-732-6643.
- *Retirement Income on the House*, by Ken Scholen, National Center for Home Equity Conversion, 7373 147th Street West, Suite 115, Apple Valley, MN 55124, 612-953-4474.

Also available for $20 each is a video, *Reverse Mortgages—Cashing In on Your Home*, put out by the Human Investment Project, Inc., 364 S. Railroad Avenue, San Mateo, CA 94401, 415-348-6660; and a book by Ken Scholen, *Your New Retirement Nest Egg: A Consumer Guide to the New Reverse Mortgages*, available from the National Center for Home Equity Conversion.

f. Borrow From Family or Friends

In times of financial crises, some people are lucky enough to have friends or relatives who can and will help out. Before asking your college roommate, Uncle Paul or someone similar, consider the following:

- Can the lender really afford to help you? If the person is on a fixed income and needs the money to get by, you should probably look elsewhere for a loan.
- Do you want to owe this person money? If the loan comes with emotional strings attached, be sure you can handle the situation before taking the money.
- Will the loan help you out or will it just delay the inevitable (most likely, filing for bankruptcy)? Don't borrow money to make payments on debts you will eventually discharge in bankruptcy.
- Will you have to repay the loan now or will the lender let you wait until you're back on your feet? If you have to make payments now, you're just adding another monthly payment to your already unmanageable pile of debts.
- If the loan is from your parents, can you treat it as part of your eventual inheritance? If so, you won't ever have to repay it. If your siblings get angry that you're getting some of mom and dad's money, be sure they understand that your inheritance will be reduced accordingly.

g. Borrow From a Finance Company

A few finance companies—the three biggest nationwide are Beneficial Corp., Household International Inc. and ITT—lend money to consumers. These companies make secured consolidation loans, requiring that you pledge your house or car as collateral. The loans are just like second mortgages or secured vehicle loans; you'll usually be charged interest between 10% and 15% and if you default on the loan, the finance company can foreclose on your home or take your car.

Finance companies and similar lenders also make unsecured consolidation loans—that is, they may lend you some money without requiring that you pledge any property as a guarantee that you'll pay. But the interest rate on these loans can be astronomical, often reaching 25%. Lenders also charge all kinds of fees—many not disclosed—bringing the effective interest rate closer to 50%.

If you want to take out a consolidation loan, you are better off borrowing from a bank or credit union than a finance company. Many finance companies engage in illegal or borderline collection practices if you default, and are not as willing as banks and credit unions to negotiate if you have trouble paying. Furthermore, loans from finance companies are viewed negatively by potential creditors who see them in your credit file. They often imply prior debt problems.

3. Get Outside Help to Design a Repayment Plan

Many people aren't well-equipped to negotiate with their creditors. Inside, they may feel that they are obliged to make full payment. Or, their creditors may be so hard-nosed that the process is too unpleasant to stomach. And some people just haven't honed their negotiation skills.

If you don't want to negotiate with your creditors, there are people and organizations available to help you. Creditors are often more than happy to work with respected organizations that work with debtors who are serious about repaying their debts. Consumer Credit Counseling Service (see Appendix 1), the United Way or a church or synagogue are all excellent prospects. These organizations will help you figure out how much you owe, how much you can afford to pay each month and what your various options are—including bankruptcy. CCCS will also talk to your creditors for you. Check your phone book's Yellow Pages under Counseling.

A lawyer can help, but lawyers charge high fees which rarely are justified, especially when you're heavily in debt. Whatever you do, don't use a credit repair clinic. (See Chapter 5, Section H.)

4. File for Chapter 7 Bankruptcy

Chapter 7 bankruptcy is the bankruptcy plan most people have heard about. It allows you to wipe out most consumer debts—credit cards, medical bills and the like. In exchange, however, you might have to surrender some of your property, such as a second car, valuable electronic equipment or a vacation home. To file, you fill out several forms that describe your property, your current income and expenses, your debts and any recent purchases and gifts. Then you file the forms with the federal bankruptcy court in your area.

Filing for bankruptcy puts into effect something called the "automatic stay." The automatic stay immediately stops your creditors from trying to collect what you owe them. So, at least temporarily, creditors cannot legally take (garnish) your wages, empty your bank account, go after your car, house or other property or cut off your utility service.

Until your bankruptcy case ends, your past financial problems are in the hands of the bankruptcy court. Nothing can be sold or paid without the court's consent. You keep control, however, of virtually all property and income you acquire after you file for bankruptcy.

At the end of the bankruptcy process, most of your debts are discharged—wiped out—by the court. You no longer legally owe the debts you owed when you filed for bankruptcy. If you incur debts after filing, however, you are still obligated to pay them. And you can't file for Chapter 7 bankruptcy again for another six years from the date of your filing.

Of course, bankruptcy isn't for everyone. One reason is that many types of debts can't be erased in Chapter 7 bankruptcy:

- child support or alimony obligations
- most student loans that first became due fewer than seven years ago (adding in any time you were granted a deferment or forbearance or were in another bankruptcy case)
- court-ordered restitution—payments you're ordered to make after a criminal conviction
- most federal, state and local income taxes less than three years past due, and any money borrowed or charged to pay those tax debts
- debts arising from intoxicated driving
- debts for dues or special assessments owed to a condominium or cooperative association
- debts from a marital settlement agreement or divorce decree unless the bankruptcy judge rules it would be impossible for you to pay or that the benefit you'd get by the discharge outweighs any harm to your ex-spouse, and
- debts that a bankruptcy judge rules were incurred as a result of a wrongful act on your part—examples include debts incurred from fraud (such as lying on a credit application or writing a bad check), based on intentional injury (such as assault, battery, false imprisonment, libel and slander), larceny (theft), breach of trust or embezzlement.

For more information on Chapter 7 bankruptcy, see Nolo's How to File for Bankruptcy, *by Stephen Elias, Albin Renauer and Robin Leonard (a detailed bankruptcy guide) or* Nolo's Law Form Kit: Personal Bankruptcy, *by Stephen Elias, Albin Renauer, Robin Leonard and Lisa Goldoftas (a streamlined bankruptcy guide).*

5. Pay Over Time With Chapter 13 Bankruptcy

If you have steady income and think you could squeeze out regular monthly payments, Chapter 13 bankruptcy may be a good option. Chapter 13 allows you to keep your property and use your disposable income (net income less reasonable expenses) to pay all or a portion of your debts over three to five years. You can use wages, benefits, investment income, business earnings or any other income to make your payments.

Most people file for Chapter 13 bankruptcy to make up missed mortgage or car payments and get back on track with their original loan, or to pay off a tax debt or student loan. These are not the only reasons people file for Chapter 13 bankruptcy, however.

If you cannot complete a Chapter 13 repayment plan—for example, you lose your job six months into the plan and can't make the payments—the bankruptcy court has the authority to change your plan. If the problem looks temporary, you may be given a grace period, an extended repayment period or a reduction of the total owed. If it's clear that you can't possibly complete the plan because

of circumstances beyond your control, the bankruptcy court might even let you discharge (cancel) your debts on the basis of hardship.

If the bankruptcy court won't let you modify your plan or give you a hardship discharge, you have the right to:

- convert to a Chapter 7 bankruptcy, or
- dismiss your Chapter 13 case. A dismissal would leave you in the same position as you were in before you filed, except that you'll owe less because of the payments you made. Your creditors will add to the debt the interest that was abated from the time you filed your Chapter 13 petition until it was dismissed.

For more information on Chapter 13 bankruptcy, see Nolo's Chapter 13 Bankruptcy: Repay Your Debts, *by Robin Leonard.* ∎

Avoiding Overspending

→ *If you'd rather clean up your credit report or pay off your debts before doing a budget, skip ahead, but be sure to return to this chapter later. You must make a budget as a part of repairing your credit.*

An essential step in repairing your credit is to understand where your money goes. With that information in hand, you can make intelligent choices about how to spend your money. If you'd rather not create a budget yourself, you can contact a local Consumer Credit Counseling Service (CCCS) office. This nonprofit organization, which primarily helps debtors negotiate with creditors, can also help you set up a budget for free or a nominal fee. Information on CCCS is located in Appendix 1.

Several excellent computer programs, such as Quicken, can help you keep track of your expenses, particularly those paid by check or credit card. Many of these programs have budget features as well. Be sure you have an opportunity to record your cash outlays, however, before relying on these budgeting features. This is because many commercial budgeting programs have you analyze your expenses paid primarily by check, and overlook the most obvious source of payment—cash.

A. Keep Track of Your Daily Expenditures

Your goal in this chapter is to create a monthly budget—to compare your average monthly expenses to your total monthly income. This section introduces *Form F-2: Daily Expenditures* (copies are below and in Appendix 3) on which you have space to record everything you spend over the course of a week, paying special attention to cash outlays. Here's how to use the form:

1. Make eight copies of the form so you can record your expenditures for two months. (To create your monthly budget, you'll want to record your expenses for two months. By doing this, you'll avoid creating a budget based on a week or a month of unusually high or low expenses.) If you are married or live with someone with whom you share expenses, make 16 copies so you each can record your expenditures.

2. Select a Sunday to begin recording your expenses.

3. Record that Sunday's date in the blank at the top of one copy of the form.

4. Carry that week's form with you at all times.

5. Record every expense you for pay by cash or cash equivalent. "Cash equivalent" means check, ATM or debit card or automatic bank withdrawal. Be sure to include bank fees. Also, don't forget savings and investments, such as deposits into savings accounts, certificates of deposit or money market accounts, or purchases of investments such as stocks or bonds.

   Do not record credit card charges, as your goal is to get a picture of where your cash goes. When you make a payment on a credit card bill, however, list the items paid for. If you don't pay the entire bill, list the older charges that total a little less than the amount paid—attribute the rest of your payment to interest.

EXAMPLE: On Sunday night, you pay your bills for the week and make a $450 payment toward your $1,000 credit card bill. The $1,000 includes a $500 balance from the previous month, a $350 airline ticket, a few restaurant meals and accrued interest. On your daily Expenditure Form for Sunday, you list $450 in the second column. In the first column, you identify corresponding expenses—and attribute some of it to interest. In this example, you have to look at your credit card statement from the previous month.

6. At the end of the week, put away the form and take out another copy. Go back to Step 3.

Daily Expenditures for Week of _____

Sunday's Expenditures	Cost	Monday's Expenditures	Cost	Tuesday's Expenditures	Cost	Wednesday's Expenditures	Cost
Daily Total:		Daily Total:		Daily Total:		Daily Total:	

Thursday's Expenditures	Cost	Friday's Expenditures	Cost	Saturday's Expenditures	Cost	Other Expenditures	Cost
Daily Total:		Daily Total:		Daily Total:		Weekly Total:	

F-2

7. At the end of the eight weeks, list on any form under the category "Other Expenditures" seasonal, annual, semi-annual or quarterly expenses you incur but did not pay during your two-month recording period. The most common are property taxes, car registration, magazine subscriptions, tax preparation fees and insurance payments. But there are others. For example, if you do your recording in the winter months, don't forget summer expenses such as camp fees for your children or pool maintenance. Similarly, in the summer or spring you probably won't account for your annual holiday gift expenses. Be creative and thorough.

B. Total Up Your Income

Your expenditures account for only half of the picture. You also need to add up your monthly income. Use *Form F-3: Monthly Income From All Sources* (copies are below and in Appendix 3).

If you are married or live with someone with whom you share expenses, include income information for both partners.

Column 1: Source of income. In Part A, list the jobs for which you receive a salary or wages. In Part B, list all self-employment for which you receive income, including farm income and sales commissions. In Part C, list any other sources of income. Here are some examples of other kinds of income.

- **Bonus pay.** List all regular bonuses you receive, such as an annual $500 end-of-year bonus.
- **Dividends and interest.** List all sources of dividends or interest—for example, bank accounts, security deposits or stocks.
- **Alimony or child support.** Enter the type of support you receive for yourself (alimony, spousal support or maintenance) or on behalf of your children (child support).
- **Pension or retirement income.** List the source of any pension, annuity, IRA, Keogh or other retirement payments you receive.
- **Other public assistance.** Enter the types of any public benefits, such as SSI, public assistance, disability payments, veterans' benefits, unemployment compensation, worker's compensation or any other government benefit which you receive.
- **Other.** Identify any other sources of income, such as a tax refund you received within the past year or expect to receive within the next year, or payments you receive from friends or relatives. If, within the past 12 months, you received any one-time lump sum payment (such as the proceeds from an insurance policy or from the sale of a valuable asset), don't list it as income.

Column 2: Amount of each payment. For each source of income you listed in Parts A and B of Column 1, enter the amount you receive each pay period. If you don't receive the same amount each period, average the last 12. Then enter your deductions for each pay period. Again, if these amounts vary, enter an average of the last 12 months. For the income you listed in Part A, you probably need to get out a pay stub to see how much is deducted from your paycheck. Subtract the

Monthly Income From All Sources

1 Source of Income		2 Amount of each payment	3 Period covered by each payment	4 Amount per month
A. Wages or Salary				
Job 1:	Gross pay, including overtime:	$ _____	_____	
_____	Subtract:			
	Federal taxes	_____		
	State taxes	_____		
	Social Security (FICA)	_____		
	Union dues	_____		
	Insurance payments	_____		
	Child support wage withholding	_____		
	Other mandatory deductions (specify):			
	_____	_____		
	Subtotal	$ _____	_____	_____
Job 2:	Gross pay, including overtime:	$ _____	_____	
_____	Subtract:			
	Federal taxes	_____		
	State taxes	_____		
	Social Security (FICA)	_____		
	Union dues	_____		
	Insurance payments	_____		
	Child support wage withholding	_____		
	Other mandatory deductions (specify):			
	_____	_____		
	Subtotal	$ _____	_____	_____
Job 3:	Gross pay, including overtime:	$ _____	_____	
_____	Subtract:			
	Federal taxes	_____		
	State taxes	_____		
	Social Security (FICA)	_____		
	Union dues	_____		
	Insurance payments	_____		
	Child support wage withholding	_____		
	Other mandatory deductions (specify):			
	_____	_____		
	Subtotal	$ _____	_____	_____

F-3

Monthly Income From All Sources (cont'd)

1 **Source of Income**	2 **Amount of each payment**	3 **Period covered by each payment**	4 **Amount per month**

B. Self-Employment Income

Job 1: Gross pay, including overtime: $ _____ _____

_____ Subtract:

    Federal taxes _____

    State taxes _____

    Self-employment taxes _____

    Other mandatory deductions (specify):

    _____ _____

| **Subtotal** | $ _____ | _____ | _____ |

Job 2: Gross pay, including overtime: $ _____ _____

_____ Subtract:

    Federal taxes _____

    State taxes _____

    Self-employment taxes _____

    Other mandatory deductions (specify): _____

    _____ _____

| **Subtotal** | $ _____ | _____ | _____ |

C. Other Sources

Bonuses _____ _____ _____ _____

Dividends and interest_____ _____ _____ _____

Rent, lease or license income_____ _____ _____ _____

Royalties_____ _____ _____ _____

Note or trust income_____ _____ _____ _____

Alimony or child support you receive_____ _____ _____ _____

Pension or retirement income_____ _____ _____ _____

Social Security_____ _____ _____ _____

Other public assistance_____ _____ _____ _____

Other (specify):_____ _____ _____ _____

_____ _____ _____ _____

_____ _____ _____ _____

_____ _____ _____ _____

_____ _____ _____ _____

| **Total monthly income** | | | $ _____ |

F-3

deductions and enter your net income in the Subtotal blank in Column 2.

In Part C, enter the amount of each payment for each source of income.

Column 3: Period covered by each payment. For each source of income, enter the period covered by each payment—such as weekly, twice monthly (24 times a year), every other week (26 times a year), monthly, quarterly (common for royalties), or annually (common for farm income).

Column 4: Amount per month. Multiply or divide the subtotals (or amounts in Part C) in Column 2 to determine the monthly amount. For example, if you are paid twice a month, multiply the Column 2 amount by two. If you are paid every other week, multiply the amount by 26 (for the annual amount) and divide by 12. (The shortcut is to multiply by 2.167.)

When you are done, total up Column 4. This is your total monthly income.

C. Make a Budget or Spending Plan

After you've kept track of your expenses and income for a couple of months, you're ready to create a budget, or spending plan. (Although most people are more familiar with the term "budget," many people find it restrictive and prefer the term "spending plan." Use whichever is more comfortable for you.)

Your twin goals in making a budget are to control your impulses to overspend and to help you start saving money—an essential part of repairing your credit. You use the figures you entered on Forms F-2 and F-3 as the basis for your budget.

To make (and use) a monthly budget, follow these steps:

1. On a blank piece of paper, write down categories into which your expenses fall. (See list, below, for suggested categories.) Also, total up your two months' (or estimated seasonal, annual, semi-annual or quarterly) expenses for the categories you create.

2. Starting on a second piece of paper, list your categories of expenses down the left side of the page. Use as many sheets as you need to list all categories. These are your budget sheets. (See the sample below.)

3. On the sheets containing your list of categories, make 13 columns. Label the first one "projected" and the remaining 12 with the months of the year. Unless today is the first of the month, start with next month.

4. Using your total actual expenses for the two months you tracked or your estimated seasonal, annual, semi-annual or quarterly expenses, project your monthly expenses for the categories you've listed. To find your projected monthly expenses, divide your actual two months' expenses by two, divide your total seasonal or annual expenses by 12, divide your semi-annual expenses by six and divide your quarterly expenses by four.

5. Enter your projected monthly expenses into the "projected" column of your budget sheets.

6. Add up all projected monthly expenses and enter the total into the "Total Expenses" category at the bottom of the projected column.

7. Enter your projected monthly income from Form F-3 below your total projected expenses.

8. Figure out the difference. If your expenses exceed your income, you will have to cut expenses or increase your income. One way to do this is to make more money—but let's assume that you are not likely to get a substantial raise, find a new (higher-paying) job, take on a second job, or make significant money by selling assets. This means you need to find ways to decrease your expenses without depriving yourself of items or services you truly need. Review your expenses with any eye toward reducing. Rather than looking to cut out categories completely, look for

categories you can comfortably reduce slightly. For example, let's say you need to cut $75 from your budget. You had planned to buy $25 in music each month, but you can reduce it by $10 easily. You had also planned on spending $55 a month to eat out dinner, but are willing to decrease that to $35, thereby saving $20. Keep looking for categories in which you can make similar, small adjustments.

9. Return to your budget and category by category make the kinds of small adjustments described above. Once you're done making your adjustments, enter your new total.

10. During the course of a month, use a pencil to write down your expenses in each category. At the end of the month, total up the amount you spent. How are you doing? Are you keeping close to your projected figures? (See the sample below.)

    Don't think of your budget as etched in stone. If you do, and you spend more on an item than you've budgeted, you'll only find yourself frustrated. Use your budget as a guide. If you constantly overspend in an area, you need to change the projected amount for that category—don't berate yourself. Keep in mind that a budget is designed to help you recognize what you can afford—not to fill in the "correct" numbers. Check your figures periodically to help you keep an eye on how you're doing. If one month an annual payment comes due (such as your car registration), you'll need to cut back in other categories that month. If you never have enough money to make ends meet (you're using credit cards and not paying the balance in full each month), it's time to adjust some more. (See Section D, below, for suggestions of ways to control your spending.)

Categories of Expenses

Home
rent/mortgage
property taxes
insurance (renter's or
    homeowner's)
homeowner's association dues
telephone
gas & electric
water & sewer
cable TV
garbage
household supplies
housewares
furniture & appliances
cleaning
yard or pool care
maintenance & repairs

Food
groceries
breakfast out
lunch out
dinner out
coffee/tea
snacks

Wearing Apparel
clothing & accessories
laundry, dry cleaning &
    mending

Self Care
toiletries & cosmetics
haircuts
massage
health club membership
donations

Health Care
insurance
medications
vitamins
doctors
dentist
eyecare
therapy

Transportation
insurance
road service club
registration
gasoline

maintenance & repairs
car wash
parking & tolls
public transit & cabs
parking tickets

Entertainment
music
movies & video rentals
concerts, theater & ballet
museums
sporting events
hobbies & lessons
club dues or membership
film development
books, magazines & news-
    papers
software

Dependent Care
child care
clothing
allowance
school expenses
toys & entertainment

Pet Care
grooming
vet
food, toys & supplies

Education
tuition or loan payments
books & supplies

Travel

Gifts & Cards
holidays
birthdays & anniversaries
weddings & showers

Personal Business
supplies
photocopying
postage
bank & credit card fees
lawyer
accountant

Taxes

Insurance

Savings & Investments

Sample Monthly Budget

Expense Category	proj.	Aug.	Sept.	Oct.	Nov.	Dec.	Jan.	Feb.	Mar.	April	May	June	July
Home													
rent	650	650	650										
renter's insurance	12	0	24										
phone	55	53	50										
gas & electric	45	49	43										
water	30	30	30										
cable	25	25	25										
household supplies	20	35	28										
furniture & appliances	30	0	0										
cleaning	30	30	30										
maintenance & repairs	35	0	25										
Food													
groceries	200	250	197										
breakfast out	10	19	0										
lunch out	25	25	40										
dinner out	60	35	55										
coffee/tea	10	8	8										
snacks	10	15	12										
Wearing Apparel													
clothing & access.	20	30	0										
laundry	15	14	21										
Self Care													
toiletries & cosmetics	25	25	25										
haircuts	40	40	40										
donations	40	40	40										
Health Care													
medications & prescriptions	10	5	0										
vitamins	20	20	23										
insurance	100	100	100										

Sample Monthly Budget (cont'd)

Expense Category	proj.	Aug.	Sept.	Oct.	Nov.	Dec.	Jan.	Feb.	Mar.	April	May	June	July
Health Care (cont'd)													
dentist	10	0	0										
eyecare	10	0	0										
Transportation													
car insurance	80	80	80										
registration	15	180	0										
gasoline	35	35	34										
maintenance & repairs	20	0	12										
parking & tolls	30	30	25										
public transit & cabs	10	0	15										
Entertainment													
music	15	16	25										
movies & video rentals	20	10	7										
books, magazines & newspapers	25	20	35										
software	10	0	15										
Pet Care													
vet	30	0	45										
food & toys	30	30	15										
Travel	25	0	0										
Gifts & Cards	20	25	35										
Personal Business													
supplies	10	5	0										
postage	16	32	0										
bank & credit card fees	25	12	18										
Savings	35	35	35										
Total Expenses	1,988	2,008	1,862										
Total Income	2,100	2,100	1,950										
Difference	112	92	88										

D. Prevent Future Financial Problems

There are no magic rules that will solve everyone's financial troubles. But nine suggestions should help you stay out of financial hot water. If you have a family, everyone will have to participate—no one person can do all the work alone. So make sure your spouse or partner, and the kids, understand that the family is having financial difficulties and agree together to take the steps that will lead to recovery.

1. **Create a realistic budget and stick to it.** This means periodically checking it and readjusting your figures and spending habits.

2. **Don't impulse buy.** When you see something you hadn't planned to buy, don't purchase it on the spot. Go home and think it over. It's unlikely you'll return to the store and buy it.

3. **Avoid sales.** Buying a $500 item on sale for $400 isn't a $100 savings if you didn't need the item to begin with. It's spending $400 unnecessarily.

4. **Get medical insurance if at all possible.** Even a stopgap policy with a large deductible can help if a medical crisis comes up. You can't avoid medical emergencies, but living without medical insurance is an invitation to financial ruin.

5. **Charge items only if you can afford to pay for them now.** If you don't currently have the cash, don't charge based on future income—sometimes future income doesn't materialize. An alternative is to toss all of your credit cards in a drawer (or in the garbage) and to commit to living without credit for a while.

6. **Avoid large rent or house payments.** Obligate yourself only to what you can now afford and increase your mortgage or rent payments only as your income increases. Consider refinancing your house if your payments are unwieldy.

7. **Avoid cosigning or guaranteeing a loan for someone.** Your signature obligates you as if you were the primary borrower. You can't be sure that the other person will pay.

8. **Similarly, avoid joint obligations with people who have questionable spending habits**—even a spouse or significant other. If you incur a joint debt, you're probably liable for all of it if the other person defaults.

9. **Don't make high-risk investments.** Invest conservatively, opting for certificates of deposit, money market funds and government bonds over riskier investments such as speculative real estate, penny stocks and junk bonds. ■

Handling Existing Debts

To repair your credit, you must pay attention to two different kinds of debts: debts that aren't overdue (such as current charges on your utility bill) and your past due accounts (such as an unpaid phone bill from last month or a doctor's bill from last year). You cannot repair your credit if you ignore your past due debts—those default notations will stand out in your credit report. In addition, if you repair your credit and later default on debts that are now current, you will have wasted the hard work you did repairing your credit in the first place.

For more detail on paying your past due bills and contacting your creditors about accounts on which you are current, see Money Troubles: Legal Strategies to Cope With Your Debts, *by Robin Leonard (Nolo Press).*

Tips For Sending Letters

Throughout this chapter, you are advised to send various letters to your creditors, depending on your situation. When you send a letter, try to adhere to the following guidelines:

- type your letters or neatly fill in the blanks of the letters in Appendix 3, if possible
- keep a copy for yourself
- send by certified mail, return receipt requested, and
- if you are enclosing money, use a cashier's check or money order if you have any debts in collection; otherwise the recipient of the check could pass your account number on to any debt collector, which will make it easier for the collector to grab your assets to collect the debt.

A. Deal With Debts Current or Not Seriously Overdue

If you've already fallen behind on your debts, jump ahead to Section C, below.

One important step in repairing and maintaining your credit is to stay current—or to not get too far behind—on your existing debts. If it looks like you can't pay, your best bet is to contact your creditors before you miss a payment.

Negotiating with your creditors for extra time or to change the terms of your agreement isn't particularly difficult. Creditors generally like to hear from people who anticipate having problems paying their bills. If you simply skip your payment, the creditor assumes the worst—that you're a deadbeat trying to get away with not paying. If you call or write in advance, however, your creditor is likely to help you through your difficulties. Merchants, lenders and other creditors have fallen on economic hard

Understand the Two Kinds of Debts

To successfully negotiate with your creditors, you must understand your options, which often depend on whether a debt is secured or unsecured.

Secured debts are linked to specific items of property, called "collateral." One way for a debt to be secured is for you to sign an agreement to create a secured debt and specify the collateral. The collateral guarantees payment of the debt. If you don't pay, the creditor has the legal right to take the collateral. The creditor does not have to take back the collateral, however, and can try other methods to collect what you owe. For example, if you owe $7,500 on a loan secured by your car, but recently totaled the vehicle, the creditor won't take it—creditors want dollars, not dents. The other way a debt becomes secured is for a creditor to record a lien (a notice that you owe the creditor money) against the property.

Common examples of secured debts include:

- mortgages and home equity loans (also called second mortgages)—loans to buy, refinance or fix up a house or other real estate
- loans for cars, boats, tractors, motorcycles, planes, RVs
- personal loans from finance companies where you pledge as collateral real estate or personal property, such as a paid-off motor vehicle
- department store charges when the store requires you to sign a security agreement in which you state that the item purchased is collateral for your repayment (most store charges are not secured), and
- tax liens, judgment liens, mechanic liens and child support liens.

Unsecured debts have no collateral. For example, you charge a television set on your Visa card. If you don't pay, the bank that issued the Visa card can't take the television from you. If it wants to be paid, it must sue you, get a judgment for the money you owe and try to collect. A creditor who wins a lawsuit typically can go after your wages, bank accounts and valuable property.

The majority of debts are unsecured. Some common ones are:

- credit and charge card purchases and cash advances (Visa, MasterCard, American Express, Discover Card)
- gasoline charges
- most department store charges
- student loans
- bills from doctors, dentists, hospitals, accountants and lawyers
- alimony and child support
- loans from friends or relatives unless you gave the person a note secured by some property you own
- rent, and
- utility bills.

times at least as much as consumers have. They are aware of unemployment rates, underemployment trends, income reductions, corporate mergers and downsizing, and other sour economic realities. And when times turn good again, they're going to want—and need—your business. So they will most likely be accommodating now.

As soon as it becomes clear to you that you're going to have trouble paying your bills, contact your creditors. Your goals are twofold: You want time to pay and you don't want the creditor to report your bill as past due to credit bureaus. Calling your creditors is faster than writing, but if you find it easier to express yourself on paper than over the phone, go ahead and write. If you call, follow up your call with a confirming letter so that you and the creditor have some evidence of what you agreed to. If you write, make sure your letter will get there before your payment is due. (Section B, below, explains how to use the form letters included in this book.)

Your success with your creditors will depend on the type of debt, the creditor's policies and your ability to negotiate. Follow these key points when dealing with your creditors:

Explain the problem clearly. Creditors can easily grasp accidents, job layoffs, emergency expenses for your child's health, costs of caring for an aged family member or a large back tax assessment.

Mention any development that points to an improving financial condition. Creditors like to hear about disability or unemployment benefits beginning, job prospects, an expense about to end (such as a child finishing school), the end of a strike, a job recall or a small inheritance on the way.

If possible, send a token payment. This tells the creditor that you are serious about paying but just can't now.

Request that the creditor not report your bill past due, if the creditor may otherwise do so. The following creditors, as a rule, report payment histories to credit bureaus each month:

- banks and other commercial lenders that issue credit cards and make mortgage, personal, car and student loans

- non-bank credit and charge card issuers (American Express, Discover and Diner's Club)
- large department stores (Sears and J.C. Penney)
- oil and gas companies, and
- other creditors receiving regular monthly installments.

These creditors can make a notation that your payment is considered timely, even if you are late. So ask them to. Most landlords, utility companies, local retailers, insurance companies, doctors, hospitals, lawyers and other professionals don't report past due bills to credit bureaus unless the bill goes to a collection agency or the creditor (or the collection agency) sues you to collect. Don't bother making the request to these creditors.

→ *Below is advice for dealing with specific types of debts: rent and mortgage payments, utility and telephone bills, car payments, secured loans, student loans, insurance policies, bills from professionals and credit card payments. Read only the sections that apply to you.*

1. Rent Payments

Many landlords will let their tenants pay rent late for a month or two, especially if the tenant has been reliable in the past. You will have the best chance of working out a payment plan if you contact the landlord promptly.

If your rent is too steep for your budget, you could try asking for a reduction. Many landlords won't agree, but in areas where property values have declined or the vacancy rate has increased (there are many empty units on the market), it might work. The landlord may agree to accept a partial payment now and the rest later. The landlord may even temporarily lower your rent, rather than have to evict you or re-rent the place if you move out.

If your landlord agrees to a rent reduction or late payments, send or hand deliver a letter confirming the arrangement. (See the sample, below.) Be sure to keep a copy for yourself. Once the understanding is written down, the landlord will have a hard time evicting you as long as you live up to your new agreement.

Sample Letter to Landlord

Frank O'Neill
1556 North Lakefront
Minneapolis, MN 67890

November 22, 19xx

Dear Frank:

Thanks for being so understanding. This letter is to confirm the telephone conversation we had yesterday.

My lease requires that I pay rent of $750 per month. You agreed to reduce my rent to $600 per month, beginning December 1, 19xx, and lasting until I find another job, but not to exceed six months. That is, even if I haven't found a new job, my rent will go back to $750 per month on June 1, 19xy.

Thank you again for your understanding and help. As I mentioned on the phone, I am following all leads in order to secure another job shortly.

Sincerely,

Abigail Landsberg
Abigail Landsberg

If your landlord refuses to help out, your options are limited. If you don't pay the amount of rent you obligated yourself to pay, your landlord can—and no doubt will—evict you. You are usually better off trying to get a roommate or moving out before any eviction takes place.

If you have a month-to-month tenancy, you merely have to give your landlord the amount of notice required under your rental agreement before you move out (often 30 days). Of course, if moving out means living on the streets, you might as well stay and see what action the landlord takes. This is especially true in areas where evictions can take several weeks.

If you have a written lease, you will violate it by moving out before the lease term expires. If you know of someone who can take over your lease, recommend that person to your landlord. The landlord must accept her unless he has another tenant in mind or her credit is bad and he's convinced she couldn't pay the rent. Even if you don't find someone to take over the lease, the landlord has a duty to "mitigate" damages—he must try to re-rent the place as soon as possible in order to collect the rent he's losing by your moving. Your landlord could, in theory, hold you responsible for the balance of rent due under the agreement. The most he should try to get you to pay is lost rent for a month or two. If you advanced one or two months' rent or paid a security deposit when you moved in, the landlord will probably put that money toward any rent you owe.

If you end up owing your landlord some money and don't pay it, your landlord might report the amount due to the credit bureaus or to tenant screening services, which provide the same function as credit bureaus but gather information for property owners and managers. Not all landlords report this information. Some do it only to be spiteful. But anytime the landlord takes court action—files an eviction lawsuit or sues you for a balance owed—you can be sure it will appear in your credit file.

2. Mortgage Payments

You have a number of options for dealing with house payments.
- If you anticipate having trouble making payments for a few months, contact the lender. Lenders often defer or waive late charges, accept interest-only payments, apply prior prepayments to the current debt or temporarily reduce or suspend payments.
- Especially if your problem looks long-term, the lender may let you refinance the loan to reduce the amount of your monthly payments.

If you refinance at a lower interest rate, you may save money in the long run, too. You'll need to show the lender that you have enough income to afford the reduced payments. Before refinancing your loan, be sure you understand the potential costs involved—points, loan fees and many of the same closing costs you paid when you bought your house. Because you're looking to refinance with your original lender, however, the lender may waive many of these costs.

- If you can't get a refinance loan with the original lender, you may be able to find another lender who will loan you money to pay off all or some of your first loan. Again, be aware of the potential costs involved.

If you can't pay your mortgage and can't work out a deal with your original or a new lender, you have three options:

- **Sell the house.** This is the best option. Many investors and savvy buyers look to buy "distressed" houses—houses in or near foreclosure. You probably won't get top dollar, but you should be able to at least save some of the equity you have built up and avoid doing serious damage to your credit.
- **Walk away from your house.** Especially if you owe more than your house is worth, you may be best off moving out and giving the keys to the lender. The lender isn't likely to foreclose—it has the house. And you won't lose your equity in the house, because you don't have any.
- **Let the lender foreclose—force a sale of your house.** If this happens, you may still owe money. In most states, if the sale price doesn't cover what you owe, the lender gets something called a "deficiency balance." A deficiency balance is the difference between the amount you owe the foreclosing lender and the amount he sells the house for.

How a Foreclosure Works

If you haven't been able to sell your house and you don't just walk away, your lender will probably foreclose. Here's what to expect. After you miss a few payments, the lender will send you a letter reminding you that your payments are late and imposing a late fee. If you don't respond, the lender will wait another 60 days or so and then send you a notice telling you that your loan is in default and that it will begin foreclosure proceedings unless payment is received.

After getting this notice, you have about 90 days to "cure" the default and reinstate the loan—pay all your missed payments, late fees and other charges. The only way to avoid foreclosure is to sell the house during this period. If you were being picky before, now is the time to accept any offer.

If you don't cure the default, the lender applies to a court for an order allowing it to sell your house at an auction. (Obtaining court approval is unnecessary when the lender issues a deed of trust, not a mortgage. The two documents are virtually the same, except that the holder of a deed of trust can forego court involvement.) Then the lender publishes a notice of the sale in a newspaper. Between the dates when the notice is published and the sale takes place, most lenders let you reinstate the loan by making up the back payments and penalties.

If you don't reinstate the loan or sell the house, the lender will "accelerate" the loan. This means you no longer can reinstate the loan. The only way you can keep your house is by paying the entire balance immediately.

If you don't pay the balance, your house will be sold at a foreclosure sale. Anyone with a financial interest in your house will attend. The house is sold to the highest bidder.

Even if your problem looks long-term, the lender may try to work with you to avoid foreclosure. In the past, lenders were quick to start foreclosure proceedings. In recent years, however, they have looked at new ways to work out mortgage delinquencies short of foreclosure.

When Your Loan Is Owned by the Federal Government

Millions of American homeowners' loans are owned by one of the giant U.S. government mortgage holders, Fannie Mae or Freddie Mac. Historically, Fannie Mae has worked with homeowners in trouble by automatically cutting interest rates or taking other steps to avoid foreclosure. On the other hand, Freddie Mac has been quick to grab a house when a loan is delinquent.

Early in 1996, Fannie Mae and Freddie Mac did a sort of role reversal. Fannie Mae is cutting its loan modifications by as much as 75%, thereby dramatically increasing the number of foreclosures. Freddie Mac, by contrast, plans to reduce foreclosures by 50% by offering rate reductions, term extension and other changes for people in financial distress. Freddie Mac is especially anxious to work with people experiencing involuntary financial problems such as an illness, death of a spouse or job loss. While Freddie Mac made only 88 loan modifications in 1994, it hopes to make at least 2,500 a year starting in 1996.

3. Utility and Telephone Bills

Most electric, gas, water and telephone companies will let you get two or three months behind before turning off your service or taking other steps to collect what you owe.

Many utility companies offer reduced rates to elderly and low income people and have emergency funds to help pay the bills of low-income people. If you face high heating bills in the winter or air conditioning bills in the summer, you may want to see if your utility company offers "level payments." This means that the annual bill is averaged and paid in equal payments over 12 months. During a designated month of the year, the actual bills are calculated against your level payments and you are either billed for the balance owed or given a refund for any overpayment.

To find out if you qualify for reduced rates, level payments or other programs offered by the utility company, call and ask. In addition, in many areas, charitable groups—especially religious organizations—offer assistance to low-income people needing help with their utility bills. You should probably take advantage of any assistance available to you. It can be a real hassle, and expensive, to get your utility service back after it's been shut off for nonpayment of your bill.

4. Car Payments

Handling car payments depends on whether you buy or lease your vehicle.

a. Purchase Payments

If you suspect you'll have trouble making your car payments for several months, your best bet is to sell the car, pay off the lender and use whatever is left to pay your other debts or to buy a used car that can get you where you need to go.

If you want to hold onto your car and you miss a payment, call the lender *immediately* and speak to someone in the customer service or collections department. Don't delay. Cars can be, and often are, repossessed within hours of the time payment was due. One reason is that the creditor doesn't have to get a court judgment before seizing the car. Another reason is that cars lose value fast—if the creditor has to auction it off, it wants the largest possible return.

Finance companies are most likely to grab a car as soon as you miss a payment. Banks will often wait a little while longer. Credit unions can be quite patient, especially if you explain your situation.

If you present a convincing explanation of why your situation is temporary, the lender will probably grant you an extension, meaning that you can make the delinquent payment at the end of your loan period. The lender probably won't grant an extension unless you've made at least six payments on time. Also, most lenders charge a fee for granting an extension, and don't grant more than one a year.

Instead of granting an extension, the lender may rewrite the loan to reduce the monthly payments. This means, however, that you'll have to pay longer and you'll have to pay more total interest.

b. Lease Payments

Nearly 30% of new car owners lease, rather than purchase, automobiles. The reasons are many—but most people like the low monthly payments which accompany vehicle lease contracts.

If you can't afford your lease payments, your first step is to review your lease agreement. If your total obligation under the lease is less than $25,000 and the lease term exceeds four months (virtually all car leases meet these two requirements), the federal Consumer Leasing Act (15 U.S.C. §§ 1667-1667e) requires that your lease include the following:

- A written statement of costs, including the amount of the down payment and any security deposit; the number, amount and dates of your regular payments; the total amount of all payments; and the amount you must pay for license, registration, taxes and other fees.
- Other terms under the lease, such as the kinds of insurance you must have, any extended warranty you are required to purchase, the penalty for defaulting or how to terminate the lease early.

(The Federal Reserve Board is considering amendments to the Consumer Leasing Act. The amendments would require, among other things, that the auto lease contain a warning that you may have to pay a "substantial charge" if you end the lease early.)

If you want to cancel your lease, look carefully at the provisions of your lease agreement describing what happens if you default and how you can terminate the lease early. Many lease agreements include formulas to determine the amount owed for early cancellation that are too difficult to understand.

If you find yourself in this situation, write to the dealer stating that you want to terminate the lease early. (Keep a copy of the letter.) The dealer will contact you telling you that you owe a certain amount of money, based on the formula. Write a second letter stating that the formula in the lease agreement is ambiguous (too complex to understand). State further that you know you are entitled to sue for damages because of the dealer's failure to use a reasonable formula. Finally, state that you are willing to waive your right to sue if the dealer will drop his claim against you. If the dealer refuses to back off, consider hiring a lawyer to write some letters. The lawyer won't really say anything different than what you said, but the lawyer's letterhead carries clout.

Sample Letter to Cancel Car Lease

Motor Credit
7300 Main Blvd.
Wayne, NJ 07400

June 17, 19xx

Re: Lease Number CL349902-43492

To Whom It May Concern:

I can no longer make the payments required under my car lease. I plan to return the vehicle to your dealership tomorrow at 10:00 am.

I have reviewed the clause in my lease agreement which dictates how much I must pay in the event I terminate the lease early. I do not understand the formula. It is ambiguous and complex. Under the federal Consumer Leasing Act (15 U.S.C. §§ 1667-1667e), I am not obligated to make additional payments after terminating a lease if the termination formula is unreasonable.

Furthermore, I know that I am entitled to sue you for damages because of your failure to use a reasonable formula. I am willing to waive my right to sue if you will waive your claim for additional payments because of my early termination.

Sincerely,

David Gold

David Gold

5. Loans Where You Pledged Collateral Other Than a Motor Vehicle

If a personal loan or store agreement is secured—for example, you pledged a refrigerator or couch as collateral for your repayment—the lender probably won't reduce what you owe. Instead, it may threaten to send a truck over and take the property. Rarely do lenders repossess personal property other than motor vehicles, however, because appliances and furniture bring in little money at auctions. Thus, if you simply stop paying, the lender will probably sue you before grabbing your new couch.

If you propose something reasonable, the lender may extend your loan or rewrite it to reduce the monthly payments. This will keep the property from being repossessed and keep you from being sued.

6. Student Loans

Under certain circumstances, you may be able to cancel your obligation to repay your student loans, defer your payments or enter into a payment schedule that fits with your income. If you're in default, you may be able to get out of default and avoid being sued, having your wages garnished or having your tax refunds taken.

The student loan scheme is quite complex, depending on the type of loan you have and when you obtained it. Before taking action on your loan, you must understand what kind of loan it is. Your ability to negotiate with your lender, defer your payments or possibly cancel your loan may depend on the type of loan you have.

Watch for one wrinkle when determining what type of loan you have. In 1994, the federal government initiated a new student loan program, called the Federal Direct Loan Program. Under the new plan, the government makes loans directly to students, eliminating the role of financial institutions in up to 40% of new loans. So if you've recently obtained a federally guaranteed Stafford, PLUS or consolidation loan, it may have come through the new program—straight from the government—rather than through a financial institution. If you have a direct loan, your repayment options may differ from those available through financial institutions.

 Further information on student loans may be found in the following:
- The Student Guide, *published by the U.S. Department of Education. You can obtain a copy from the Department of Education's*

Federal Student Aid Information Center (800-433-3243) or the Department of Education's Debt Collection Services Office (800-621-3115).

- Money Troubles: Legal Strategies to Cope With Your Debts, *by Robin Leonard (Nolo Press). This book has an entire chapter on student loans.*
- Take Control of Your Student Loans, *by Robin Leonard and Shae Irving (Nolo Press), available spring 1997.*

a. Canceling a Student Loan

You may be able to cancel a federal student loan under one of the following circumstances:

- You become totally and permanently disabled.
- The former student dies.
- You serve in the U.S. military.
- You're a full-time elementary or secondary school teacher in a designated area serving low-income students.
- You're a full-time teacher of children with disabilities in a public or other nonprofit elementary or secondary school.
- You're a full-time professional provider of early intervention services for the disabled.
- You're a full-time teacher of math, science, foreign languages, bilingual education or other fields designated as teacher-shortage areas.
- You're a full-time employee of a public or nonprofit agency providing services to low-income, high-risk children and their families.
- You're a full-time nurse or medical technician.
- You're a full-time law enforcement or corrections officer.
- You're a full-time staff member in a Head Start program.
- You're a Peace Corps or VISTA volunteer.
- Your school closed before you could complete your program of study.
- Your school falsely certified that you were eligible for a student loan.

To cancel a student loan—or to determine if you qualify for cancellation—call the holder of your loan or the Department of Education's Debt Collection Services Office at the 800-621-3115.

b. Obtaining a Deferment of Your Student Loan Payments

You may be able to defer (postpone) repayment of a federal student loan if you are not in default—that is, you have made your payments on time, are in the grace period after graduation or have been granted other deferments. For more details about obtaining deferments on the types of loans listed below as well as other types (such as loans for health professionals), see the two Nolo Press resources listed above.

Any Federal Loan Disbursed After July 1, 1993

- You are enrolled in school at least half-time.
- You are enrolled in an approved graduate fellowship program or a rehabilitation program for the disabled.
- You are unable to find full-time employment.
- You are suffering from economic hardship.

In addition, you can defer a Perkins loan for any reason listed in Section a, above, except the first and the last two.

Stafford, SLS and Consolidation Loans Disbursed Before July 1, 1993

- You are in school full-time.
- You are disabled and enrolled in full-time rehabilitation training.
- You, your spouse, or one of your dependents are temporarily totally disabled.
- You are in the military.
- You are a full-time volunteer in a tax-exempt organization, the Peace Corps or an ACTION program.
- You are on active duty with the National Oceanic and Atmospheric Administration Corps.
- You are a full-time teacher in a government-identified teacher shortage area.

- You are completing a professional internship.
- You are unemployed, but looking for work.
- You are the mother of preschool children, are entering or reentering the work force and are earning no more than $1 per hour above the federal minimum wage.
- You are on parental leave.

PLUS Loans Disbursed Before July 1, 1993

- You are in school full-time.
- You are disabled and enrolled in full-time rehabilitation training.
- You are temporarily totally disabled.
- You are in the military.
- You are a full-time volunteer in a tax-exempt organization, the Peace Corps or an ACTION program.
- You are a commissioned officer in the U.S. Public Health Service.
- You are completing a professional internship.
- You are unemployed, but are looking for work.

Perkins Loans Disbursed Before July 1, 1993

- You are in school full-time.
- You are disabled and enrolled in full-time rehabilitation training.
- You are temporarily totally disabled.
- You are in the military.
- You are a full-time volunteer in a tax-exempt organization, the Peace Corps or an ACTION program.
- You are on active duty with the National Oceanic and Atmospheric Administration Corps.
- You are completing a professional internship.
- You are the mother of preschool children, are entering or reentering the work force and are earning no more than $1 per hour above the federal minimum wage.
- You are on parental leave.

To obtain a deferment of a federal student loan, contact the current holder of your loan. If you don't know who currently holds your loan, contact the financial or educational institution you initially borrowed from. If that institution has sold your loan or sent it elsewhere, it will tell you.

Ask the holder of your loan to send you a deferment application form. Fill it out thoroughly. The holder of your loan may require that you submit supporting documentation, such as periodic verifications of your job search if you obtain an unemployment deferment. Be sure to comply.

c. Obtaining a Forbearance of Your Student Loan Payments

If you don't qualify for a deferment, but are facing hard times financially, your lender may still allow you to postpone payments or temporarily reduce them. An arrangement of this sort is called a forbearance. Forbearances are easier to obtain than deferments—you may be able to obtain a forbearance even if your loan is in default—but forbearance is less attractive because interest continues to accrue during the time when you are not making payments, no matter what type of loan you have.

Lenders typically have the authority to grant forbearances in six-month increments for up to two years. There is no stated condition for qualifying; it's simply up to the lender. Call your lender and ask.

d. Consolidating Your Student Loans

If you want to repay your loans but can't afford the payments and don't qualify for cancellation, deferment or forbearance, you may be able to consolidate your loans.

When you consolidate, you lower your monthly payments by combining multiple loans into one packaged loan and extending your current repayment period. You may also be able to refinance several loans, or just one loan, at a lower interest rate. But be aware that if you extend your repayment period, you will increase the amount of money you pay in interest over the life of your loan—sometimes dramatically. Even so, consolidation is one way to keep your head above water and avoid default. And if you've already defaulted, consolidation can help you get back on track.

1. Extending the Time to Repay

You can stretch the term of your loan from its original length—typically ten years—to 12-30 years, depending on how much money you owe. You can choose a fixed monthly payment for the life of your loan or "step-up" payments that start low and increase over time.

If you still can't afford your payments, you can request a repayment plan based on your income level. Under the government's direct lending program, you can obtain an income-contingent repayment plan that bases your monthly payments on your annual income and loan amount. As your income rises and falls, so do your payments. Payments may be as low as 4% of your adjusted gross income. If, after 25 years, you're still making payments, the government will wipe out your remaining debt (though present tax laws would require that you report your forgiven debt as taxable income).

Inspired by the federal competition, private lenders have recently developed income-sensitive plans. These plans are similar to the government's income-contingent plan, but there are no provisions for forgiveness after 25 years.

2. Lowering Your Interest Rate

The government's direct lending program offers a unique reason to consider its loan consolidation program rather than a consolidation program with a private lender: a variable interest rate that will never exceed 8.25% (9% on PLUS loans). If your loans carry a higher interest rate, it may be to your advantage to consolidate them or refinance. You can still extend the payment period, too, if you can't make the payments at the lower interest rate.

If you consolidate your loans with a private lender, you'll get only a small interest rate reduction, if any. Your new loan will carry a fixed rate, based on the average rate of all the loans you consolidate. But ask your lender about other ways to reduce the rate. For example, Sallie Mae—one of the largest private loan consolidators—will cut your interest rate by 1/4% if you authorize automatic payments from your bank account, and will knock a full percentage point off the rate if you make your loan payments on time for 48 consecutive months.

e. Requesting a Flexible Payment Option

If you have a federal direct Stafford loan, you can pay it back in any of the four ways listed below. If you have a federal direct PLUS loan, you can pay it back in any of the first three ways:

- the standard ten-year repayment schedule
- an extended repayment schedule—the length of your payback period depends on the amount of your loan—from 12 years for loans under $10,000 to 30 years for loans over $60,000
- a graduated repayment schedule—you can pay off your loan in as many as 30 years by making lower payments in the early years of the loan and higher payments later, and
- an income-contingent repayment plan—your payments change each year based on the amount of your income and student loan.

While these payment options can offer much relief, opting for one could cost you a lot. For example, if you stretch your payments out for 20 or 30 years, you will wind up paying thousands—possibly tens of thousands—of dollars more in interest than you would have if you paid your loans off in ten years. While financial institutions are not obligated to offer extended, graduated or income-contingent repayment plans, many do so in order to remain competitive with the government direct lending program.

f. Getting Out of Default

You can get out of default through the government's "reasonable and affordable" payment program (you and the agency holding your loan decide what is reasonable and affordable based on your income and expenses), even if you've been sued and there is a court judgment against you. It is a once-in-a-lifetime opportunity. If you default again, the government will not grant you another reasonable and affordable plan.

If you make six consecutive monthly payments under your reasonable and affordable plan, you will be out of default sufficient enough to be eligible for a new student loan if you want to return to school. You will also be eligible for deferment.

Once you make 12 consecutive reasonable and affordable monthly payments, the agency holding your loan can sell it to a company that handles payments and collections of student loans, and can remove the default notation from your credit record. Once your loan is sold, you will be given ten years to repay it. If you've been paying very small amounts for 12 months, the new monthly payments probably will rise dramatically. If you can't afford them, you will need to request one of the flexible repayment options described above.

7. Insurance Policies

Most insurance policies have 30-day grace periods—that is, if your payment is due on the tenth of the month and you don't pay until the ninth of the following month, you won't lose your coverage. A few companies won't terminate your policy as long as you pay your premium within 60 days of when it's due. If you don't pay within 60 days, your policy will surely be canceled.

If you want to keep your insurance coverage, contact your insurance agent. You can reduce the amount of your coverage or increase your deductible, thereby reducing your premiums. This can usually be done easily for auto, medical, dental, renter's, life and disability insurance. It will be harder for homeowner's insurance, because you'll probably have to get authorization from your mortgage lender, who won't want your house to be under-insured.

If you have a life insurance policy with a cash value—an amount of money building up that you'll receive if you cancel the policy before it pays out—you usually can apply the money that represents the cash value toward your premiums. The company will treat the use of the cash value as a loan. Your policy's cash value won't decrease, but you are theoretically required to repay the money. (If you don't repay it, when you die, the proceeds your beneficiaries receive will be reduced by what you borrowed.) Or, you can simply ask that the cash reserves be used to pay the premiums. This will reduce your cash value, but you won't have to repay anything.

Perhaps the best way to keep life insurance coverage while reducing the payments is to convert a whole or universal policy (with relatively high premiums and a cash value build-up) into a term policy (with low premiums and no cash value.) You may lose a little of the existing cash value as a conversion fee, but it may be worthwhile if you get a policy that costs far less to maintain.

8. Doctors', Dentists', Lawyers' and Accountants' Bills

Many doctors, dentists, lawyers and accountants are accommodating if you communicate how difficult your financial problems are and try to get their sympathy. They may accept partial payments, reduce the total bill, drop interest or late fees and delay sending bills to collection agencies.

9. Credit and Charge Card Bills

If you can't pay your credit card bill (including a department store or gasoline card bill), contact the credit card company. Most will insist that you make the minimum monthly payment, usually 5% of the outstanding bill, but in no event less than $20. If you convince the company that your financial situation is bleak, it may reduce your payments to 2%-2.5% of the outstanding balance. And if you have an excellent payment history, the company may let you skip a month or two altogether.

⚠ *By paying less than the full bill, you incur interest charges. At an average annual interest rate of 17%, this is a strategy you will want to employ only temporarily. Otherwise, your balance will increase faster than you will be able to pay it off.*

While you are paying off your balance, some credit card companies will help by waiving late fees. It's almost impossible to get a credit card company to reduce interest that has already accumulated. Some will stop the addition of future interest charges, however, if you get assistance from Consumer Credit Counseling Service. (See Appendix 1.) The company will also probably freeze your credit line—that is, not let you incur any more charges—if you pay less than the minimum.

Ask the company to report your payments to a credit bureau as on time while you pay off your balance. If you keep to the new schedule, the credit card company shouldn't report the debt as past due.

If you can't pay a charge card—such as American Express or Diners' Club—you must approach the creditor differently than with a credit card. Normally, you are required to pay off your entire charge card balance when your bill arrives. If you don't, you'll get one month's grace, when no interest is charged. After that, you'll be charged interest in the neighborhood of 20%. Call the charge card company and ask that you be given a monthly repayment plan for paying off the bill. Offer to pay only what you can afford—but remember, if you pay only a very small amount, interest will accumulate—and your balance will go up—faster than you're able to pay it off. The company usually doesn't report this arrangement to credit bureaus if you pay the monthly amount you agreed to.

a. If You Dispute a Credit or Charge Card Bill

If you use a credit or charge card and don't receive a product, receive a defective item or get substandard service, you can legally refuse to pay if all of the following are true:

- You attempt in good faith to resolve the dispute with the merchant who refuses to replace, repair or otherwise correct the problem.
- Your credit card or charge card was not issued by the seller—for example, you used a Visa, MasterCard, American Express or Discover card, not a Sears or Chevron card.
- The purchase was for more than $50 and was made within the state in which you live or within 100 miles of your home. The 100-mile limit is easy to calculate when purchases are made in person. For example, if you live in northern New Jersey and buy a suit in New York City (about 25 miles away), you can refuse to pay if the suit falls apart and the seller won't make good. But if you live in Georgia and order that same suit from the New York store over the telephone, is the purchase made in Georgia or New York (more than 100 miles away)?

It's unclear. Tell the credit card company that the purchase was made in Georgia and assert your right to refuse to pay. The credit card company will ask the seller for its version of the dispute. Usually, the seller won't push the issue, as it would rather keep you as a customer, even if it means writing off the bill. If the seller refuses to compromise, the credit card company will include the charge on your monthly bill and add interest each month. After several months, the company may threaten to cancel your credit card account if you don't pay. Some companies will let you keep the account, as long as you make payments on the undisputed balance. If you conclude that you are entitled to withhold payment, write to the credit card company at the billing address and explain why you aren't paying. Detail how you tried to resolve the problem with the merchant. Use *Form F-4: Dispute Credit Card Bill* in Appendix 3. Always keep a copy for your own records.

b. If Your Bill Contains an Error

If you find an error in your credit or charge card statement, immediately write a letter to the company that issued the card; don't just scribble a note on the bill. The credit or charge card company must receive your letter within 60 days after it mailed the bill to you. You can use *Form F-5: Error on Credit Card Bill* in Appendix 3. Give your name, account number, an explanation of the error and the amount involved. Also enclose copies of supporting documents, such as receipts showing the correct amount of the charge. Send the letter to the customer service department—look on the back of the bill—not to the billing address.

The credit or charge card company must acknowledge receipt of your letter within 30 days, unless it corrects the bill within that time. The card issuer must, within two billing cycles (but in no event more than 90 days from when it receives your letter), correct the error or explain why it believes the amount to be correct. If the card company does not comply with these time limits, you don't have to pay $50 of the disputed balance, even if you are wrong.

During the two-billing-cycle/90-day period, the card issuer cannot report to a credit bureau or other creditors that the disputed amount is delinquent. Likewise, the card issuer cannot threaten or actually take any collection action against you for the disputed amount. But it can include the disputed amount on your monthly billing statements. And it can apply the amount in dispute to your credit limit, thereby lowering the total credit available to you. Furthermore, the credit or charge card company can add interest to your bill on the amount you dispute, but if the company later agrees you were correct, it must drop the interest accrued.

If the card company sends you an explanation but doesn't correct the error and you are not satisfied with its reason, you have ten days to respond. Send a second letter explaining why you still refuse to pay. If the card company then reports your account as delinquent to a credit bureau or anyone else, it must also state that you dispute that you owe the money.

⚠️ *Check your credit file following a billing dispute or error. Despite laws designed to protect consumers, a credit card company may negligently report an outstanding balance it removed from your card or fail to report that you dispute a charge. Be sure to check your credit file. (See Chapter 4, Sections B, C and D.)*

B. Use the Form Negotiation Letters Provided in This Book

Negotiating with your creditors to request a reduction, extension or other repayment program can be somewhat intimidating. Fortunately, sending a short letter can simplify the process considerably. Appendix 3 includes several form letters you can send to creditors. Use these to confirm telephone conversations or to start the negotiation process. You can fill in the blanks and send the forms, or, if you prefer, retype the letters. Be sure to keep a copy of whatever you send.

At the top of the form you're using, above the "Attn: Collections Department" line, type or write the creditor's name and address. Most items on the forms are self-explanatory. At the bottom, be sure to sign your name and provide the address that appears on your bill. If you are asking the creditor to get in touch with you, include your home phone number.

If you use Forms F-6, F-7, F-8, F-9 or F-10 you will need to state reasons why you can't make the full payment. Here are what creditors and lenders look for:

- job layoff, reduction in hours, sporadic employment or pay cut, coupled with a good faith effort to find work or increase income
- large and unexpected tax assessment

- divorce or separation—your responsibility for paying bills or your ex-spouse fails to pay bills the court ordered him or her to pay
- permanent or temporary disability—temporary disabilities may include a heart attack, stroke or cancer, or something less drastic like repetitive motion syndrome, or
- inadequate medical insurance coverage following a major illness or accident.

C. Deal With Creditors on Past Due Accounts

It's important to know if the person trying to collect your past due debt works for the business or person who first extended you credit (the creditor) or for a company or lawyer hired by a creditor to collect the creditor's debt (a collection agency). A collection agency also includes a creditor who sets up a separate office (operated under a different name) to collect its debts. Depending on who is trying to collect, you have different legal rights and may want to employ different strategies. If any of your debts are being pursued by a collection agency, read Section D, below.

⚠️ *Don't assume you must deal with a collector. If you have no money, plan to file for bankruptcy or just don't feel like paying right now, you can opt to not speak with the collector at all. Or you may want to seek outside help. Depending on the complexity of your situation and your negotiation skills, negotiating with your creditors on your own may not always be wise. A savvy lender who refuses to rewrite your car loan may think twice if he hears from a credit counselor or lawyer. (See Appendix 1.)*

If you have past due accounts, you may be able to take care of the debts and start repairing your credit. Here are two requests you can make to a creditor using *Form F-6: Make Payment If Negative Removed or Account Re-aged* in Appendix 3:

- Ask that an unpaid debt and negative information in your credit file associated with the debt be removed from your credit file in exchange for full or partial payment. Some creditors will agree to report your account as "nonevaluated" rather than as past due or formerly past due.
- If the creditor puts you on a new schedule for repaying the debt, ask the creditor to "re-age" your account, meaning it makes the current month the first repayment month and shows no late payments. Sometimes, the creditor won't re-age the account until you make two or three monthly payments first.

Not all creditors remove negative marks or re-age accounts, but it never hurts to ask. Contact the creditor's collections or customer service department and make an offer. Tell whomever you speak to that you cannot afford to pay more, but that you'd really like to pay a good portion of the bill. Explain your financial problems—be bleak, but never lie. Get the creditor's agreement in writing (send your own confirming letter if need be) before sending any money.

When negotiating, it's helpful to know at what stage you stand in the collection process. Collection efforts almost always begin with past due invoices or letters. One day, you open your mail box and find a polite letter from a creditor reminding you that you seemed to have overlooked the company's most recent bill. "Perhaps it's already in the mail. If so, please accept our thanks. If not, we'd appreciate prompt payment," the letter or invoice states.

This "past due" form letter is the kind that almost every creditor sends to a customer with an overdue account. If you ignore it, you'll get a second one, also automatically sent. In this letter, most creditors remain friendly, but want to know what the problem is. "If you have some special reason for withholding payment, please let us know. We are here to help." Some creditors also suspend your credit at this point; the only way to get it back is to send a payment.

Tips on Negotiating With Creditors

You are most vulnerable at this time. Be sure you truly understand any new loan terms and can afford to make the payments under a new agreement.

- Get outside help negotiating if you need or want it.
- If you're told "no" in response to any request, ask to speak to a supervisor.
- Adopt a plan and stick with it. If you owe $1,100 but can't afford to pay more than $600, don't agree to pay more.
- Try to identify the creditor's bottom line. For example, if a bank offers to waive two months' interest if you pay the principal due on your loan, perhaps the bank will actually waive three or four months of interest. If you need to, push it.
- Don't split the difference. If you offer a low amount to settle a debt and the creditor proposes that you split the difference between a higher demand and your offer, don't agree to it. Treat the split-the-difference number as a new top and propose an amount between that and your original offer.
- Don't be intimidated by your creditors. If they think you can pay $100, they will insist that $100 is the lowest amount they can accept. Don't believe them. It's fine to hang up and call back a day later. Some of the best negotiations may take weeks.
- Try to settle with a lump sum. Many creditors will settle for less than the total debt if you pay in a lump sum, but will insist on 100% if you pay over time. If so, try to get the money to settle the matter. (See Chapter 1, Section C.2.)
- Get a signed release. If you settle for less than the full amount owed, make sure the creditor signs a release stating that your partial payment excuses you from the remaining balance.
- Be careful not to give up more than you get. A creditor may waive interest, reduce your payments or let you skip a payment and tack it on at the end. But tread cautiously. She is likely to ask for something in exchange, such as getting a cosigner (who will be liable for the debt if you don't pay, even if you erase the debt in bankruptcy), waiving the statute of limitations (the number of years the lender has to sue you if you stop making payments), paying higher interest, paying for a longer period or giving a security interest in your house or car.

Forms for Negotiating With Creditors

No.	Form Name	Use if ...
F-7	Request Short-Term Small Payments	You need a few months to make reduced payments but then intend to resume full payments.
F-8	Request Long-Term Small Payments	You need to make reduced payments indefinitely.
F-9	Request Short-Term Pay Nothing	You can't make any payment for a few months but intend to resume full payments shortly.
F-10	Request Long-Term Pay Nothing	You've concluded that your situation is bleak and you cannot make any payment for an indefinite period.
F-11	Request Rewrite of Loan Terms	You would like the lender to rewrite the loan to permanently reduce the amount of each payment.
F-12	Offer to Give Secured Property Back	You want the lender to take the collateral back, making sure you won't owe any balance on the debt after the property is taken back.
F-13	Cashing Check Constitutes Payment in Full (Outside of California)	You live outside of California and plan to send the creditor part of what you owe with a notation on the check, "cashing this check constitutes payment in full."
F-14 & F-15	Cashing Check Constitutes Payment in Full (California)	You live in California and want to send the creditor part of what you owe with a notation on the check, "cashing this check constitutes payment in full."
		You must send two forms. The first (Form F-14) is to let the creditor know you intend to send a partial check. In that letter you must identify a dispute you have with the creditor. If the creditor does not object within 15 days, you send the second (Form F-15) along with the check. The second must be sent between 15 and 90 days after the first.
F-16	Inform Creditor of Judgment Proof Status	You have no property that can be taken by your creditors to pay what you owe them, even if you file for bankruptcy or they sue you. (This is called being judgment proof.) You are judgment proof if your only source of income is government benefits or disability, you have little or no equity in a house or car, and you have limited personal property.
F-17	Inform Creditor of Plan to File for Bankruptcy	You plan to file for bankruptcy. Incur no more charges on the account after sending the letter. If you do, you will not be able to erase those debts in bankruptcy, because the creditor will argue that you knew you were going to file and incurred debts anyway, never intending to pay.

If you don't answer the second letter, you'll probably receive three to five more form letters. Each will get slightly firmer. By the last letter, expect a threat: "If we do not receive payment within ten days, your credit privileges will be canceled. Your account will be sent to a collection agency and your delinquency will be reported to a credit reporting agency. You could face a lawsuit, wage attachment or lien on your property."

After you've received a series of collection letters, you may conclude that you no longer have leverage to negotiate. Nonsense. You always have leverage because you have what they want—money.

Appendix 3 includes several form letters you can use to send to creditors for your past due accounts. The forms are described below. Find the form that fits your situation and send it off.

If the creditor rejects your proposal or wants more evidence that you are genuinely unable to pay, consider asking a credit counselor with Consumer Credit Counseling Service to intervene on your behalf. (See Appendix 1.)

Or, if the debt is quite large, or one of many, consider hiring a lawyer to write a second letter asking for additional time. The lawyer won't say anything different than you would, but a lawyer's stationery carries clout. And it especially may be worth the few hundred dollars if you have many outstanding debts and need substantial help. When a creditor learns that a lawyer is in the picture, the creditor may be willing to compromise, assuming that you'll file for bankruptcy if he isn't accommodating.

⚠ *Be specific with the lawyer about what you want done. If you're not clear that you want the lawyer only to write a letter to your creditors on your behalf, the lawyer may do much more and send you a bill for work you didn't authorize and can't afford, giving you one more debt to add to your pile.*

D. Deal With Collection Agencies

If you ignored (or didn't receive) the creditor's letters and phone calls, or you failed to make payments as promised on a new repayment schedule, your bill was probably turned over to a collection agency.

Start by understanding a major point. A person who works at a collection agency is not your friend and does not have your best interest at heart. *He wants your money.* To get it, he may ask you to take him into his confidence regarding your personal problems. He may claim that he's trying to save you from ruining your credit. Or he may pose as your friend and counselor. Don't believe him. A collection agent doesn't really care about your problems or your credit rating. His only goal is to get you to send him money.

By taking some time to understand how collection agencies operate, you'll know how to respond when they contact you.

Point 1. A collection agency takes its cues from the creditor that hired it. The collection agency can't sue you without the creditor's authorization, although that authorization is routinely granted. Similarly, if the creditor insists that the agency collect 100% of the debt, the agency cannot accept less from you, although it can agree to accept installment payments. To reduce the total amount you pay, the collection agency must get the creditor's okay, or you'll have to contact the creditor yourself.

Contacting the creditor directly can often be to your benefit because the creditor has broader discretion in negotiating than does the collection agency. Unfortunately, however, some creditors won't deal with you after your debt has been sent to a collection agency, unless you raise a legitimate dispute with the creditor or make three consecutive monthly payments to the collection agency first. (See Point 5, below.) Even if you don't have a dispute, try negotiating with the creditor before negotiating with a collection agency. Send *Form F-18: Request Direct Negotiation With Creditor* in

Appendix 3 to the collection agency, with a copy to the creditor.

Point 2. A collection agent will try to contact you very soon after the creditor hires the agency. Professional debt collectors know that the earlier they strike, the higher their chance of collecting. For example, if an account is three months overdue, bill collectors typically have a 75% chance of collecting it. If it's six months late, the chances of collecting drop to 50%. And if the bill's been owed for more than a year, collectors have only a one in four chance of recovering the debt.

Point 3. Bill collecting is a serious—and lucrative—business. Collection agents are good at what they do. One owner of an agency bragged that before offering a job to someone, he observed the person's body language, had the person make mock collection calls, administered IQ and polygraph tests, and checked employment agency and credit bureau reports.

Point 4. A collection agency usually keeps between 25% and 60% of what it collects. The older the account, the higher the agency's fee. Sometimes, the agency charges per letter it writes or phone call it places—usually about 50¢ per letter or $1 per call. Thus, some collection agencies are very aggressive about contacting debtors.

Point 5. If you're contacted by a collection agency, you can delay collection efforts if you raise legitimate questions about the debt. For example, if you question the accuracy of the balance owed or the quality of the goods you received, the agency will have to verify the information with the creditor. If you raise a legitimate concern, the collection agency will send the debt back to the creditor—collection agencies don't pursue debtors who have a beef with creditors. Getting the debt sent back to the creditor should remove any "sent to collection agency" notation in your credit file.

Use *Form F-19: Dispute Amount of Bill or Quality of Goods or Services Received* in Appendix 3 to raise a legitimate concern about the amount of a bill or the quality of goods or services received with a collection agency.

1. Getting a Collection Agency Off Your Back

You have the legal right to tell a collection agency to leave you alone. Simply write to the collection agency and tell it to cease all communications with you. Use *Form F-20: Collection Agency: Cease All Contact* in Appendix 3. By law, the agency must then stop contacting you, except to tell you that:

- collection efforts against you have ended, or
- the collection agency or creditor will invoke a specific remedy against you, such as suing you.

If a collection agent contacts you to tell you that she intends to invoke a specific remedy, she must truly plan to do so. She cannot simply write to you several times saying "we're going to sue you" and then drop the matter.

2. Negotiating With a Collection Agency

Although most creditors initially insist that collection agencies collect 100% of a debt, if you make a sweet enough offer, the collection agency may convince the creditor to accept less. Often, the creditor has all but given up on you and will be thrilled if the collection agency can collect anything. Knowing that, keep in mind the following:

- The collection agency didn't lay out the money initially. It doesn't care if you owe $250 or $2,500. It just wants to maximize its return, which is usually a percentage of what it collects.
- Time is money. Every time the collection agency writes or calls you, it spends money. The agency has a strong interest in getting you to pay as much as you can as fast as possible. It has less interest in collecting 100% over five years.

3. Offering a Lump-Sum Settlement

A collection agency has more incentive to settle with you if you can pay all at once. If you owe $500 and offer $300 on the spot to settle the matter, the agency can take its fee, pass the rest on to the creditor (who writes off the difference on its tax return as a business loss) and close its books.

If you decide to offer a lump sum, understand that no two collection agencies accept the same amount to settle a debt. Some want 75%-80%. Others—especially when they are the second or third agency to try to collect your debt—will take 50¢ on the dollar. But be careful. Once the agency sees you are willing to pay something, it will assume it can talk you into paying more. Which of course is a good reason to start by offering less than you know you can pay.

Although you don't want to agree to pay more than what you initially decided was your top amount, if you can get the debt removed from your credit file in exchange for paying a little more, it may be worth it. But don't let the collection agency know where that money is coming from. If you mention a parent, friend or distant relative who "may be able to help" you out, the collection agent will sit back and wait for the entire amount. And never agree to more than you can truly pay. Whatever you agree to over the phone, be sure to send a confirming letter and keep a copy for your records. You could use *Form F-13: Cashing Check Constitutes Payment in Full* and describe your agreement in the blank space above "Sincerely." For example, "This check is being sent per our agreement of October 2, 19xx, in which you agreed to accept $565 as payment in full for my outstanding bill."

4. Offering to Make Payments

If you offer to make monthly payments, the agency has little incentive to compromise for less than the full amount. It still must chase you for payment, and statistically there's a good chance that after a month or two, you'll stop paying. And you risk hurting your credit again. If you succeed in convincing the creditor (through the collection agency) to remove the "past due" notation in your credit file in exchange for paying off the debt or to re-age your account in agreement for paying under a new schedule, as soon as you miss a payment under your new agreement the past due notation goes back into your file.

But if you have no choice—you simply can't afford a lump sum—offer installments. If the creditor (through the collection agency) won't remove the negative credit file notation right away, get back in touch after you've made six months of payments and ask again for them to remove the notation. State that the negative marks are keeping you from getting good credit, a place to live, a good job or anything else you've been denied, and that with better credit/place to live/job, you will be more secure and better able to pay off the debt. Be sure to keep a copy of the letter for your records.

5. When the Collection Agency Gives Up

If collection efforts by the collection agency fail, the creditor and agency will put their heads together and decide whether or not to pass your debt on to an attorney for collection. They will consider the following:

- the likelihood of winning
- the likelihood of collecting—are you currently employed or apt to become employed, or do you have other assets from which the creditor could collect (such as a bank account or a house on which the creditor could record a lien)
- whether the contract calls for the collection of the lawyer's fees (most loan agreements and credit contracts do)—which means the collection agency can tack its lawyer's fee onto the judgment against you, and
- whether or not you recently filed for bankruptcy (you may have to wait six years to file again).

6. Illegal Debt Collection Practices

The federal Fair Debt Collections Practices Act (FDCPA) prohibits a collection agency from engaging in many kinds of activities. (15 U.S.C. § 1692 et seq.) If a collection agency violates the law, you have the right to sue both the agency and the creditor that hired the agency. If the behavior is truly outrageous, the creditor may waive the debt and remove the negative marks from your credit file in exchange for your not suing.

Under the FDCPA, a collection agency cannot legally engage in any of the following:

Communications with third parties. If you have an attorney, a collection agent must deal with your lawyer unless you give the agent permission to contact you. A collection agent cannot contact other people except to locate you. When contacting other people, the agent must state her name and that she's confirming or correcting location information about you. She cannot:

- give the collection agency's name, unless asked
- state that you owe a debt, or
- contact the person more than once unless he requests it or the agent believes his first response was wrong or incomplete.

Communications with you. A collection agent cannot contact you:

- at an unusual or inconvenient time or place—calls before 8 a.m. and after 9 p.m. are not allowed, or
- at work, if she knows that your employer prohibits you from receiving collections calls at work—if you are contacted at work, tell the collector that your boss prohibits such calls.

Harassment or abuse. A collection agent cannot engage in conduct meant to harass, oppress or abuse you. The agent cannot:

- use or threaten to use violence or to harm you, another person, or your or another person's reputation or property
- use obscene or profane language
- publish your name as a person who doesn't pay bills, such as in a "deadbeats" list

- list your debt for sale to the public
- call you repeatedly, or
- place telephone calls to you or any other person without identifying herself.

False or misleading representations. A collection agent cannot:

- claim to be a law enforcement officer, suggest that she is connected with the government or send you a document that looks like it's from a court or government agency
- falsely represent the amount you owe or the amount of compensation she will receive
- falsely claim to be an attorney or send you a document that looks like it's from a lawyer
- threaten to take action that isn't intended or can't be taken
- communicate false credit information, including failing to tell someone you dispute a debt
- use a false business name, or
- claim to be employed by a credit bureau, unless the collection agency and the credit bureau are the same company.

Unfair practices. A collection agent cannot engage in any unfair or outrageous method to collect a debt. Specifically, she can't:

- add interest, fees or charges not authorized in the original agreement or by state law
- solicit a postdated check by threatening you with criminal prosecution
- accept a check postdated by more than five days unless she notifies you between three and ten days in advance of when she will deposit it
- deposit a postdated check prior to the date on the check, or
- call you collect or otherwise cause you to incur communications charges.

7. If a Collection Agency Violates the Law

More than a few collection agencies engage in illegal practices when attempting to collect debts. Low income and non-English speaking debtors are especially vulnerable. Some collectors send fake legal papers and visit debtors, pretending to be sheriffs. The collectors tell debtors to pay immediately or threaten to take the debtors' personal possessions. Other collectors use vulgarity and profanity to threaten debtors. Another favorite tactic is to harass the debtor's parents or adult children.

If a collection agent violates the law—be it a large or small violation—complain loud and clear. If you're loud enough about the abuse you suffered—and you've got a witness backing you up—you have a chance to get the whole debt canceled in exchange for dropping the matter. Use *Form F-21: Complain of Collection Agency Harassment* in Appendix 3 to write and complain about a collection agency.

Here are some suggestions of where to send your complaint letter:

- **The creditor.** The creditor may be disturbed by the collection agency's tactics and concerned about its own reputation, and might prefer to have you come back some day as a customer than have you be abused by a collection agency.
- **The Federal Trade Commission.** (Addresses and phone numbers are in Chapter 4, Section D.)

- **Your state attorney general's or other office that regulates collection agencies.** (See Appendix 1.)

You also have the right to sue a collection agency for harassment. You can represent yourself in small claims court or hire an attorney; you can recover attorney fees and court costs if you win. You're entitled to any actual damages (including pain and suffering) and up to $1,000 in punitive damages. To win, you'll probably need to have a witness and to produce documentation of repeated abusive behavior. If the collector calls five times in one day and then you never hear from him again, you probably don't have a case.

If you sue a collection agency, you should also name the creditor as a defendant in the lawsuit. Unless the creditor sold the debt to the collection agency, the creditor may be held liable for the collection agency's actions.

For more information on debt collectors—including state laws that govern collection agencies and creditors collecting their own debts—see Money Troubles: Legal Strategies to Cope With Your Debts, *by Robin Leonard (Nolo Press).*

Cleaning Up Your Credit File

Credit bureaus are profit-making companies that gather and sell information about a person's credit history. They sell credit files to banks, mortgage lenders, credit unions, credit card companies, department stores, insurance companies, landlords and even a few employers. (Beginning September 30, 1997, employers will have to obtain your consent before requesting a copy of your credit file.) These companies and individuals use the credit files to supplement applications for credit, insurance, housing and employment.

Credit bureaus may also provide identifying information concerning a consumer—including name, address, former address, place of employment and former place of employment—to government agencies. And of course, if a government agency is considering extending credit, reviewing the status of an account or attempting to collect a debt, the agency is entitled to the complete credit report.

There are three major credit bureaus—Equifax, Trans Union and Experian (formerly known as TRW). There are also thousands of smaller credit bureaus, known as "affiliates." Open up your Yellow Pages and look under "Credit Reporting Agencies." You may see none, one, two or all three of the three major credit bureaus. You will probably also see dozens of affiliates. The affiliated companies get their information from Equifax, Trans Union and TRW/Experian, so this chapter focuses on the reports issued by those companies.

Laws Regulating Credit Bureaus

The rules regulating credit bureaus are contained in the federal Fair Credit Reporting Act (FCRA). A copy is in Appendix 2. In addition, California, Colorado, Kentucky, Maine, Michigan, Minnesota, Montana, New Hampshire, New Mexico, New York, Oklahoma, Rhode Island, Utah and Vermont have enacted laws related to credit reporting and credit bureaus. Excerpted portions of these state laws are also in Appendix 2.

⚠ *Beginning September 30, 1997, credit reporting laws will change when the Consumer Credit Reporting Reform Act of 1996 takes effect. Throughout this book, we provide you with both the law as it is and the law as it will be after September 30, 1997. Read carefully to avoid confusion. Appendix 2 is in two parts: 2a, to be used before September 30, 1997, and 2b, to be used after the laws change. One provision of the Consumer Credit Reporting Reform Act nullifies certain state laws. Therefore, if you're looking up the law after September 30, 1997, be sure to read Appendix 2b to find out if your state law was affected by the federal law changes.*

A. The Contents of a Credit Report

Information in your credit report can be broken down into five main categories:
- personal information about you
- accounts reported monthly
- accounts reported when in default
- public records, and
- inquiries.

Let's take a look at these one at a time.

1. Personal Information

A credit file usually includes your name and any former names, past and present addresses, Social Security number and employment history (including salary). If you're married, the same information may be in your file for your spouse. Credit bureaus get this information from creditors, who get it from you every time you fill out a credit application. For this reason, it is very important that your credit applications be accurate and complete.

2. Accounts Reported Monthly

The bulk of information in your credit file is your credit history. Certain creditors (see below) provide monthly reports to credit bureaus showing the status of your account with them. Your credit report will contain the following information on these accounts:

- name of the creditor
- type of account
- account number
- when the account was opened
- your payment history for the previous 24-36 months—that is, whether you take 30, 60, 90 or 120 days to pay, whether the account has been turned over to a collection agency, whether the account has been discharged in bankruptcy or whether you are disputing any charges
- your credit limit or the original amount of a loan, and
- your current balance.

Creditors who provide monthly reports generally include:

- banks, savings and loans, credit unions, finance companies and other commercial lenders that issue credit cards and make mortgage, personal, car and student loans
- non-bank credit and charge card issuers (such as American Express, Discover and Diner's Club)

- large department stores (such as Sears, J.C. Penney, Macy's and Nordstrom)
- oil and gas companies, and
- other creditors receiving regular monthly installments.

3. Accounts Reported When in Default

Many businesses provide information to credit bureaus only when an account is past due or the creditor has taken collection action against you, including turning the account over to a collection agency. In these situations, your credit report will generally include the following:

- name of the creditor
- type of account
- account number, and
- your delinquency status—whether you're 60, 90 or 120 days late, whether the account has been turned over to a collection agency or you've been sued, or whether the account has been discharged in bankruptcy.

Creditors who generally report accounts only when they are past due or in collection include:

- landlords and property managers
- utility companies
- local retailers
- insurance companies
- magazines and newspapers
- doctors and hospitals, and
- lawyers and other professionals.

4. Public Records

Public records are maintained by government agencies and accessible to anyone. Local, state and federal court filings are public records. So is the data kept at land record's offices. Credit bureaus use private companies to search public records for information such as:

- lawsuits (including a divorce)
- court judgments and judgment liens

- foreclosures
- bankruptcy filings
- tax liens
- mechanic's liens, and
- criminal arrests and convictions.

In addition, federal law requires child support enforcement agencies to report child support delinquencies of $1,000 or more to credit bureaus. Many agencies report all delinquencies, regardless of the amount.

5. Inquiries

The final items in your credit report are called "inquiries." These are the names of creditors and others (such as a potential employer) who requested a copy of your report during the previous six months (one year beginning September 30, 1997), although credit bureaus usually report inquiries for up to two years.

Credit inquiries generally fall into two categories. Some creditors request credit reports for promotional purposes—if you've ever received a pre-approved credit card application or an invitation to apply for a credit card, your credit report was reviewed and you "passed" the creditor's test. (It's usually a test of income, payment history and outstanding credit.) Other creditors review credit files periodically to check up on their customers. As a result of the check, you might have your credit line increased or your credit privileges revoked.

Creditors don't like to see a file containing a lot of inquiries. It is often a sign of a person desperately applying for credit. A creditor might assume you will be an irresponsible user of credit, or worse, a scam artist planning to commit fraud.

B. Get a Copy of Your Credit Report

The major step in repairing your credit is cleaning up your credit report. You can't do that unless you know exactly what's in it. You start by getting a copy. Then you review it and challenge the incorrect items.

You can get your credit report by asking one of the three credit bureaus listed above to send you one.

Tips for Sending Letters

Throughout the rest of this chapter, you are advised to send various letters to credit bureaus, and in some cases, your creditors. When you send a letter, try to adhere to the following guidelines:

- type your letters or neatly fill in the blanks of the letters in Appendix 3, if possible
- keep a copy for yourself
- send by certified mail, return receipt requested, and
- if you are enclosing money, use a cashier's check or money order if you have any debts in collection; otherwise the recipient of the check could pass your account number to any debt collector, which will make it easier for the collector to grab your assets to collect the debt.

---

1. How Much Does a Credit Report Cost?

You are entitled to a copy of your credit report for free if:

- **You've been denied credit because of information in your credit file.** You are entitled to a free copy of your file from the bureau that reported the information. (A creditor that denies you credit in this situation will tell you the name and address of the credit bureau reporting the information that led to the denial.) You must request your copy within 60 days of being denied credit.

- **You haven't requested a copy in the last year.** You can get a free copy of your credit report once a year from any credit bureau if you live in Georgia, Maryland, Massachusetts or Vermont. If you live in any other state, you can get a free copy of your credit report once a year from TRW/Experian.
- **Additional reasons beginning September 30, 1997.** Under the Consumer Credit Reporting Reform Act of 1996, you'll also be entitled to a free copy of your credit report if you are unemployed and planning to apply for a job within the 60 days following your request for a credit report, you receive public assistance or you believe your credit file contains errors due to fraud.

For additional copies—or to obtain a report from Trans Union or Equifax if you don't qualify for a free copy and you don't live in Georgia, Maryland, Massachusetts or Vermont—you'll have to pay a fee of $8, except in Colorado (Trans Union only, $4), Connecticut ($5 for the first report requested in a year and $7.50 for subsequent reports) and Maine (Equifax $2 and Trans Union $3). You should receive the report in a week to ten days.

2. From Which Company Should I Get My Credit Report?

You can request your credit report from one, two or all three bureaus. Here's how to decide:

- If you've been denied credit, get a copy of your credit report from the bureau that reported the information leading to the denial. If you find errors in that credit file, obtain copies of your file from the other two bureaus.
- If you're just beginning to repair your credit, get a copy of your file for free from TRW/ Experian. Again, if there are mistakes in it, you'll want to get copies of your file from the other two bureaus.

Use *Form F-22: Request Credit File* in Appendix 2 to request your credit file. The following instruc-

tions explain what information must be provided and whether any of it is optional.

Full name. A credit bureau cannot process your request without your name. It's important that you provide your full name, including generations (Jr., Sr., III) and any other versions of your name that you use, such as "Trevor J. (aka T.J.) Williams."

Date of birth. A credit bureau may provide your report without your date (or at least year) of birth. But this information helps distinguish you from anyone else with a similar name, so you should include it.

Social Security number. Many people refuse to give out their Social Security numbers to anyone other than their employers, banks and the IRS. That's fine, but realize you may have trouble getting credit or an accurate credit report. If you obtain your credit report without giving your Social Security number and it doesn't include accounts for other people, go ahead and keep your Social Security number to yourself. If, however, your file contains accounts for other people, you'll want to add your Social Security number to clear up the inaccuracies.

Spouse's name. It's not absolutely necessary, but again, it helps distinguish you from anyone else with a similar name.

Telephone number. You may not get your report if you don't include your telephone number. You may hesitate to include it, knowing that bill collectors can get it by getting a copy of your credit file. But unless it's unlisted, they can also call Directory Assistance and get it. If you're trying to repair your credit, you will want to make sure your phone number is in your file. It is one sign of stability your future creditors look for.

Current address. You won't get a copy of your credit report if you don't include your address.

Previous addresses. Credit bureaus ask for this if you've been at your current address fewer than two to five years. Again, it helps distinguish you from other people with similar names. If you don't want the bureau to have this information, you can leave it off, but your request may be rejected.

(Check one.) Check only the box that applies:

☐ I was denied credit on __. Fill in the date that you received the rejection letter and enclose a copy of it.

☐ I am requesting my annual complimentary TRW credit report. Check this box only if you are requesting your free annual report from TRW. You will need to enclose a copy of your driver's license or other document showing your full name and address.

☐ I have not been denied credit within the preceding 60 days. Check here if you haven't been denied credit and you're requesting your report from Trans Union or Equifax. Also check this box if you haven't been denied credit and you're requesting your second report within a year from TRW/Experian. Enclose a cashier's check or money order for the fee, as well as a copy of your driver's license or other document identifying you.

☐ *[After September 30, 1997]* I hereby certify that I am unemployed and intend to apply for a job within the next 60 days. Check this box only if you truly are unemployed and job searching.

☐ *[After September 30, 1997]* I hereby certify that I receive public assistance/welfare. Check this box only if you are currently receiving public aid, general assistance, aid to the blind or disabled or another form of welfare.

☐ *[After September 30, 1997]* I hereby certify that I believe there is erroneous information in my file due to fraud. Check this box if you know or think someone has applied for credit in your name, used your Social Security number or otherwise victimized you using your credit information.

Credit Bureaus' Addresses and Phone Numbers

Experian Complimentary Report
P.O. Box 8030
Layton, UT 84041-8030
(annual free copy)

or

Experian
National Consumers Assistance Center
P.O. Box 949
Allen, TX 75013
800-682-7654 or
800-422-4879
(subsequent copies or copy after credit denial)

Trans Union
P.O. Box 390
Springfield, PA 19064
601-933-1200

Equifax
P.O. Box 740241
Atlanta, GA 30374-0241
404-612-3321
404-612-3150 (fax)

One-Stop Shopping
First American Credco
9444 Balboa Avenue
San Diego, CA 92113
800-443-9342

For $30.95 (includes shipping), Confidential Credit, a service of First American Credco, will obtain your credit reports from Trans Union, TRW/Experian and Equifax, and send you one compiled report. The report indicates which information was reported by which bureau. To challenge incorrect information, you must contact the credit bureau reporting the information, not Confidential Credit. For expedited 24-hour service, send $49.95 and Confidential Credit will send the report by Airborne Express Delivery.

C. Review Your Credit Report

Review your report carefully. One of the biggest problems with credit files is that they contain incorrect or out-of-date information. TRW/Experian admits to handling 360,000 monthly complaints about errors in reports. Trans Union concedes that 50% of the people who get a copy of their report question or dispute their credit history. Sometimes credit bureaus confuse names, addresses, Social Security numbers or employers. If you have a common name, say John Brown, your file may contain information on other John Browns, John Brownes or Jon Browns. Your file may erroneously contain information on family members with similar names.

On the pages that follow are copies of credit reports from Equifax, Trans Union and TRW/Experian (the report was requested while the company was still called TRW) for the same consumer. (The consumer's name, address, phone number, Social Security number, account numbers and other identifying information have been deleted.) You will notice that the three credit bureaus report the information in very different formats, and furthermore, contain different information. For example, this consumer's Equifax report contains 21 credit entries, her Trans Union report includes 30 and her TRW/Experian report contains 27. Also, this consumer filed for—and dismissed—a bankruptcy case. Although she listed all of her debts in her bankruptcy papers, only a few specific debts are listed as having been included in her bankruptcy case—and those debts differ among the credit reports.

Here's how to read each credit report.

Equifax. Equifax is the only credit reporting agency that provides consumers with a credit report in list form filled with codes. (All three credit bureaus used to report the information this way.) Nevertheless, the Equifax report is not difficult to read. At the top of the first page, you'll find your name and address, the date, your Social Security number and your age (or in some cases, date of birth).

The only other information is your credit history. The report begins by listing each account reported to Equifax. Here's what you see:

- **Company Name** is the name of the business reporting the information. In many cases, just below the company name, Equifax includes a description of the type of account (such as student loan, credit card or line of credit), some payment history and/or the account's status (such as charge off, collection account, payment deferred, account transferred or account closed by consumer.)
- **Account Number** is your account number with the company reporting the information. (These have been deleted on the sample report.)
- **Whose Acct** indicates who is responsible for the account and the type of obligation you have. The possibilities are:
  - A = Authorized user (of someone else's account)
  - B = On behalf of another person
  - C = Comaker/Cosigner
  - I = Individual
  - J = Joint
  - M = Maker
  - S = Shared
  - T = Terminated
  - U = Undesignated
- **Date Opened** is the month and year you opened the account.
- **Months Reviewed** is the number of months for which your account payment history has been reported to Equifax.
- **Date of Last Activity** is the most recent month and year that something happened on the account. This may be the last time you made a payment (if you are currently paying) or when the account was charged off or sent to collections. This date is important because negative information (other than bankruptcies) can stay on your report for up to seven years after the date of the last activity.
- **High Credit** is the amount of any loan you took out, your credit limit or possibly the

highest amount you have ever charged on the account.

- **Terms** indicates either the number of installments you have (indicated by an M) to pay off the debt or the amount of your monthly payment.
- **Balance** is the amount you owed on the account when the creditor last provided Equifax with information.
- **Past Due** is the amount past due on the account when the creditor last provided Equifax with information.
- **Status** indicates both the type of account and your payment history.

Type of Account

I = Installment (payment amount is fixed each month)

O = Open (entire balance is due each month)

R = Revolving (payment amount is variable each month)

Payment History

0 = Too new to review

1 = Paid as agreed

2 = 30+ days past due

3 = 60+ days past due

4 = 90+ days past due

5 = 120+ days past due or account sent to collection

7 = Making regular payments under wage earner plan (Chapter 13 bankruptcy) or similar arrangement

9 = Charged off to bad debt

- **Date Reported** is the date the creditor last provided Equifax with information.

After the listing of accounts, your credit report may contain any of the following information:

- **Accounts with collection agencies.** Equifax often separates out accounts with collection agencies. Equifax has not done this on the sample credit report.
- **Public records.** The section includes information obtained from local, state and federal courts and offices, such as lawsuits, bankruptcies and liens.

- **Additional information.** This section includes former addresses and any known employers.
- **Inquiries.** Creditors who have requested a copy of your report are listed in the final section with the date they requested your report. Some of these creditors are coded (under Equifax's own policies, coded inquiries are given only to you; other creditors don't see them):

ACIS = This indicates that Equifax responded to your request for a copy of your credit report or to verify information in your account.

AM = This is one of your existing creditors who requested your file for periodic review. This inquiry remains for six months.

AR = Same as AM.

EQUIFAX = Same as ACIS.

INQ = This is a business that was given a copy of your file. This inquiry remains for six months.

PRM = This indicates that a creditor wanted your file to send you an application for credit. Only your name and address was given out. This inquiry remains for six months.

UPDATE = Same as ACIS.

Uncoded credit inquiries can stay on your report for up to two years.

Trans Union. Trans Union did a major overhaul of its credit reports in 1995, eliminating the column format, codes and other features that made the report difficult to read. As you can see from the samples, however, the Trans Union report contains the same basic information as the Equifax report. But here is how Trans Union reports it:

First, you will notice that the Trans Union report is actually two reports—the first is two pages and the second is five pages. This is because the consumer changed her name in 1995; Trans Union conducted two searches and generated two reports. (By contrast, Equifax and TRW/Experian combined all accounts that matched the consumer's former name or present name into one report.)

The top of each Trans Union report contains identifying information, most of which has been deleted on the sample. This information includes the consumer's name, address, former addresses, employment, Social Security number and birthdate. The top of the report also indicates how far back Trans Union has information on the consumer. (Notice that on the top of all subsequent pages, Trans Union includes the consumer's name and Social Security number.)

Trans Union breaks down the credit information into several subsections:

- **Public records.** This section includes information obtained from local, state and federal courts and offices, such as lawsuits, bankruptcies and liens.
- **Accounts with negative notations.** Trans Union separates out accounts that "contain information which some creditors may consider to be adverse" and further highlights the negative information (for you, not your creditors) by enclosing it in >brackets<. The bracketed information usually includes the account's status, any past due amount and information on late payments.
- **Accounts without negative notations.** Immediately following the negative accounts, Trans Union lists the accounts that are "reported with no adverse information."

    Both the accounts with negative notations the accounts without negative notations contain the following information:
    - name of the company
    - account number (these are deleted on the sample report)
    - type of credit extended:
        - ▲ Check credit (line of credit drawn on by writing checks)
        - ▲ Installment (payment amount is fixed each month)
        - ▲ Mortgage (installment credit extended to purchase a home)
        - ▲ Open (entire balance is due each month)
        - ▲ Revolving (payment amount is variable each month)
    - the date the creditor last provided Trans Union with information (updated)
    - the amount you owed on the account when the creditor last provided Trans Union with information (balance)
    - who is responsible for the account, such as individual account, joint account, account relationship terminated, cosigner account
    - the month and year you opened the account (opened)
    - the amount of any loan you took out or the highest amount you have ever charged on the account (most owed)
    - your credit limit on a revolving or open account (credit limit) or the amount of your monthly payments and number of months you have to pay off an installment debt (pay terms)
    - the month and year you or the creditor closed the account (closed)
    - the status of your account as of the date the account was updated:
        - ▲ charged off as bad debt
        - ▲ collection account
        - ▲ paid as agreed
        - ▲ payment after charge off/collection (you began repaying the debt after the creditor had already written it off) unrated (a creditor usually does not rate accounts for which they have no payment history—for example, when your payments have been deferred or an account which has been transferred to another creditor or closed)
- **Inquiries—full disclosure.** Trans Union divides your inquiries into two sections. The first section lists the companies that received your full credit report in response to your request for credit. These inquiries stay on your credit report for two years. (An inquiry with a

"Consum Discl" notation indicates that Trans Union responded to your request for a copy of your credit report or to verify information in your account. These inquiries are not seen by other creditors.)

- **Inquiries—partial disclosure.** Some companies received only your name and address for the purpose of making you a credit offer or to review your account. These inquiries stay on your credit report for six months and are not seen by other creditors.

TRW/Experian. TRW/Experian (when it was TRW) was the first credit bureau to redesign its credit reports and eliminate the column format, codes and other features that made the report difficult to read.

At the top of each odd-numbered page of the TRW/Experian report is an identification number in a box (this number has been deleted on the sample), along with your name and address (this, too, has been deleted on the sample).

Following your name and address on the first page are two paragraphs called "How to Read this Report" and "Your Credit History." "How to Read this Report" refers to an explanatory enclosure which has not been reproduced below. "Your Credit History" explains that information in your report comes from public records or organizations that have granted you credit. This section further explains that credit entries marked with an asterisk (*) "may require further review by a prospective creditor," which generally means that the information is negative.

The bulk of the rest of the report is your credit history. TRW/Experian provides more account information than does Equifax or Trans Union. In the account column, TRW/Experian includes the creditor's name and full address, a description of the type of creditor (such as national credit card, oil company, banking, education or undefined), and the account or court case number. In the description column, you'll find complete sentences indicating the type of account, when it was opened, your payment terms, who is responsible for paying, and the original amount borrowed, your credit limit or

your highest balance. Finally, the account status paragraph (below the account and description columns) tells you how many months were reviewed, whether you are current or delinquent, the date of any delinquency and whether the account has been sent out to collections or written off.

Following the list of credit accounts, TRW/Experian separates out credit inquiries into two sections: creditors who reviewed your report for the purpose of offering you credit (these inquiries are included in the credit report provided to other creditors) and creditors reviewing their own accounts or who reviewed your report for marketing purposes (these inquiries are not included in the credit report provided to other creditors).

The end of the report contains identification information, including a repeat of your name and address, followed by other information, such as your Social Security number, year of birth, previous addresses, current and previous employers and former names.

One additional feature of the TRW/Experian report not found in the Equifax and Trans Union reports is the repeated request that you tell the company if any information is inaccurate or incomplete. Most consumer advocates admit that this is not an empty request—that is, TRW/Experian is generally recognized as the credit bureau most interested in providing you (and your creditors) with a correct credit file.

Once a credit bureau gathers information about you, it can report that information (that is, include it in a credit report) as follows:

- Bankruptcies from the date of the last activity may be reported for no more than ten years. Although the date of the last activity for most bankruptcies is the date you receive your discharge, credit bureaus usually start counting the ten-year period from the earlier date of filing. Also, most credit bureaus report successfully-completed Chapter 13 bankruptcies for only seven years.

- Lawsuits and judgments may be reported from the date of the entry of judgment against you up to seven years or until the governing statute of limitations has expired, whichever is longer. (See sidebar, below.) As a practical matter, credit bureaus usually delete all lawsuits and judgments after seven years.

- Paid tax liens, accounts sent out for collection, criminal records and any other adverse information may be reported from the date of the last activity on the account up to seven years. The date of last activity has generally been considered to be when the creditor charged off the account or sent it to a collection agency. Making a payment does not cause the seven-year period to run from that date. Beginning September 30, 1997, "date of last activity" will be defined as 180 days after the account is sent to collections (internal at the company or to a collection agency), charged off or subjected to a similar action.

- Bankruptcies, lawsuits, paid tax liens, accounts sent out for collection, criminal records and any other adverse information may be reported indefinitely if you apply for $50,000 ($150,000 beginning September 30, 1997) or more of credit or insurance, or if you apply for a job with an annual income of at least $20,000 ($75,000 beginning September 30, 1997). As a practical matter, however, credit bureaus usually delete all items after seven or ten years.

Statutes of Limitations

The statute of limitations is the length of time someone has to sue you if you do something wrong, such as cause an auto accident or break (breach) a contract, including an obligation to pay a debt. In the following states, for the kinds of contracts listed, the statute of limitations exceeds seven years. This means that if you are sued on any of these types of accounts, theoretically the lawsuit or judgment notation could remain in your credit report for up to the time listed.

State	Written Contracts	Oral Contracts	Promissory Notes	Open-Ended Accounts (Revolving Credit Card Accounts)
Illinois	10 years		10 years	
Iowa	10 years		10 years	
Kentucky	15 years		15 years	
Louisiana	10 years	10 years		
Missouri	10 years	10 years	10 years	
Montana	8 years		8 years	
Ohio	15 years		15 years	
Rhode Island	10 years	10 years	10 years	10 years
West Virginia	10 years		10 years	
Wyoming	10 years	8 years	10 years	8 years

Please address all future
correspondence to this address ◆

EQUIFAX CREDIT INFORMATION SERVICES
P O BOX 740256
ATLANTA, GA 30374

(800)216-1035

DATE: 08/21/96
SOCIAL SECURITY NUMBER
AGE 30

CREDIT HISTORY

Company Name	Account Number	Whose Acct.	Date Opened	Months Re-viewed	Date Of Last Activity	High Credit	Terms	Items as of Date Reported			Date Reported
								Balance	Past Due	Status	
SALLIE MAE STUDENT LOAN		I	11/94	01	07/96	44K	1	189		I1	07/96
CHOICE		I	06/90		03/95	5200	89	4056	1K	R9	07/96
>>> PRIOR PAYING HISTORY - 30(00)60(01)90+(01) 02/95-R5,11/94-R3 <<< CHARGE OFF - MAKING PAYMENTS											
AMERICAN EXPRESS TRA		I	03/90	01	07/96	149		149		01	07/96
AMERICAN EXPRESS TRA COLLECTION ACCOUNT		I	03/90	01	06/93	0		0		05	07/96
EDUSERV NATL DIR STU		I	08/92	34	06/96	1000	30	661		I1	06/96
>>> PRIOR PAYING HISTORY - 30(03)60(00)90+(00) 01/96-I2,10/95-I2,08/95-I2 <<< STUDENT LOAN											
U S DEPARTMENT OF ED STUDENT LOAN STUDENT LOAN - PAYMENT DEFERRED		I	10/95		02/96	51K	395	51K	0	IO	06/96
CHEVRON USA CREDIT CARD		I	01/94	28	06/96	50		16		R1	06/96
WELLS FARGO ACCOUNT CLOSED BY CONSUMER CREDIT CARD		I	11/91	52	09/93	1000		0		R1	04/96
EDUSERV TECHNOLOGIES STUDENT LOAN				30	12/95	22K	313	29K		I1	02/96
CITIBANK - VISA		I	01/88	50	09/95	14K				R1	09/95
STUDENT LOAN MARKETI STUDENT LOAN ACCOUNT TRANSFERRED OR SOLD		I	11/94		08/95	44K	381	0		IO	08/95
USAA CREDIT CARDS CREDIT CARD AMOUNT IN H/C COLUMN IS CREDIT LIMIT		I	06/91		11/94	INCLUDED IN BANKRUPTCY					12/94
EDUSERV TECHNOLOGIES ACCOUNT TRANSFERRED OR SOLD STUDENT LOAN		I	08/88		12/94	11K		0		IO	12/94
FIRST DEPOSIT CORP LINE OF CREDIT		I	09/94		11/94	INCLUDED IN BANKRUPTCY					11/94
MACY'S		I	02/88	74	03/90	502		0		R1	05/94
WELLS FARGO		I	04/89	46	02/91	1500		0		R1	02/93
BANK OF AMERICA		I	07/89	05	11/91	1800		0		R1	11/91
BANK OF AMERICA		I	07/88	31	02/91	3300		0		R1	03/91
AMERICAN EXPRESS /S		A	05/75	20	01/91	0		0		R1	01/91
NORDSTROMS		S	10/88	04	10/90	428		0		R1	10/90
AMERICAN EXPRESS TRA ACCOUNT CLOSED BY CONSUMER		I	03/90		04/90	0		0		00	04/90

```
********** PUBLIC RECORDS OR OTHER INFORMATION **********

>>> BANKRUPTCY FILED 11/94; US DISTRICT BANKRUPT; CASE OR OTHER ID NUMBER-
    LIABILITIES-$93211; PERSONAL; INDIVIDUAL; DISMISSED CH-7; ASSETS-$11842


********** ADDITIONAL INFORMATION **********

FORMER/OTHER ADDRESS

FORMER/OTHER ADDRESS

LAST REPORTED EMPL -

********** COMPANIES THAT REQUESTED YOUR CREDIT HISTORY **********

08/21/96 EQUIFAX - DISCLOSURE        07/20/96 AR  AMERICAN EXPRESS
05/13/96 AR  AMERICAN EXPRESS         04/28/96 AR  WELLS FARGO
03/01/96 PRM FINGERHUT CORPORATIO    03/31/95 WELLS FARGO BANK CCD
```

G90

⊡ *TRANS UNION*

1561 E. ORANGETHORPE AVENUE
FULLERTON, CA 92831-5207

YOUR TRANS UNION FILE NUMBER:
PAGE 1 OF 2 (INTL USE:
DATE THIS REPORT PRINTED: 08/22/96

SOCIAL SECURITY NUMBER:

YOU HAVE BEEN IN OUR FILES SINCE: 05/95

CONSUMER REPORT FOR:

‖⃦⃒⃒‖⃒⃒‖⃒⃒‖⃒‖⃒⃒‖⃒‖⃒

YOUR CREDIT INFORMATION

THE FOLLOWING ACCOUNTS ARE REPORTED WITH NO ADVERSE INFORMATION

```
CHEVRON      - #                        REVOLVING ACCOUNT
   UPDATED  07/96   BALANCE:        $43  INDIVIDUAL ACCOUNT
   OPENED   01/94   MOST OWED:      $50
   IN PRIOR  8 MONTHS FROM LAST UPDATE NEVER LATE
   STATUS AS OF 07/96: PAID AS AGREED

AMERICAN EXP - #                        OPEN ACCOUNT
                                        CREDIT CARD
   UPDATED  07/96   BALANCE:       $149  INDIVIDUAL ACCOUNT
   OPENED   03/90   MOST OWED:     $149
   IN PRIOR 16 MONTHS FROM LAST UPDATE NEVER LATE
   STATUS AS OF 07/96: PAID AS AGREED

EDUSERV TECH - #                        INSTALLMENT ACCOUNT
                                        STUDENT LOAN
   UPDATED  02/96   BALANCE:     $28762  INDIVIDUAL ACCOUNT
   OPENED   08/90   MOST OWED:   $22236  PAY TERMS: 655 MONTHLY $313
   IN PRIOR  1 MONTH  FROM LAST UPDATE NEVER LATE
   STATUS AS OF 02/96: PAID AS AGREED

US DEP ED    - #                        INSTALLMENT ACCOUNT
STUDENT LOAN NOT IN REPAYMENT           STUDENT LOAN
   UPDATED  06/96   BALANCE:     $50512  INDIVIDUAL ACCOUNT
   OPENED   10/95   MOST OWED:   $50512  PAY TERMS: 298 MONTHLY $395
   IN PRIOR  9 MONTHS FROM LAST UPDATE NEVER LATE
   STATUS AS OF 06/96: UNRATED
```

THE FOLLOWING COMPANIES HAVE RECEIVED YOUR CREDIT REPORT. THEIR INQUIRIES
REMAIN ON YOUR CREDIT REPORT FOR TWO YEARS. (NOTE: "CONSUM DISCL" REFERS TO
TRANS UNION CONSUMER RELATIONS AND ARE NOT VIEWED BY CREDITORS).

```
                         INQUIRY TYPE                        INQUIRY TYPE
   CONSUM DISCL 08/22/96  INDIVIDUAL
```

60823 39248

REPORT ON   PAGE 2 OF 2
SOCIAL SECURITY NUMBER: TRANS UNION FILE NUMBER:

THE FOLLOWING COMPANIES DID NOT GET YOUR FULL REPORT, BUT INSTEAD RECEIVED ONLY
YOUR NAME AND ADDRESS INFORMATION FOR THE PURPOSE OF MAKING YOU A CREDIT OFFER,
OR TO REVIEW YOUR ACCOUNT. THEIR INQUIRIES ARE NOT SEEN BY CREDITORS.

HHLD CRD SER 04/96   WELL FARG BK 06/96

60823 39249

⊡ TRANS UNION
1561 E. ORANGETHORPE AVENUE
FULLERTON, CA 92831-5207

YOUR TRANS UNION FILE NUMBER:
PAGE 1 OF 5 (INTL USE:
DATE THIS REPORT PRINTED: 08/22/96

SOCIAL SECURITY NUMBER:
BIRTH DATE:
YOU HAVE BEEN IN OUR FILES SINCE: 02/88

PHONE: 841-5808

CONSUMER REPORT FOR:

FORMER ADDRESSES REPORTED:

EMPLOYMENT DATA REPORTED:

YOUR CREDIT INFORMATION

THE FOLLOWING ITEMS OBTAINED FROM PUBLIC RECORDS APPEAR ON YOUR REPORT. YOU MAY
BE REQUIRED TO EXPLAIN PUBLIC RECORD ITEMS TO POTENTIAL CREDITORS. ANY BANK-
RUPTCY INFORMATION WILL REMAIN ON YOUR REPORT FOR 10 YEARS FROM THE DATE OF
FILING. ALL OTHER PUBLIC RECORD INFORMATION, INCLUDING DISCHARGED CHAPTER 13
BANKRUPTCY AND ANY ACCOUNTS CONTAINING ADVERSE INFORMATION, REMAIN FOR 7 YEARS.

DOCKET #   FEDERAL DISTRICT   CHAPTER 7 BANKRUPTCY DISMISSED
PLAINTIFF ATTORNEY: N A   ENTERED: 11/94
                                      ASSETS: $0 PAID: 03/95
                                                        LIAB: $0

THE FOLLOWING ACCOUNTS CONTAIN INFORMATION WHICH SOME CREDITORS MAY CONSIDER TO
BE ADVERSE. THE ADVERSE INFORMATION IN THESE ACCOUNTS HAS BEEN PRINTED IN
>BRACKETS< FOR YOUR CONVENIENCE, TO HELP YOU UNDERSTAND YOUR REPORT. THEY ARE
NOT BRACKETED THIS WAY FOR CREDITORS. (NOTE: THE ACCOUNT # MAY BE SCRAMBLED BY
THE CREDITOR FOR YOUR PROTECTION).

 PROVIDIAN   - #   REVOLVING ACCOUNT
>PROFIT AND LOSS WRITEOFF<
    UPDATED 07/96   BALANCE: $5054   INDIVIDUAL ACCOUNT
    OPENED   09/94   MOST OWED: $5054   CREDIT LIMIT: $5000
    CLOSED   11/94 >PAST DUE: $5054<
    >STATUS AS OF 11/94: CHARGED OFF AS BAD DEBT<

                                           60823   39250

```
REPORT ON                                             PAGE  2 OF  5
SOCIAL SECURITY NUMBER:              TRANS UNION FILE NUMBER:


 USAA CRDT CD - #                        REVOLVING ACCOUNT
>PROFIT AND LOSS WRITEOFF<               CREDIT CARD
    UPDATED  06/96   BALANCE:      $3539  INDIVIDUAL ACCOUNT
    OPENED   06/91                        CREDIT LIMIT:    $3500
    CLOSED   11/94  >PAST DUE:     $3539<
    >STATUS AS OF 11/94: CHARGED OFF AS BAD DEBT<

 AMERICAN EXP - #                        OPEN ACCOUNT
>PLACED FOR COLLECTION<                  CREDIT CARD
    UPDATED  07/96   BALANCE:        $0   INDIVIDUAL ACCOUNT
    OPENED   03/90   MOST OWED:      $0
    CLOSED   06/93
    >STATUS AS OF 06/93: COLLECTION ACCOUNT<

 CHOICE       - #                        REVOLVING ACCOUNT
>PROFIT AND LOSS WRITEOFF<               CREDIT CARD
    UPDATED  07/96   BALANCE:     $4056   INDIVIDUAL ACCOUNT
    OPENED   06/90   MOST OWED:    $122   CREDIT LIMIT:    $5200
    CLOSED   07/94  >PAST DUE:    $1053<
    >STATUS AS OF 07/94: PAYMENT AFTER CHARGE OFF/COLLECTION<

 EDUSRV/      - #                        INSTALLMENT ACCOUNT
                                         STUDENT LOAN
    UPDATED  07/96   BALANCE:      $633   INDIVIDUAL ACCOUNT
    OPENED   08/92   MOST OWED:   $1000   PAY TERMS: 30 MONTHLY $30
    >IN PRIOR 36 MONTHS FROM LAST UPDATE  3 TIMES 30 DAYS LATE<
    STATUS AS OF 07/96: PAID AS AGREED

 EDUSERV      - #                        INSTALLMENT ACCOUNT
>BANKRUPTCY<                             STUDENT LOAN
    UPDATED  01/96   BALANCE:       $32   INDIVIDUAL ACCOUNT
    OPENED   09/93   MOST OWED:   $2750   PAY TERMS: 120 MONTHLY $33
    CLOSED   12/94
    IN PRIOR  1 MONTH  FROM DATE CLOSED NEVER LATE
    STATUS AS OF 12/94: UNRATED

 EDUSERV      - #                        INSTALLMENT ACCOUNT
>BANKRUPTCY<                             STUDENT LOAN
    UPDATED  01/96   BALANCE:       $55   INDIVIDUAL ACCOUNT
    OPENED   08/93   MOST OWED:   $4750   PAY TERMS: 120 MONTHLY $57
    CLOSED   12/94
    IN PRIOR  1 MONTH  FROM DATE CLOSED NEVER LATE
    STATUS AS OF 12/94: UNRATED


THE FOLLOWING ACCOUNTS ARE REPORTED WITH NO ADVERSE INFORMATION

 SLMA/LSCTX   - #                        INSTALLMENT ACCOUNT
                                         STUDENT LOAN
    UPDATED  07/96   BALANCE:      $189   INDIVIDUAL ACCOUNT
    OPENED   11/94   MOST OWED:  $43504   PAY TERMS:   MONTHLY $1
    IN PRIOR 12 MONTHS FROM LAST UPDATE NEVER LATE
    STATUS AS OF 07/96: PAID AS AGREED




                                              60823  39251
```

```
REPORT ON                                              PAGE  3 OF  5
SOCIAL SECURITY NUMBER:              TRANS UNION FILE NUMBER:


  EDUSERV       - #                      INSTALLMENT ACCOUNT
                                         STUDENT LOAN
    UPDATED  07/96    BALANCE:       $0   INDIVIDUAL ACCOUNT
    OPENED   08/92    MOST OWED:   $4000  PAY TERMS: 119 MONTHLY $51
    CLOSED   12/94
    IN PRIOR  1 MONTH  FROM DATE CLOSED NEVER LATE
    STATUS AS OF 12/94: PAID AS AGREED

  EDUSERV       - #                      INSTALLMENT ACCOUNT
                                         STUDENT LOAN
    UPDATED  07/96    BALANCE:       $0   INDIVIDUAL ACCOUNT
    OPENED   08/91    MOST OWED:   $4000  PAY TERMS: 119 MONTHLY $54
    CLOSED   12/94
    IN PRIOR  1 MONTH  FROM DATE CLOSED NEVER LATE
    STATUS AS OF 12/94: PAID AS AGREED

  EDUSERV       - #                      INSTALLMENT ACCOUNT
                                         STUDENT LOAN
    UPDATED  07/96    BALANCE:       $0   INDIVIDUAL ACCOUNT
    OPENED   08/91    MOST OWED:   $7500  PAY TERMS: 120 MONTHLY $91
    CLOSED   12/94
    IN PRIOR  1 MONTH  FROM DATE CLOSED NEVER LATE
    STATUS AS OF 12/94: PAID AS AGREED

  EDUSERV       - #                      INSTALLMENT ACCOUNT
                                         STUDENT LOAN
    UPDATED  07/96    BALANCE:       $0   INDIVIDUAL ACCOUNT
    OPENED   08/90    MOST OWED:   $4000
    CLOSED   05/93
    IN PRIOR 33 MONTHS FROM DATE CLOSED NEVER LATE
    STATUS AS OF 05/93: PAID AS AGREED

  EDUSERV       - #                      INSTALLMENT ACCOUNT
                                         STUDENT LOAN
    UPDATED  07/96    BALANCE:       $0   INDIVIDUAL ACCOUNT
    OPENED   08/90    MOST OWED:   $7500  PAY TERMS: 120 MONTHLY $91
    CLOSED   12/94
    IN PRIOR  1 MONTH  FROM DATE CLOSED NEVER LATE
    STATUS AS OF 12/94: PAID AS AGREED

  WELL FARG MC - #                       REVOLVING ACCOUNT
  ACCOUNT CLOSED BY CONSUMER             CREDIT CARD
    UPDATED  04/96    BALANCE:       $0   INDIVIDUAL ACCOUNT
    OPENED   11/91    MOST OWED:   $1000  CREDIT LIMIT:    $1000
    CLOSED   07/93
    IN PRIOR 21 MONTHS FROM DATE CLOSED NEVER LATE
    STATUS AS OF 07/93: PAID AS AGREED

  CHEVRON       - #                      REVOLVING ACCOUNT
    UPDATED  11/95    BALANCE:       $6   INDIVIDUAL ACCOUNT
    OPENED   01/94    MOST OWED:     $44
    IN PRIOR 22 MONTHS FROM LAST UPDATE NEVER LATE
    STATUS AS OF 11/95: PAID AS AGREED




                                         60823   39252
```

```
REPORT ON                                                    PAGE  4 OF  5
SOCIAL SECURITY NUMBER:                   TRANS UNION FILE NUMBER:


   CITIBK VISA  - #                            REVOLVING ACCOUNT
                                               CREDIT CARD
      UPDATED  09/95   BALANCE:      $9691     ACCOUNT RELATIONSHIP TERMINATED
      OPENED   01/88                           PAY TERMS:  MINIMUM $140
                                               CREDIT LIMIT:    $13500
      IN PRIOR 48 MONTHS FROM LAST UPDATE NEVER LATE
      STATUS AS OF 09/95: PAID AS AGREED

   AMERICAN EXP  - #                           OPEN ACCOUNT
                                               CREDIT CARD
      UPDATED  02/95                           INDIVIDUAL ACCOUNT
      OPENED   03/90   MOST OWED:      $35
      IN PRIOR 20 MONTHS FROM LAST UPDATE NEVER LATE
      STATUS AS OF 02/95: PAID AS AGREED

   EDUSERV TECH  - #                           INSTALLMENT ACCOUNT
   ACT CLOSD-TRNSFR OR REFINANCE               STUDENT LOAN
      UPDATED  12/94   BALANCE:        $0      INDIVIDUAL ACCOUNT
      OPENED   08/88   MOST OWED:   $10500     PAY TERMS: 126 MONTHLY $148
      IN PRIOR 38 MONTHS FROM LAST UPDATE NEVER LATE
      STATUS AS OF 12/94: PAID AS AGREED

   EDUSERV TECH  - #                           INSTALLMENT ACCOUNT
                                               STUDENT LOAN
      UPDATED  11/94                           INDIVIDUAL ACCOUNT
      OPENED   08/90   MOST OWED:   $22236     PAY TERMS: 638 MONTHLY $299
      IN PRIOR  8 MONTHS FROM LAST UPDATE NEVER LATE
      STATUS AS OF 11/94: PAID AS AGREED

THE FOLLOWING ITEM IS SUPPRESSED:
   EMPORIUM       - #                          REVOLVING ACCOUNT
   CLOSED
      UPDATED  05/94   BALANCE:        $0      INDIVIDUAL ACCOUNT
      OPENED   02/88   MOST OWED:     $502     CREDIT LIMIT:      $500
      PAID OFF 03/90
      IN PRIOR  5 MONTHS FROM DATE PAID NEVER LATE
      STATUS AS OF 03/90: PAID AS AGREED

   WELL FARG BK  - #                           REVOLVING ACCOUNT
      UPDATED  02/93   BALANCE:        $0      INDIVIDUAL ACCOUNT
      OPENED   04/89   MOST OWED:    $1500
      PAID OFF 02/91
      IN PRIOR 16 MONTHS FROM DATE PAID NEVER LATE
      STATUS AS OF 02/91: PAID AS AGREED

   BK OF AMER   - #                            REVOLVING ACCOUNT
      UPDATED  10/91   BALANCE:        $0      INDIVIDUAL ACCOUNT
      OPENED   07/89                           CREDIT LIMIT:     $1800
      PAID OFF 10/91
      IN PRIOR  4 MONTHS FROM DATE PAID NEVER LATE
      STATUS AS OF 10/91: PAID AS AGREED




                                               60823  39253
```

```
REPORT ON                                                  PAGE  5 OF  5
SOCIAL SECURITY NUMBER:                 TRANS UNION FILE NUMBER:


  BK OF AMER    - #                       REVOLVING ACCOUNT
     UPDATED   03/91    BALANCE:       $0  INDIVIDUAL ACCOUNT
     OPENED    07/88                       CREDIT LIMIT:    $3300
     PAID OFF  02/91
     IN PRIOR 16 MONTHS FROM DATE PAID NEVER LATE
     STATUS AS OF 02/91: PAID AS AGREED

  NORDSTROM    - #                         REVOLVING ACCOUNT
     UPDATED   10/90    BALANCE:       $0  JOINT ACCOUNT
     OPENED    10/88    MOST OWED:    $428
     PAID OFF  01/90
     IN PRIOR  3 MONTHS FROM DATE PAID NEVER LATE
     STATUS AS OF 01/90: PAID AS AGREED

  SLMA / LSCV  - #                         INSTALLMENT ACCOUNT
  TRANSFER                                 STUDENT LOAN
     UPDATED   08/95    BALANCE:       $0  INDIVIDUAL ACCOUNT
     OPENED    11/94    MOST OWED:  $43504 PAY TERMS:  MONTHLY $381
     CLOSED    08/95
     IN PRIOR 10 MONTHS FROM DATE CLOSED NEVER LATE
     STATUS AS OF 08/95: UNRATED

  AMERICAN EXP - #                         OPEN ACCOUNT
  ACCOUNT CLOSED BY CONSUMER               CREDIT CARD
     UPDATED   01/94    BALANCE:       $0  ACCOUNT RELATIONSHIP TERMINATED
     OPENED    05/75    MOST OWED:     $0
     CLOSED    11/93
     IN PRIOR 48 MONTHS FROM DATE CLOSED NEVER LATE
     STATUS AS OF 11/93: UNRATED
```

THE FOLLOWING COMPANIES HAVE RECEIVED YOUR CREDIT REPORT. THEIR INQUIRIES REMAIN ON YOUR CREDIT REPORT FOR TWO YEARS. (NOTE: "CONSUM DISCL" REFERS TO TRANS UNION CONSUMER RELATIONS AND ARE NOT VIEWED BY CREDITORS).

```
                        INQUIRY TYPE                      INQUIRY TYPE
  CONSUM DISCL 08/22/96 INDIVIDUAL    PAC COAST CO 06/23/95 INDIVIDUAL
  AMEX         10/24/94 INDIVIDUAL    PROVIDIAN    09/01/94 INDIVIDUAL
```

THE FOLLOWING COMPANIES DID NOT GET YOUR FULL REPORT, BUT INSTEAD RECEIVED ONLY YOUR NAME AND ADDRESS INFORMATION FOR THE PURPOSE OF MAKING YOU A CREDIT OFFER, OR TO REVIEW YOUR ACCOUNT. THEIR INQUIRIES ARE NOT SEEN BY CREDITORS.

```
  CITIBK VISA   10/95    HHLD CRD SER  04/96    CITIBK VISA   06/96
  CHOICE        06/96
```

IF YOU BELIEVE ANY OF THE INFORMATION IN YOUR CREDIT REPORT IS INCORRECT, PLEASE LET US KNOW. FOR YOUR CONVENIENCE, AN INVESTIGATION FORM IS INCLUDED. PLEASE COMPLETE IT AND MAIL TO:

TRANS UNION CONSUMER RELATIONS
1561 E. ORANGETHORPE AVENUE
FULLERTON, CA 92831-5207
1-800-858-8336

```
                                          60823   39254
```

TRW

This is your TRW consumer identification number. Please refer to this number when you call or write TRW.

ID #

HOW TO READ THIS REPORT:

AN EXPLANATORY ENCLOSURE ACCOMPANIES THIS REPORT. IT DESCRIBES YOUR CREDIT RIGHTS AND OTHER HELPFUL INFORMATION. IF THE ENCLOSURE IS MISSING, OR YOU HAVE QUESTIONS ABOUT THIS REPORT, PLEASE CONTACT THE OFFICE LISTED ON THE LAST PAGE.

YOUR CREDIT HISTORY:

THIS INFORMATION COMES FROM PUBLIC RECORDS OR ORGANIZATIONS THAT HAVE GRANTED CREDIT TO YOU. AN ASTERISK BY AN ACCOUNT INDICATES THAT THIS ITEM MAY REQUIRE FURTHER REVIEW BY A PROSPECTIVE CREDITOR WHEN CHECKING YOUR CREDIT HISTORY. IF YOU BELIEVE ANY OF THE INFORMATION IS INCORRECT, PLEASE LET US KNOW.

	ACCOUNT	DESCRIPTION
1	* US BKPT CT CA OAKLAND P O BOX 2070 OAKLAND CA 94612 Docket #	BANKRUPTCY CHAPTER 7 DISMISSED 03/16/95. ORIGINAL PETITION ON 11/15/94.
2	* AMERICAN EXPRESS CO P O BOX 7871 SROC FORT LAUDERDALE FL 33329 NATL CREDIT CARDS ACCT #	THIS CREDIT CARD ACCOUNT WAS OPENED 03/01/90 AND HAS REVOLVING REPAYMENT TERMS. YOU HAVE CONTRACTUAL RESPONSIBILITY FOR THIS ACCOUNT AND ARE PRIMARILY RESPONSIBLE FOR ITS PAYMENT.

AS OF 1994, THIS ACCOUNT IS SERIOUSLY PAST DUE AND REFERRED TO A CREDIT GRANTOR'S INTERNAL COLLECTION DEPARTMENT, ATTORNEY OR COLLECTION AGENCY. BALANCE UNKNOWN ON 09/20/96. MONTHS REVIEWED: 33.
PAYMENT HISTORY: 9------------ ------------- -------9
TIMES LATE: 30=0, 60=0, 90+=0, DEROG=2.

| ACCOUNT | DESCRIPTION |

3   AMERICAN EXPRESS CO   THIS CREDIT CARD ACCOUNT WAS OPENED 03/01/90 AND HAS
     P O BOX 7871 SROC   REVOLVING REPAYMENT TERMS. YOU HAVE CONTRACTUAL
     FORT LAUDERDALE FL 33329   RESPONSIBILITY FOR THIS ACCOUNT AND ARE PRIMARILY
     NATL CREDIT CARDS   RESPONSIBLE FOR ITS PAYMENT. HIGH BALANCE: $353.
     ACCT #

AS OF 03/01/90, THIS OPEN ACCOUNT IS CURRENT AND ALL PAYMENTS ARE BEING MADE ON TIME.
BALANCE $166 ON 08/30/96. MONTHS REVIEWED: 79.

4   AMERICAN EXPRESS CO   THIS CREDIT CARD ACCOUNT WAS OPENED 05/01/75 AND HAS
     P O BOX 7871 SROC   REVOLVING REPAYMENT TERMS. YOU ARE AN AUTHORIZED USER
     FORT LAUDERDALE FL 33329   OF THIS ACCOUNT; ANOTHER INDIVIDUAL HAS CONTRACTUAL
     NATL CREDIT CARDS   RESPONSIBILITY. HIGH BALANCE: $85.
     ACCT #

AS OF 07/01/93, THIS ACCOUNT IS PAID. PREVIOUSLY WAS CURRENT AND ALL PAYMENTS WERE MADE ON
TIME. BALANCE $0 ON 07/02/93. MONTHS REVIEWED: 99.
** CREDIT LINE CLOSED/CONSUMER REQUEST/REPORTED BY SUBSCRIBER **

5   BANK OF AMERICA   THIS CREDIT CARD ACCOUNT WAS OPENED 07/12/89 AND HAS
     1825 EAST BUCKEYE ROAD   REVOLVING REPAYMENT TERMS. YOU HAVE CONTRACTUAL
     PHOENIX AZ 85034   RESPONSIBILITY FOR THIS ACCOUNT AND ARE PRIMARILY
     BANKING   RESPONSIBLE FOR ITS PAYMENT. CREDIT LIMIT: $1,800.
     ACCT #

AS OF 11/01/91, THIS ACCOUNT IS PAID. PREVIOUSLY WAS CURRENT AND ALL PAYMENTS WERE MADE ON
TIME. BALANCE $0 ON 11/30/91. MONTHS REVIEWED: 29.

6   BANK OF AMERICA   THIS CREDIT CARD ACCOUNT WAS OPENED 07/15/88 AND HAS
     1825 EAST BUCKEYE ROAD   REVOLVING REPAYMENT TERMS. YOU HAVE CONTRACTUAL
     PHOENIX AZ 85034   RESPONSIBILITY FOR THIS ACCOUNT AND ARE PRIMARILY
     BANKING   RESPONSIBLE FOR ITS PAYMENT. CREDIT LIMIT: $3,300.
     ACCT #

AS OF 03/01/91, THIS ACCOUNT IS PAID. PREVIOUSLY WAS CURRENT AND ALL PAYMENTS WERE MADE ON
TIME. BALANCE $0 ON 03/30/91. MONTHS REVIEWED: 33.

7   CHEVRON U S A   THIS CREDIT CARD ACCOUNT WAS OPENED 01/06/94 AND HAS
     P O BOX 5010   REVOLVING REPAYMENT TERMS. YOU HAVE CONTRACTUAL
     CONCORD CA 94524   RESPONSIBILITY FOR THIS ACCOUNT AND ARE PRIMARILY
     OIL COMPANIES   RESPONSIBLE FOR ITS PAYMENT. HIGH BALANCE: $61.
     ACCT #

AS OF 1994, THIS OPEN ACCOUNT IS CURRENT AND ALL PAYMENTS ARE BEING MADE ON TIME. BALANCE
$50 ON 08/31/96. MONTHS REVIEWED: 33.

TRW

This is your TRW consumer identification
number. Please refer to this number when
you call or write TRW.

ID #

ACCOUNT   DESCRIPTION

8   CITIBANK VISA   THIS CREDIT CARD ACCOUNT WAS OPENED IN 1988 AND HAS
     PO BOX 6500   REVOLVING REPAYMENT TERMS. YOU ARE AN AUTHORIZED USER
     SIOUX FALLS SD 57117   OF THIS ACCOUNT; ANOTHER INDIVIDUAL HAS CONTRACTUAL
     BANKING   RESPONSIBILITY. CREDIT LIMIT: $15,500. HIGH BALANCE:
     ACCT # $9,272.

AS OF 1988, THIS OPEN ACCOUNT IS CURRENT AND ALL PAYMENTS ARE BEING MADE ON TIME. LAST
PAYMENT REPORTED TO TRW: 07/22/96. BALANCE $1,407 ON 07/31/96. MONTHS REVIEWED: 99.

9 * CITICORP/CHOICE   THIS CREDIT CARD ACCOUNT WAS OPENED 06/01/90 AND HAS
     701 EAST 60TH STREET NOR   REVOLVING REPAYMENT TERMS. YOU HAVE CONTRACTUAL
     SIOUX FALLS SD 57117   RESPONSIBILITY FOR THIS ACCOUNT AND ARE PRIMARILY
     NATL CREDIT CARDS   RESPONSIBLE FOR ITS PAYMENT. CREDIT LIMIT: $5,200. HIGH
     ACCT #   BALANCE: $5,431. CHARGE OFF: $5,431.

AS OF 04/01/96, THIS OPEN ACCOUNT IS NOW BEING PAID BUT WAS WRITTEN OFF AS A LOSS.
ORIGINAL DELINQUENCY DATE 11/03/94. SCHEDULED MONTHLY PAYMENT: $85. LAST PAYMENT REPORTED
TO TRW: 07/29/96. BALANCE $4,056 ON 08/31/96. PAST DUE: $1,142. MONTHS REVIEWED: 76.
TIMES LATE: 30=0, 60=0, 90+=0, DEROG=1.

10   EDUSERV TECHNOLOGIES INC   THIS EDUCATIONAL LOAN WAS OPENED 08/02/91 AND HAS 120
     1128 WEST 2400 SOUTH   MONTH REPAYMENT TERMS. YOU HAVE CONTRACTUAL
     SALT LAKE CITY UT 84119   RESPONSIBILITY FOR THIS ACCOUNT AND ARE PRIMARILY
     UNDEFINED FIRM TYPE   RESPONSIBLE FOR ITS PAYMENT. ORIGINAL AMOUNT: $7,500.
     ACCT #

AS OF 07/01/96, THIS ACCOUNT IS PAID. PREVIOUSLY WAS CURRENT AND ALL PAYMENTS WERE MADE ON
TIME. MONTHS REVIEWED: 60.
PAYMENT HISTORY: B-0---------- ------9
TIMES LATE: 30=0, 60=0, 90+=0, DEROG=1.

11   EDUSERV TECHNOLOGIES INC   THIS EDUCATIONAL LOAN WAS OPENED 08/02/91 AND HAS 119
     1128 WEST 2400 SOUTH   MONTH REPAYMENT TERMS. YOU HAVE CONTRACTUAL
     SALT LAKE CITY UT 84119   RESPONSIBILITY FOR THIS ACCOUNT AND ARE PRIMARILY
     UNDEFINED FIRM TYPE   RESPONSIBLE FOR ITS PAYMENT. ORIGINAL AMOUNT: $4,000.
     ACCT #

AS OF 07/01/96, THIS ACCOUNT IS PAID. PREVIOUSLY WAS CURRENT AND ALL PAYMENTS WERE MADE ON
TIME. MONTHS REVIEWED: 60.
PAYMENT HISTORY: B-0---------- ------9
TIMES LATE: 30=0, 60=0, 90+=0, DEROG=1.

ACCOUNT   DESCRIPTION

12 EDUSERV TECHNOLOGIES INC   THIS EDUCATIONAL LOAN WAS OPENED 08/15/90 AND HAS 120
    1128 WEST 2400 SOUTH   MONTH REPAYMENT TERMS. YOU HAVE CONTRACTUAL
    SALT LAKE CITY UT 84119   RESPONSIBILITY FOR THIS ACCOUNT AND ARE PRIMARILY
    UNDEFINED FIRM TYPE   RESPONSIBLE FOR ITS PAYMENT. ORIGINAL AMOUNT: $7,500.
    ACCT #

AS OF 07/01/96, THIS ACCOUNT IS PAID. PREVIOUSLY WAS CURRENT AND ALL PAYMENTS WERE MADE ON
TIME. MONTHS REVIEWED: 72.
PAYMENT HISTORY: B-0---------- ------9
TIMES LATE: 30=0, 60=0, 90+=0, DEROG=1.

13 EDUSERV TECHNOLOGIES INC   THIS EDUCATIONAL LOAN WAS OPENED 08/15/90 AND HAS
    1128 WEST 2400 SOUTH   UNSPECIFIED REPAYMENT TERMS. YOU HAVE CONTRACTUAL
    SALT LAKE CITY UT 84119   RESPONSIBILITY FOR THIS ACCOUNT AND ARE PRIMARILY
    UNDEFINED FIRM TYPE   RESPONSIBLE FOR ITS PAYMENT. ORIGINAL AMOUNT: $4,000.
    ACCT #

AS OF 05/01/93, THIS ACCOUNT IS PAID. BALANCE $0 ON 05/30/93. MONTHS REVIEWED: 34.

14 EDUSERV TECHNOLOGIES INC   THIS EDUCATIONAL LOAN WAS OPENED 08/27/93 AND HAS 120
    1128 WEST 2400 SOUTH   MONTH REPAYMENT TERMS. YOU HAVE CONTRACTUAL
    SALT LAKE CITY UT 84119   RESPONSIBILITY FOR THIS ACCOUNT AND ARE PRIMARILY
    UNDEFINED FIRM TYPE   RESPONSIBLE FOR ITS PAYMENT. ORIGINAL AMOUNT: $4,750.
    ACCT #

AS OF 07/01/96, THIS ACCOUNT IS PAID. PREVIOUSLY WAS CURRENT AND ALL PAYMENTS WERE MADE ON
TIME. MONTHS REVIEWED: 35.
PAYMENT HISTORY: B-0---------- ------9
TIMES LATE: 30=0, 60=0, 90+=0, DEROG=1.

15 EDUSERV TECHNOLOGIES INC   THIS EDUCATIONAL LOAN WAS OPENED 09/14/93 AND HAS 120
    1128 WEST 2400 SOUTH   MONTH REPAYMENT TERMS. YOU HAVE CONTRACTUAL
    SALT LAKE CITY UT 84119   RESPONSIBILITY FOR THIS ACCOUNT AND ARE PRIMARILY
    UNDEFINED FIRM TYPE   RESPONSIBLE FOR ITS PAYMENT. ORIGINAL AMOUNT: $2,750.
    ACCT #

AS OF 07/01/96, THIS ACCOUNT IS PAID. PREVIOUSLY WAS CURRENT AND ALL PAYMENTS WERE MADE ON
TIME. MONTHS REVIEWED: 35.
PAYMENT HISTORY: B-0---------- ------9
TIMES LATE: 30=0, 60=0, 90+=0, DEROG=1.

16 EDUSERV TECHNOLOGIES INC   THIS EDUCATIONAL LOAN WAS OPENED 08/11/92 AND HAS 119
    1128 WEST 2400 SOUTH   MONTH REPAYMENT TERMS. YOU HAVE CONTRACTUAL
    SALT LAKE CITY UT 84119   RESPONSIBILITY FOR THIS ACCOUNT AND ARE PRIMARILY
    UNDEFINED FIRM TYPE   RESPONSIBLE FOR ITS PAYMENT. ORIGINAL AMOUNT: $4,000.
    ACCT #

AS OF 07/01/96, THIS ACCOUNT IS PAID. PREVIOUSLY WAS CURRENT AND ALL PAYMENTS WERE MADE ON
TIME. MONTHS REVIEWED: 48.
PAYMENT HISTORY: B-0---------- ------9
TIMES LATE: 30=0, 60=0, 90+=0, DEROG=1.

TRW

This is your TRW consumer identification
number. Please refer to this number when
you call or write TRW.

ID #

ACCOUNT   DESCRIPTION

17   EDUSERV TECHNOLOGIES   THIS EDUCATIONAL LOAN WAS OPENED 08/29/90 AND HAS
      P O BOX 99   UNSPECIFIED REPAYMENT TERMS. YOU HAVE CONTRACTUAL
      MINNEAPOLIS MN 55440   RESPONSIBILITY FOR THIS ACCOUNT AND ARE PRIMARILY
      EDUCATION   RESPONSIBLE FOR ITS PAYMENT. ORIGINAL AMOUNT: $22,236.
      ACCT #

AS OF 09/01/90, THIS OPEN ACCOUNT IS CURRENT AND ALL PAYMENTS ARE BEING MADE ON TIME.
SCHEDULED MONTHLY PAYMENT: $313. LAST PAYMENT REPORTED TO TRW: 12/22/95. BALANCE $28,762
ON 02/01/96. MONTHS REVIEWED: 66.

18 * EDUSRV/UC BERKLEY   THIS EDUCATIONAL LOAN WAS OPENED 08/31/92 AND HAS 30
      P O BOX 3176   MONTH REPAYMENT TERMS. YOU HAVE CONTRACTUAL
      WINSTON-SALEM NC 27102   RESPONSIBILITY FOR THIS ACCOUNT AND ARE PRIMARILY
      EDUCATION   RESPONSIBLE FOR ITS PAYMENT. ORIGINAL AMOUNT: $1,000.
      ACCT #

AS OF 02/01/96, THIS OPEN ACCOUNT IS CURRENT AND PAYMENTS ARE BEING PAID ON TIME BUT WAS
DELINQUENT 30 DAYS 2 OTHER TIMES. SCHEDULED MONTHLY PAYMENT: $30. LAST PAYMENT REPORTED TO
TRW: 06/18/96. BALANCE $661 ON 06/30/96. MONTHS REVIEWED: 47.
PAYMENT HISTORY: CC-CC1CC-C1CC CCCCCCCCCCCC CCC
TIMES LATE: 30=2, 60=0, 90+=0

19   NORDSTROM   THIS CHARGE ACCOUNT WAS OPENED 10/15/88 AND HAS
      P O BOX 6554   REVOLVING REPAYMENT TERMS. YOU HAVE USE OF THIS
      ENGLEWOOD CO 80155   ACCOUNT. HIGH BALANCE: $428.
      DEPARTMENT STORES
      ACCT #

AS OF 10/01/88, THIS OPEN ACCOUNT IS CURRENT AND ALL PAYMENTS ARE BEING MADE ON TIME.
BALANCE $0 ON 09/01/96. MONTHS REVIEWED: 96.

20 * PROVIDIAN BANCORP   THIS LINE OF CREDIT WAS OPENED 09/29/94 AND HAS
      2301 CAMINO RAMON   REVOLVING REPAYMENT TERMS. YOU HAVE CONTRACTUAL
      SAN RAMON CA 94583   RESPONSIBILITY FOR THIS ACCOUNT AND ARE PRIMARILY
      BANKING   RESPONSIBLE FOR ITS PAYMENT. CREDIT LIMIT: $5,000. HIGH
      ACCT #   BALANCE: $5,933. CHARGE OFF: $5,618.

AS OF 11/01/94, THIS ACCOUNT IS SERIOUSLY PAST DUE AND WRITTEN OFF AS A LOSS. PREVIOUSLY
WAS INCLUDED IN OR DISCHARGED THROUGH BANKRUPTCY CHAPTER 7, 11, OR 12. ORIGINAL
DELINQUENCY DATE 11/01/94. LAST PAYMENT REPORTED TO TRW: 12/21/95. BALANCE $5,933 ON
08/30/96. PAST DUE: $1,300. MONTHS REVIEWED: 24.
PAYMENT HISTORY: 9999--------- --------9
TIMES LATE: 30=0, 60=0, 90+=0, DEROG=5.

ACCOUNT   DESCRIPTION

21   STUDENT LOAN MKT ASSN   THIS EDUCATIONAL LOAN WAS OPENED 11/18/94 AND HAS
      365 HERNDON PARKWAY   UNSPECIFIED REPAYMENT TERMS. YOU HAVE CONTRACTUAL
      HERNDON VA 22070   RESPONSIBILITY FOR THIS ACCOUNT AND ARE PRIMARILY
      EDUCATION   RESPONSIBLE FOR ITS PAYMENT. ORIGINAL AMOUNT: $43,504.
      ACCT #

AS OF 08/01/95, THIS TRANSFERRED ACCOUNT IS CURRENT AND ALL PAYMENTS ARE BEING MADE ON
TIME. BALANCE $0 ON 08/27/95. MONTHS REVIEWED: 10.
** TRANSFERRED TO OTHER LENDER OR CLAIM PURCHASE **

22   STUDENT LOAN MKT ASSN   THIS EDUCATIONAL LOAN WAS OPENED 11/18/94 AND HAS
      777 TWIN CREEK DRIVE   UNSPECIFIED REPAYMENT TERMS. YOU HAVE CONTRACTUAL
      KILLEEN TX 76543   RESPONSIBILITY FOR THIS ACCOUNT AND ARE PRIMARILY
      EDUCATION   RESPONSIBLE FOR ITS PAYMENT. ORIGINAL AMOUNT: $43,504.
      ACCT #

AS OF 11/01/94, THIS OPEN ACCOUNT IS CURRENT AND ALL PAYMENTS ARE BEING MADE ON TIME.
SCHEDULED MONTHLY PAYMENT: $1. LAST PAYMENT REPORTED TO TRW: 08/23/96. BALANCE $181 ON
08/31/96. MONTHS REVIEWED: 22.

23   FEDERAL DIRECT STUDENT L   THIS EDUCATIONAL LOAN WAS OPENED 10/04/95 AND HAS 298
      501 BLEECKER ST   MONTH REPAYMENT TERMS. YOU HAVE CONTRACTUAL
      UTICA NY 13501   RESPONSIBILITY FOR THIS ACCOUNT AND ARE PRIMARILY
      EDUCATION   RESPONSIBLE FOR ITS PAYMENT. ORIGINAL AMOUNT: $50,512.
      ACCT #

AS OF 10/01/95, THIS OPEN ACCOUNT IS CURRENT AND ALL PAYMENTS ARE BEING MADE ON TIME.
BALANCE $50,512 ON 05/31/96. MONTHS REVIEWED: 9.
** STUDENT LOAN PAYMENT DEFERRED **

24 * USAA FEDERAL SAVINGS   THIS CREDIT CARD ACCOUNT WAS OPENED 06/25/91 AND HAS
      PO BOX 47504   REVOLVING REPAYMENT TERMS. YOU HAVE CONTRACTUAL
      SAN ANTONIO TX 78288   RESPONSIBILITY FOR THIS ACCOUNT AND ARE PRIMARILY
      BANKING   RESPONSIBLE FOR ITS PAYMENT. CREDIT LIMIT: $3,539. HIGH
      ACCT #   BALANCE: $3,968. CHARGE OFF: $3,539.

AS OF 11/01/94, THIS ACCOUNT IS SERIOUSLY PAST DUE AND WRITTEN OFF AS A LOSS. PREVIOUSLY
WAS INCLUDED IN OR DISCHARGED THROUGH BANKRUPTCY CHAPTER 7, 11, OR 12. LAST PAYMENT
REPORTED TO TRW: 11/07/94. BALANCE $3,539 ON 07/31/96. MONTHS REVIEWED: 62.
PAYMENT HISTORY: 999---------- -------9
TIMES LATE: 30=0, 60=0, 90+=0, DEROG=4.

25 * WELLS FARGO BANK   THIS CREDIT CARD ACCOUNT WAS OPENED 11/01/91 AND HAS
      P O BOX 29476   REVOLVING REPAYMENT TERMS. YOU HAVE CONTRACTUAL
      PHOENIX AZ 85038   RESPONSIBILITY FOR THIS ACCOUNT AND ARE PRIMARILY
      BANKING   RESPONSIBLE FOR ITS PAYMENT. CREDIT LIMIT: $1,000.
      ACCT #

AS OF 04/01/94, THIS CLOSED ACCOUNT IS CURRENT AND ALL PAYMENTS ARE BEING MADE ON TIME.
BALANCE $0 ON 04/30/96. MONTHS REVIEWED: 55.
** CREDIT LINE CLOSED/CONSUMER REQUEST/REPORTED BY SUBSCRIBER **

TRW

This is your TRW consumer identification
number. Please refer to this number when
you call or write TRW.

ID #

ACCOUNT

DESCRIPTION

26   WELLS FARGO BANK
      P O BOX 29476
      PHOENIX AZ 85038
      BANKING
      ACCT #

THIS CREDIT CARD ACCOUNT WAS OPENED 11/01/91 AND HAS
REVOLVING REPAYMENT TERMS. YOU HAVE CONTRACTUAL
RESPONSIBILITY FOR THIS ACCOUNT AND ARE PRIMARILY
RESPONSIBLE FOR ITS PAYMENT. CREDIT LIMIT: $1,000. HIGH
BALANCE: $15.

AS OF 03/01/93, THIS ACCOUNT IS PAID. PREVIOUSLY WAS CURRENT AND ALL PAYMENTS WERE MADE ON
TIME. BALANCE $0 ON 03/31/93. MONTHS REVIEWED: 18.
** CREDIT LINE CLOSED/REPORTED BY SUBSCRIBER **

27 * WELLS FARGO BANK
      P O BOX 29476
      PHOENIX AZ 85038
      BANKING
      ACCT #

THIS CREDIT CARD ACCOUNT WAS OPENED 04/01/89 AND HAS
REVOLVING REPAYMENT TERMS. YOU HAVE CONTRACTUAL
RESPONSIBILITY FOR THIS ACCOUNT AND ARE PRIMARILY
RESPONSIBLE FOR ITS PAYMENT. CREDIT LIMIT: $1,500.

AS OF 02/01/93, THIS CLOSED ACCOUNT IS CURRENT AND ALL PAYMENTS ARE BEING MADE ON TIME.
BALANCE $0 ON 04/30/96. MONTHS REVIEWED: 86.
** CREDIT LINE CLOSED/REPORTED BY SUBSCRIBER **

YOUR CREDIT HISTORY WAS REVIEWED BY:

THE FOLLOWING INQUIRIES ARE REPORTED TO THOSE WHO ASK TO REVIEW YOUR CREDIT HISTORY

ACCOUNT

DESCRIPTION

28   FIRST USA BANK
      201 N WALNUT ST/6TH FL
      WILMINGTON DE 19801
      BANKING

11/03/95 INQUIRY MADE FOR EXTENSION OF CREDIT, REVIEW
OR OTHER PERMISSIBLE PURPOSE..

29   THE TRAVELERS BANK
      100 COMMERCE DRIVE
      NEWARK DE 19713
      BANKING

09/16/96 INQUIRY MADE FOR EXTENSION OF CREDIT, REVIEW
OR OTHER PERMISSIBLE PURPOSE..

THE FOLLOWING INQUIRIES ARE NOT REPORTED TO THOSE WHO ASK TO REVIEW YOUR CREDIT HISTORY. THEY ARE INCLUDED SO THAT YOU HAVE A COMPLETE LIST OF INQUIRIES.

	ACCOUNT	DESCRIPTION
30	CHEVRON U S A 2001 DIAMOND BLVD CONCORD CA 94524 OIL COMPANIES	08/09/96 INQUIRY MADE FOR A REVIEW OF YOUR CREDIT HISTORY BY YOUR CREDITOR.
31	CITICORP CREDIT SVCS INC PO BOX 6000 SIOUX FALLS SD 57117 BANKING	01/10/96 INQUIRY MADE FOR PRESCREEN PROGRAM. YOUR FILE WAS MATCHED AGAINST THIS CREDITOR'S CRITERIA TO DEVELOP A LIST OF NAMES FOR A CREDIT OFFER OR SERVICE.
32	CITICORP CREDIT SVCS INC PO BOX 6000 SIOUX FALLS SD 57117 BANKING	03/07/96 INQUIRY MADE FOR A REVIEW OF YOUR CREDIT HISTORY BY YOUR CREDITOR.
33	CITICORP CREDIT SVCS INC PO BOX 6000 SIOUX FALLS SD 57117 BANKING	03/27/96 INQUIRY MADE FOR A REVIEW OF YOUR CREDIT HISTORY BY YOUR CREDITOR.
34	CITICORP CREDIT SVCS INC PO BOX 6000 SIOUX FALLS SD 57117 BANKING	04/12/96 INQUIRY MADE FOR PRESCREEN PROGRAM. YOUR FILE WAS MATCHED AGAINST THIS CREDITOR'S CRITERIA TO DEVELOP A LIST OF NAMES FOR A CREDIT OFFER OR SERVICE.
35	PROVIDIAN BANCORP 150 SPEAR STREET 9TH FLR SAN FRANCISCO CA 94105 BANKING	02/29/96 INQUIRY MADE FOR A REVIEW OF YOUR CREDIT HISTORY BY YOUR CREDITOR.

PLEASE HELP US HELP YOU:

AT TRW WE KNOW HOW IMPORTANT YOUR GOOD CREDIT IS TO YOU. IT IS EQUALLY IMPORTANT TO US THAT OUR INFORMATION BE ACCURATE AND UP TO DATE. LISTED BELOW IS THE INFOMATION YOU GAVE US WHEN YOU ASKED FOR THIS REPORT. IF THE INFORMATION IS NOT CORRECT OR YOU DID NOT SUPPLY US WITH YOUR FULL NAME, ADDRESS FOR THE PAST 5 YEARS, SOCIAL SECURITY NUMBER AND YEAR OF BIRTH, THIS REPORT MAY NOT BE COMPLETE. IF THIS INFORMATION IS INCOMPLETE OR NOT ACCURATE, PLEASE LET US KNOW.

YOUR NAME: SOCIAL SECURITY #:
                                                    YEAR OF BIRTH: 1962
ADDRESS:

As you read through your credit report, make a list of everything that is incorrect, out-of-date or misleading. In particular, look for the following:

- incorrect or incomplete name, address or phone number
- incorrect Social Security number or birthdate
- incorrect, missing or outdated employment information
- incorrect marital status—a former spouse listed as your current spouse
- bankruptcies older than ten years or not identified by the specific chapter of the bankruptcy code
- lawsuits or judgments reported beyond seven years or beyond the expiration of the statute of limitations (see above)
- paid tax liens, accounts sent out for collection, criminal records and any other adverse information older than seven years
- credit inquiries older than two years
- unauthorized credit review (not promotional) inquiries—credit bureaus usually do not remove these at a consumer's request, but it never hurts to ask
- commingled accounts—credit histories for someone with a similar or the same name
- duplicate accounts—for example, a debt is listed twice, once under the creditor and a second time under a collection agency
- premarital debts of your current spouse attributed to you
- lawsuits you were not involved in
- incorrect account histories—such as a late payment notation when you've paid on time or a debt shown as past due when it's been discharged in bankruptcy
- paid tax, judgment, mechanic's or other liens listed as unpaid
- a missing notation when you disputed a charge on a credit card bill
- closed accounts incorrectly listed as open—it may look as if you have too much open credit, and

- accounts you closed that don't indicate "closed by consumer"—it looks like your creditors closed the accounts.

D. Dispute Incorrect, Outdated and Misleading Information in Your Credit File

Under the Fair Credit Reporting Act, you have the right to dispute all incorrect, out-of-date and misleading information in your credit file. Once the credit bureau receives your letter, it must reinvestigate the items you dispute and get back in touch with you within a "reasonable time," usually interpreted as 30 days. (The Consumer Credit Reporting Reform Act of 1996 specifies this as 30 days.) Colorado (Revised Statutes § 12-14.3-106), Connecticut (General Statutes Annotated § 36a-696) and Massachusetts (Annotated Laws § 93-58) require reinvestigation within five days. Maine (Revised Statutes Annotated § 9-A-8-403) and Maryland (Commercial Code § 12-918(a)(3)(ii)) require reinvestigation within ten days. Louisiana permits 45 days. (Revised Statutes § 9:3571.1(3).) The new law specifies that these state laws will not be nullified on September 30, 1997.

The five- and ten-day requirements are not hard for a credit bureau to meet. Credit bureaus and 6,000 of the nation's creditors are linked by computer, which speeds up the verification process. Furthermore, if you let a credit bureau know that you're trying to obtain a mortgage or car loan, they can do a "rush" verification. If the credit bureau cannot verify the information, it must remove it. Often credit bureaus will remove an item on request without an investigation if rechecking the item is more bother than it's worth.

Requesting a reinvestigation shouldn't cost you anything except in New Mexico, where a credit bureau can charge up to $5 for a reinvestigation. (Statutes Annotated § 56-3-2.) (This charge will be prohibited beginning September 30, 1997.)

If You're the Victim of Fraud

If your credit card is stolen or you are otherwise the victim of credit fraud, you can ask the credit bureaus to add a "fraud alert" to your credit file. Here's how the different credit bureaus handle it:

TRW/Experian. Experian lets you put a security alert in your credit file for 90 days (during which time no new credit will be approved) and a victim statement for seven years. In the statement, you can ask that a creditor call you for oral confirmation of your application before approving further credit. To put a fraud notation in your credit file, call Experian at 800-422-4879.

Trans Union. Trans Union's fraud alert lets you specify that no new credit should be approved until the creditor calls you to verify the application. It lasts for seven years unless you ask that it be removed earlier. To put a fraud notation in your credit file, call Trans Union at 714-738-3800, ext. 9449.

Equifax. Equifax requires that you first obtain a copy of your credit, which will include a toll-free telephone number where you can call to ask that the fraud alert be added to your file. Like the other bureaus, Equifax's fraud alert lets you specify that no new credit should be approved until the creditor obtains a verification from you that the application is legitimate.

Once you've compiled a list of all information you want changed or removed, complete the "request for reinvestigation" form which was enclosed with your credit report. If the bureau did not enclose such a form, use *Form F-23: Request Reinvestigation* in Appendix 3. Don't simply handwrite a letter. Handwritten letters on plain paper often are given minimal attention. Also, try not to dispute your file during the winter holiday season, when credit bureaus are often understaffed.

Incorrect information does not have to be negative to be challenged. In fact, one court ruled that a consumer could sue a credit bureau that reported erroneous but neutral information after the consumer asked that the information be removed. (*Guimond v. Trans Union*, 45 F.3d 1329 (9th Cir. 1995).) The consumer objected to the inclusion of accounts that were not hers, an incorrect assertion that she used a second name, and an erroneous notation that she was married (including the phantom spouse's Social Security number).

Below are some examples of the types of responses you might include on Form F-23:

[X] The following personal information about me is incorrect:

Erroneous Information	Correct Information
Spouse: Ramsey Weiser	I divorced Ramsey Weiser on
	8/23/xx. I'm now married to
	Brian Jones.

[X] The following accounts are not mine:

Creditor's Name	Account Number	Explanation
Dept. of Education	123456789	Pre-marital debt of my
		husband, Brian Jones.
Strong's Dept. Store	0987654321	I've never had a
		Strong's account.

[X] The account status is incorrect for the following accounts:

Creditor's Name	Account Number	Correct Status
Big Bank	1234 5678 9012	Discharged in
MasterCard		bankruptcy; balance
		owed is $0.

[X] The following inquiries were not authorized:

Creditor's Name	Date of Inquiry	Explanation
Wowza Bank Visa	2/14/xx	I did not apply for credit
		with Wowza Bank nor
		authorize them to conduct
		a credit check of me.

[X] Other incorrect information:

Explanation

(1) My credit report states that I filed a Chapter 13 bankruptcy on July 23, 19xx. That is not correct. In fact, I filed a Chapter 7 case and received a discharge of my debts on October 19, 19xx.

(2) American Express account is listed twice—one listing indicates the account was discharged in bankruptcy (this is correct); the other listing shows the account with Tenacious Collection Services (incorrect).

Send your letter to the address provided by the credit bureau for disputing information. Also, enclose copies of any documents you have that support your claim.

If you don't hear from the credit bureau within 30 days, send a follow-up letter using *Form F-24: Request Follow-Up After Reinvestigation* in Appendix 2. Send a copy of Form F-24 to the Federal Trade Commission (addresses are listed below), the agency that oversees credit bureaus. Again, keep a copy for your records.

Credit bureaus have not been legally required to do much more than contact the creditor reporting the information within a reasonable time when they receive a dispute from a consumer. Beginning September 30, 1997, a credit bureau will have to do a bit more, including:

- complete its investigation within 30 days of receiving your complaint (extended to 45 if the bureau receives information from you during the 30-day period)
- contact the creditor reporting the information you dispute within five days of receiving your dispute
- review and consider all relevant information submitted by you
- remove all inaccurate and unverified information
- adopt procedures to keep the information from reappearing
- reinsert removed information only if the provider of the information certifies that the

information is accurate and you are notified within five days of the reinsertion, and
- provide you with the results of its reinvestigation within five days of completion, including a new credit report.

If the credit bureau responds that the creditor reporting the information verified its accuracy and that therefore the information will remain in your file, you will need to take more aggressive action in cleaning up your credit report. Understand that this may be frustrating and time-consuming. A U.S. Public Interest Research Group study concluded that consumers who eventually contacted the FTC for help had spent an average of 32 weeks first trying to resolve the problem themselves. Here are some ideas to help you:

1. Contact the creditor associated with the incorrect information and demand that it tell the credit bureau to remove the information. Write to the customer service department, vice president of marketing, and president or CEO. If the information was reported by a collection agency, send the agency a copy of your letter, too. Use *Form F-25: Request Removal of Incorrect Information by Creditor* in Appendix 3 to make your request. Be sure to keep a copy of your letter. If the creditor is locally based, pay a visit. Sit down in the office of the customer service department, vice president of marketing, or president or CEO. Do not leave until someone agrees to meet with you and hear your problem. *Remember: You have the right to demand attention; this creditor has verified incorrect information and it should be removed from your credit report.*

Beginning September 30, 1997, creditors who report information to credit bureaus will be obligated to do the following:

- refrain from reporting information they know is incorrect
- refrain from ignoring information they know contradicts what they have on file
- refrain from reporting incorrect information when they learn that the information is, in fact, incorrect
- provide credit bureaus with correct information when they learn that the information they have been reporting is incorrect

- notify credit bureaus when you dispute information
- note when accounts are "closed by the consumer"
- provide credit bureaus with the month and year of the delinquency of all accounts placed for collection, charged off or similarly treated, and
- finish their investigation of your dispute within the 30-day or 45-day periods the credit bureau must complete its investigation.

2. If the creditor agrees that the information is incorrect and should be removed from your credit file, send a copy of the creditor's letter to you (or the name, title and phone number of the person with whom you met) to the credit bureau reporting the information. Use *Form F-26: Creditor Verification* found in Appendix 3.

3. If a creditor cannot or will not assist you in removing the incorrect information, you will have to call the credit bureau directly for help. Credit bureaus have 800 numbers to handle consumer disputes about incorrect items in their credit files that are not removed via the normal reinvestigation process. Use the credit bureau's toll-free 800 number as follows:

Experian	800-392-1122
Trans Union	800-851-2674
Equifax	800-685-1111

4. If you were seriously harmed by the credit bureau—for example, it continued to give out false information after you requested corrections—you may want to sue. The FCRA lets you sue a credit bureau for negligent or willful noncompliance with the law within two years after the bureau's harmful behavior first occurred. You can sue for actual damages, such as court costs, attorney's fees, lost wages and, if applicable, intentional infliction of emotional distress. In the case of truly outrageous behavior, you can recover punitive damages—damages meant to punish for malicious or willful conduct. Under the FCRA, the court decides the amount of the punitive damages.

5. If all else fails, consider calling your congressional representative or senator. That person can call the FTC and demand some action.

Federal Trade Commission

You can call or write the FTC to file a complaint against a credit bureau.

National Office
6th & Pennsylvania Avenue, NW
Washington, DC 20580
202-326-2222

Regional Offices
1718 Peachtree Street, NW, Suite 1000
Atlanta, GA 30367
404-347-4836

10 Merrimac Street, Suite 810
Boston, MA 02114-4719
617-424-5960

55 East Monroe Street, Suite 1437
Chicago, IL 60603
312-353-4423

668 Euclid Avenue, Suite 520-A
Cleveland, OH 44114
216-522-4207

100 N. Central Expressway, Suite 500
Dallas, TX 75201
214-767-5501

1405 Curtis Street, Suite 2900
Denver, CO 80202-2393
303-844-2271

11000 Wilshire Boulevard, Suite 13209
Los Angeles, CA 90024
310-575-7575

150 William Street, Suite 1300
New York, New York 10038
212-264-1207

901 Market Street, Suite 570
San Francisco, CA 94103
415-744-7920

2806 Federal Building
915 Second Avenue
Seattle, WA 98174
206-220-6363

E. Consider Adding a 100-Word Statement to Your Credit File

If you feel a credit bureau is including the wrong information in your file, or you want to explain a particular entry, you have the right to put a 100-word statement in your file. Don't always assume that adding a 100-word statement is the best approach. In fact, it's often wiser to simply explain the negative mark to creditors in person than to try to explain it in 100 words or fewer.

If you do add a 100-word statement, the credit bureau may give only a summary—written by the credit bureau—to anyone who requests your file. To avoid this, be clear and concise; keep it as short as you can. If you request it, the bureau must also give the statement or summary to anyone who received a copy of your file within the past six months—or two years if your file was given out for employment purposes.

Unfortunately, many statements or summaries are ineffective. Few creditors who receive credit files read the statements or summaries. In any David (consumer) vs. Goliath (credit bureau) dispute, creditors tend to believe Goliath. Finally, your statement might stay in your file even longer than the disputed information.

F. Add Positive Account Histories to Your Credit File

Often, credit reports don't include accounts that you might expect to find. Some major commercial lenders don't report mortgages or car loans. Local banks or credit unions often don't provide information to credit bureaus.

If your credit file is missing credit histories for accounts you pay on time, send the credit bureaus a copy of a recent account statement and copies of canceled checks (never originals) showing your payment history. Ask the credit bureaus to add the information to your file. While the bureaus aren't required to add account histories, they often do—but may charge you a fee for doing so. Use Form F-27: Request Addition of Account Histories from Appendix 3 to make your request.

It may be that credit histories for accounts you pay on time are missing from only one or two credit reports—the third report may have included all accounts when you received it, or you may have focused on cleaning up that report first. In this situation, a simple way to request that the bureaus not reporting the information add it to your file is to send them a copy of the credit report that includes all your accounts.

G. Add Information Showing Stability to Your Credit File

Creditors like to see evidence of stability in your file. If any of the items listed below are missing from your file, you may want to send a letter to the credit bureaus asking that the information be added. Use *Form F-28: Request Addition of Information Showing Stability* in Appendix 3 to make your request.

You may want to add:

- **Your current employment**—employer's name, employer's address and your job title. You may wisely decide not to add this if you think a creditor may sue you or a creditor has a judgment against you. Current employment information may be a green light for a wage garnishment.
- **Your previous employment,** especially if you've had your current job fewer than two years. Include your former employer's name and address and your job title.
- **Your current residence,** and if you own it, say so. (Not all mortgage lenders report their accounts to credit bureaus.) Again, don't do this if you've been sued or you think a creditor may sue you. Real estate is an excellent collection source.

Sample 100-Word Statements

As mentioned, be judicious in your use of 100-word statements. But if the information in your file is clearly wrong and can be simply explained, consider adding a statement. Here are a few samples:

"I am not unemployed. Since 19xx, I have worked as a freelance technical writer, and have earned an average of $35,000 per year. My work has appeared in *Data, ComPuter, Plug In, Delicious, BIM PC,* and many other computer magazines."

"Although I was sued by Randy Roofer, I did not pay her because the roof she put on my house is not sealed and she refuses to fix it. Three times I have come home and found drowned squirrels in my toilet. I refuse to pay Randy until she repairs the roof. I filed a complaint with the state contractor's board, which is pending."

"I am disputing the debt I owe to Country Electronics. I purchased a CD player which does not work correctly. The store refuses to take the merchandise back, refund my money or give me a replacement CD player. I am trying to resolve the problem with the manufacturer."

"It is technically accurate that I was sued by Jones and Jones Department Store on June 11, 19xx. Jones and Jones dismissed the lawsuit, however, when they realized that they had confused my account with another customer's. My account with Jones and Jones has never been delinquent."

"I was hospitalized following a car accident. I sent the medical bills to my insurance company, but the company took over six months to pay the bills. In the meantime, the hospital began collection efforts against me. Those efforts ended when the insurance company paid the bill."

"The late payment notations for NorthBank should not be on my file. I moved and sent NorthBank a change of address, which it did not process correctly. It took NorthBank nearly three months to catch up with me. All that time, I received no bills from the bank."

"The late payment notation for SouthBank should not be on my file. SouthBank moved and did not send me a change of address in a timely manner. I made my payment early, but it went to SouthBank's old address. By the time SouthBank received it at its new address, it was nearly a month late."

"I was not aware that I owed any money to my ex-landlord, Juanita Morales. Beginning on June 1, 19xx, I rented an apartment from her with a roommate, Mark Graves. I moved out on May 15, 19xx and Ms. Morales told me that I owed no more money. Apparently, Mr. Graves remained for a few weeks and caused damage to the place. When he refused to pay, Ms. Morales came after me because our lease didn't legally end until May 30, 19xx. I didn't learn about the problem until years later."

- **Your previous residence,** especially if you've lived at your current address fewer than two years.

- **Your telephone number,** especially if it's unlisted. If you haven't yet given the credit bureaus your phone number, consider doing so now. A creditor who cannot verify a telephone number is often reluctant to grant credit.

- **Your date of birth.** A creditor will probably not grant you credit if it does not know your age. It is especially important to add your age if you are over 50. People over 50 tend to be low credit risks because their incomes are usually higher than people under age 50, their children are grown (no college costs) and their mortgages are paid off.

- **Your Social Security number.**

- **Bank checking or savings account number** —it's an excellent sign of stability. Again, however, you won't want to add this information

if you've been sued or you think a creditor may sue you. A creditor with a judgment against you will likely use this information to try to collect.

Again, credit bureaus aren't required to add any of this information, but they often do. They are most likely to add information on jobs and residences, as that information is used by creditors in evaluating applications for credit. They will also add your telephone number, date of birth and Social Security number because those items help identify you and lessen the chances of "mixed" credit files—that is, getting other people's credit histories in your file. (Expect to pay a small fee when a credit bureau adds information to your file.)

Enclose any documentation that verifies information you're providing, such as your driver's license, a canceled check, a bill addressed to you, a pay stub showing your employer's name and address or anything else similar. Remember to keep photocopies of all correspondence. ■

CHAPTER

5

Establishing and Keeping a Good Credit Record

stablishing and keeping a good credit file is the final step in repairing your credit. Creditors evaluate credit files based on a point system used by credit bureaus to indicate payment history. In a typical case, each payment entry contains a rating point between 0 and 9. This is what is meant by a "credit rating." Ratings 0-6 pertain to payment timeframes. That is, rating 0 means you pay within 30 days, rating 1 within 60 days, rating 2 within 90 days, and so forth. Rating 7 means the creditor repossessed an item, rating 8 means the account has been sent to collection (including if you were sued) and rating 9 means the debt was discharged in bankruptcy.

Rating systems differ among credit bureaus. Some reverse their systems—that is, give a rating of 9 for accounts paid within 30 days and 0 for a debt discharged in bankruptcy. Others use a 9 to indicate any serious creditor action such as repossessions, foreclosures, collections or bankruptcies.

How the negative items in your file affect your ability to get credit depends on each creditor. Most creditors are relatively conservative—they take few risks. If your credit file shows that you routinely take 120 days to pay your bills, most creditors won't lend you money or will insist on a very large down payment or high interest rate to greatly lower their risk. Some creditors will deny you credit if you have any rating in your file other than 0s or 1s.

It's impossible to say whether taking 180 days to pay (rating 5) is better than defaulting and having your account sent to a collection agency (rating 8). Frankly, neither will raise you to "most favored borrower status." If your file shows that you've taken many steps to improve your credit, however, many creditors won't put too much weight on the negative entries.

This chapter shows you many steps you can take to improve your credit—beyond what you've done in the previous chapters—including getting credit in your own name, combining your credit history with your spouse's, getting and using different kinds of credit and avoiding being the victim of credit discrimination.

Should You Repair Your Credit?

Habitual overspending can be just as hard to overcome as excessive gambling or drinking. If you think you may be a compulsive spender, one of the worst things you can do is repair your credit. Instead, you need to get a handle on your spending habits.

Debtors Anonymous, a 12-step support program similar to Alcoholics Anonymous, has programs nationwide. If a Debtors Anonymous group or a therapist recommends that you stay out of the credit system for a while, follow that advice. Even if you don't feel you're a compulsive spender, paying as you spend may still be the way to go—because of finance charges, transaction fees and other charges, buying on credit costs between 20% and 25% more than paying with cash.

Debtors Anonymous groups meet all over the country. If you can't find one in your area, send a self-addressed, stamped envelope to Debtors Anonymous, General Services Board, P.O. Box 400, New York, NY 10163-0400. Or call their message machine at 212-642-8220 and leave your name, address and a request for information.

Concern about habitual overspending isn't the only reason to stay outside the credit system. Followers of a movement known as "voluntary simplicity" suggest that reliance on credit is one of the reasons people are overworked, overstressed and have trouble slowing down. Credit gives us the chance to consume—and often we consume far more than we need to live comfortably and at an easy pace.

Much has been written about voluntarily downshifting. Advocates are not suggesting that we all move to the wilderness, quit our jobs and live without electricity and running water. But they do suggest that we take a hard look at our reliance on money—and credit—to bring us happiness.

For more information on voluntary simplicity, take a look at any of these resources:

- *Simplify Your Life: 100 Ways to Slow Down and Enjoy the Things That Really Matter*, by Elaine St. James (Hyperion).
- *Get a Life: You Don't Need a Million to Retire Well*, by Ralph Warner (Nolo Press).
- *Your Money or Your Life*, by Joe Dominguez and Vicki Robin (Penguin Books).
- *The Pocket Change Investor* (quarterly consumer newsletter), by Marc Eisenson and Nancy Castleman (Good Advice Press, Box 78, Elizaville, NY 12523, 800-255-0899).
- "Down Shifters," *Kiplinger's Personal Finance Magazine*, by Kristin Davis (August 1996).

➡️ *If you've never been married, skip ahead to Section C.*

you want to obtain credit in your own name, complete credit applications in your name only.

A. Get Credit in Your Own Name

If you are married, separated or divorced, you are entitled to have a credit report issued in your own name. This is an excellent strategy for repairing your credit if:

- all or most of your financial problems can be attributed to your spouse or former spouse, or
- you and your spouse have gone through financial difficulties together, but most credit was in your spouse's name only.

Even if both of you have had financial problems, separating your credit histories can help you both repair your credit.

> **EXAMPLE:** Carol and Ray used several credit cards in Carol's name and two cards in both names to run up thousands of dollars in bills. They missed payments, had their cards canceled and were sued. By separating their credit histories, they can eliminate all of Carol's cards from Ray's credit file. They can then concentrate on repairing each of their credit histories. Because Ray's credit record is better, he qualifies for credit in a short time. Once things improve, they apply for credit as a couple. The positive information generated is added to both Ray and Carol's files, thereby improving Carol's credit too.

Contact all three credit bureaus and ask that a credit file be created in your name only. Then insist that the credit bureaus remove all accounts belonging to your spouse alone. (Information on marital status discrimination is in Section H, below.) Use *Form F-29: Request Credit in Own Name* in Appendix 3 to make your request to the credit bureaus. If

B. Combine Your Credit History With Your Spouse's

If you are married, you and your spouse are entitled to have the same credit information in each of your credit reports. If you have no credit history or have a few negative marks, and your spouse has A-1 credit, getting his credit histories into your file may be just what you need.

Write to all three credit bureaus and request that they merge your file with your spouse's file. Use *Form F-30: Request Merged Credit Reports* in Appendix 3 to make your request to the credit bureaus.

Once your request is complete, your file will contain your negative marks and your spouse's positive ones. Your spouse must then write the credit bureaus to have your credit accounts removed from his file. (See Section A, just above.) If your spouse doesn't make this request, your negative marks will remain in his file.

C. Understand How Credit Applications Are Evaluated

When you apply for credit, creditors use two primary methods to evaluate your request:

- weigh your three "Cs"—capacity, collateral and character, and
- create a "risk score" based on the information in your credit file.

1. Your Three "Cs"

A creditor needs information to determine the likelihood that you will repay a loan or pay charges you incur on a line of revolving credit. This is done by evaluating the three "Cs."

Capacity. This refers to the amount of debts you can realistically pay given your income. Creditors look at how long you've been on your job, your income level and the likelihood that it will increase over time. They also look to see that you're in a stable job or at least a stable job industry. It's important when you fill out a credit application to make your job sound stable, high-level and even "professional." Are you a secretary or are you an executive secretary or the office manager?

Finally, creditors examine your existing credit relationships, such as credit cards, bank loans and mortgages. They want to know your credit limits (you may be denied additional credit if you already have a lot of open credit lines), your current credit balances, how long you've had each account and your payment history—whether you pay late or on time.

Collateral. Creditors like to see that you have assets that they can take from you if you don't pay your debt. Owning a home or liquid assets such as a mutual fund may offer considerable comfort to a creditor reviewing an application. This is especially true if your credit report has negative notations in it, such as late payments.

Character. Creditors develop a feeling of your financial character through objective factors that show stability. These include the length of your residency, the length of your employment, whether you rent or own your home (you're more likely to stay put if you own), and whether you have checking and savings accounts.

2. Your Risk Score

Credit bureaus do not "rate" your creditworthiness other than to assign objective numbers along the 0-9 scale described at the beginning of this chapter.

But credit bureaus often provide a statistical summary of the information in your credit report—called a risk score. Risk scores are calculated using elaborate scoring models developed by a few companies in the U.S. There are thousands of models (Sears, alone, uses several hundred models), which

differ depending on the type of credit involved, where the consumer lives (car ownership is less important in large cities than other areas), the creditor's marketing plans and business niche, and other factors. Furthermore, risk scoring models don't necessarily use the same scoring system: one model's range of scores is 0 to 1,000, while another's range is 363 to 840. Even when creditors use the same scoring system, the same number may mean different things to different creditors.

Companies that develop risk score models (the primary developer is Fair Isaac and Company, in San Rafael, California) do not disclose these models to the public. It's anyone's guess how the information in a credit report is truly evaluated. (In 1992, the Federal Trade Commission ruled that a risk score was part of a consumer's credit file and had to be disclosed to a consumer. The credit industry was outraged and demanded that the FTC reconsider its decision. It did, and reversed itself in 1995. The FTC concluded that you have no right to any risk score associated with your credit file. And the Consumer Credit Reporting Reform Act of 1996, effective September 30, 1997, expressely states that a credit bureau is under no obligation to dislose risk scores.)

D. Get Credit Cards and Use Them Wisely

If you survived your financial disaster and managed to hold onto one of your credit cards or a department store or gasoline card, use it and pay your bills on time. Your credit history will improve quickly. As mentioned Chapter 4, most credit reports show payment histories for 24-36 months. If you charge something every month, no matter how small, and pay at least the minimum required every month, your credit report will show steady and proper use of revolving credit.

⚠️ *Charge only a small amount each month and pay it in full. By paying in full, you will avoid incurring interest, as long as you have a card with a* *grace period. Consumer groups such as Bankcard Holders of America (see Appendix 1) point out that the average consumer who pays the minimum each month ends up paying hundreds of dollars in interest charges alone. Their example: If you charge $1,000 on a 19.8% credit card and pay it off by making the minimum payments each month, you'll take over eight years to pay off the loan and will pay almost $850 in interest. This is crazy. Repairing your credit might cost you a little, but you don't have to throw your money away in the process.*

1. Applying for Credit Cards

If you don't currently have a credit card, apply for one. Keep in mind the general guidelines under the three "Cs" discussion, above, when completing your credit application. Don't lie, but present yourself in the best possible light.

It's often easiest to obtain a card from a department store or gasoline company. These companies usually open your account with a very low credit line. If you start with one credit card, charge items and pay the bill on time, other companies will issue you a card. When you use department store and gasoline cards, try not to carry a balance from one month to the next. The interest rate on these cards is as high as 22%.

Next, apply for a regular credit card from a bank, such as a Visa, MasterCard or Discover card. Interest rates and annual fees on these cards have dropped some over the past few years and you may be able to find a card with relatively low rates. Depending on how bad your credit history is, you may be eligible only for a low credit line or a card with a high interest rate. If you use the card and make your payments, however, after a year or so you can apply for an increase in your line of credit or a reduction of the credit rate.

Many people who have had serious financial problems misused or overused their credit cards. The following tips will help you when you apply for credit cards or an increased credit limit:

Be consistent with the name you use. Use your middle initial always or never. Always use your generation (Jr., Sr., II, III, etc.).

Take advantage of preapproved credit for department store, gasoline and bank credit cards. If your credit is shot, you may not have the luxury of shopping around.

Be honest, but forgiving. On applications, paint a picture of yourself in the best light. Lenders are especially apt to give less weight to past credit problems that were out of your control—such as a job layoff or illness.

Apply for credit when you are most likely to get it. For example, apply when you are working, when you've lived at the same address for at least a year and when you haven't had an unusually high number of inquiries on your credit report in the last two years.

Apply for credit from creditors with whom you've done business. For example, if you had a Sears charge card from a store in New Jersey and you moved to California, apply for a Sears card from a store near your new home.

Don't get swept up by credit card gimmicks. Before applying for a credit card that gives you rebates, credit for future purchases or other perks, make sure you will benefit by the offer. Some are good deals, especially cards that give you cash back. But in general, a card with no annual fee and/or low interest usually beats the cards with deals.

Scrutinize any preapproval solicitations for nonbank cards. A "gold" or "platinum" card with a high credit limit may be nothing more than a card that lets you purchase items through catalogues provided by the company itself. No other merchant accepts these cards and the company won't report your charges and payments to the credit bureaus. Also, the items in the catalogues are usually high priced and of low quality.

Once you receive a credit card, protect yourself and your efforts to repair your credit by following these suggestions:

Send your creditors a change of address when you move. Many creditors provide change of address boxes on their monthly bills. For your other creditors, you can send a letter, call the customer service phone number or use a post office change of address postcard.

If you need an increase in your credit limit, ask for it. Many creditors will close accounts or charge late fees on customers who exceed their credit limits. But pay close attention; if you're charging to the limit on your credit card, you may be heading for financial trouble.

Take steps to protect your cards. Sign your cards as soon as they arrive. If you have a personal identification number (PIN) that allows you take cash advances, keep the number in your head and never write it down near your credit card. Make a list of your credit card issuers, the account numbers and the issuer's phone numbers so you can quickly call if you need to report a lost or stolen card.

Don't give you credit card number to anyone over the phone unless you placed the call and are certain of the company's reputation. Never, never, never give your credit card number to someone who calls you and tries to sell you something or claims to need your credit card number to send you a "prize." *These are scam artists.*

Cosigners and guarantors should fully understand their obligations before they sign on. For example, if the primary debtor doesn't pay and erases the debt in bankruptcy, the cosigner or guarantor remains fully liable. The Federal Trade Commission's Credit Practices Rule requires that cosigners of credit issued by a financial institution be given the following notice:

> You are being asked to guarantee this debt. Think carefully before you do so. If the borrower doesn't pay the debt, you will have to. Be sure you can afford to pay if you have to, and that you want to accept this responsibility.
>
> You may have to pay up to the full amount of the debt if the borrower does not pay. You may also have to pay late fees or collection costs, which increase this amount.
>
> The creditor can collect this debt from you without first trying to collect from the borrower. The creditor can use the same collection methods against you that can be used against the borrower, such as suing you, garnishing your wages, etc. If this debt is ever in default, that fact may become a part of your credit record.

2. Cosigners and Guarantors

A cosigner is someone who promises to repay a loan or credit card charges if the primary debtor defaults. Similarly, a guarantor promises the credit grantor that he will pay if the primary debtor does not. Usually, neither the cosigner's nor the guarantor's name appears on the credit account.

Cosigned and guaranteed accounts differ in one way. With a cosigned account, the primary debtor's credit rating does not improve. Only the cosigner's credit is affected. With a guaranteed account, however, both the primary debtor's and the guarantor's credit rating are affected. If a credit grantor insists that you have a cosigner, ask instead if you can use a guarantor. It should make no difference to the credit grantor.

3. Authorized User Accounts

Another way to repair your credit using a credit card relies on the generosity of a friend or relative you trust.

If you can find someone who is willing to add you to an account as an "authorized user," you can use the credit line but you are not responsible for repaying the charges. The account holder must request that your name be added to the account and can ask that a card be issued in your name. Once your name is on the account, information about the account will probably be added to your file—and you'll be listed as an authorized user.

Of course, because the information concerning the account is reported in your credit file, this technique requires that the account holder not default.

If she does, that information will appear in your credit report, exactly what you don't want.

4. Secured Credit Cards

Many people with poor credit histories are denied regular credit cards. If your application is rejected, consider whether you truly need a credit card. Millions of people get along just fine without them. If you decide that you really need a card—for example, you travel quite a bit and need a card to reserve hotel rooms and rent cars—then you can apply for a secured credit card. With a secured credit card, you deposit a sum of money with a bank and are given a credit card with a credit limit for a percentage of the amount you deposit—as low as 50% and as high as 120%. Depending on the bank, you'll be required to deposit as little as a few hundred dollars or as much as a few thousand.

Unfortunately, secured credit cards can be expensive. Many banks charge application and processing fees in addition to an annual fee. Also the interest rate on secured credit cards is often close to 22%, while you earn only 2% or 3% on the money you deposit. And some banks have eliminated the grace period—that is, interest on your balance begins to accrue on the date you charge, not 25 days later. If you find a card with a grace period and pay your bill in full each month, you can avoid the interest charges.

Many secured credit cards have a conversion option. This lets you convert the card into a regular credit card after several months or a year, if you use the secured card responsibly. Because regular credit cards typically have lower interest rates and annual fees than secured credit cards, it's usually preferable to obtain a card with a conversion option.

To find a bank offering a secured credit card:
- call some local banks
- send $4 to Bankcard Holders of America and request "Building Credit: Banks Across the Nation Offering Secured Credit Cards," (see Appendix 1 for BHA's address), or

- contact a local Consumer Credit Counseling Service office (see Appendix 1 for more information on CCCS).

Avoid 900-number advertisements for "instant credit" or other come-ons. Obtaining a secured credit card through one of these programs will probably cost you a lot—in application fees, processing fees and phone charges. Sometimes you call one 900 number and are told you must call a second or third number. These ads also frequently mislead consumers into thinking their line of credit will be higher than it actually will be. If you have to deposit $5,000 to get a card, your credit line may be only $2,500 to $4,000 (50% to 80%).

How Many Credit Cards Should You Carry?

Once you succeed in getting a credit card, you might be hungry to apply for many more cards. Not so fast. Having too much credit may have contributed your debt problems in the first place. Ideally, you should carry one bank credit card, one department store card and one gasoline card. Your inclination may be to charge everything on your bank card and not bother using a department store or gasoline card. When creditors look in your credit file, however, they want to see that you can handle more than one credit account at a time. You don't need to build up interest charges on these cards, but use them and pay the bill in full.

Creditors frown on applicants who have a lot of open credit. So keeping many cards may mean that you'll be turned down for other credit—perhaps credit you really need. And if your credit applications are turned down, your file will contain inquiries from the companies that rejected you. Your credit file will look like you were desperately trying to get credit, something creditors never like to see.

5. Closing Credit Card Accounts

If you want to close some accounts, here are some rules to follow:

- Close accounts you don't need. Send a letter—and the card cut up—to the customer service department of the card issuer. You can close an account even if you haven't paid off the balance. The card issuer will close your account, cancel your privileges and send you monthly statements until you pay off your balance. Or contact the bank whose card you are keeping and ask it to transfer your remaining balance on the account you are closing to the account you are keeping.

- Close accounts on which you are delinquent—otherwise, the credit card issuer may close them for you. If you're delinquent on all your accounts, keep open the most current account.

- If you pay your bill in full each month—that is, you don't carry a balance—close the accounts with the highest annual fees. Make sure that the accounts you keep open have a grace period—a 20-25 day period each month in which you can pay off your bill and not incur any interest.

- If you carry a balance, close the accounts with the highest interest rates and shortest grace periods. Also, read your contract to understand the credit card company's billing practice. Interest may be calculated on the previous two months' balance, the average daily balance for the month or your balance at the end of the billing cycle. Keep the cards that charge interest on the balance at the end of the billing cycle.

E. Open Deposit Accounts

Creditors look for bank accounts as a sign of stability. Quite frankly, they also look for bank accounts as a source of how you will pay your bills. The overwhelming majority of financial transactions in our society are done by check. If you fill out a credit application and cannot provide a checking account number, you probably won't be given credit.

A savings or money market account, too, will improve your standing with creditors. Even if you never deposit additional money into the account, creditors assume that people who have savings or money market accounts use them. Having an account reassures creditors of two things: You are making an effort to build up savings, and if you don't pay your bill and the creditor must sue you to collect, it has a source to collect its judgment.

Just because you've had poor credit history, you shouldn't be denied an account. Shop around and compare fees, such as check writing fees, ATM fees, monthly service charges, the minimum balance to waive the monthly charge, interest rates on savings and the like.

F. Work With Local Merchants

Another way to repair your credit is to approach a local merchant (such as an electronics or furniture store) and arrange to purchase an item on credit. Many local stores will work with you in setting up a payment schedule, but be prepared to put down a deposit of up to 30% or to pay a high rate of interest. If you still don't qualify, the merchant might agree to give you credit if you get someone to cosign or guarantee the loan. (See Section D.2, above.) Or you may be able to get credit by first buying an item on layaway.

Even if a local merchant won't extend you credit, it may very well let you make a purchase on a layaway plan. When you purchase an item on layaway, the seller keeps the merchandise until you fully pay for it. Only then are you entitled to pick it up. One advantage of layaway is that you don't pay interest. One disadvantage is that it may be months before you actually get the item. This might be fine if you're buying a dress for your cousin's wedding that is eight months away. This isn't so fine if your mattress is so shot that you wake up with a back-ache every morning.

Layaway purchases are not reported to credit bureaus. If you purchase an item on layaway and make all the payments on time, however, the store may be willing to issue you a store credit card or store credit privileges.

G. Obtain a Bank Loan

One way to repair your credit is to take some money you've saved and open a savings account. You ask the bank to give you a loan against the money in your account. In exchange, you have no access to your money—you give your passbook to the bank and the bank won't give you an ATM card for the account—so there's no risk to the bank if you fail to make the payments. If the bank doesn't offer these types of loans, apply for a personal loan and offer either a cosigner or to secure it against some collateral you own.

No matter what kind of loan you get, be sure you know the following:

- **Does the bank report these loan payments to credit bureaus?** This is key; the whole reason you take out the loan is to repair your credit. If a bank doesn't report your payments to a credit bureau, there's no reason to take out a loan.
- **What is the minimum deposit amount required for a loans?** Some banks won't give you a loan unless you have $3,000 in an account; others will lend you money on $50. Find a bank that fits your budget.
- **What is the interest rate?** The interest rate on the loan is usually much higher than what people with good credit pay. You will probably pay between 8% and 12% interest on the loan. Yes, this means you'll lose a little money on the transaction, but it can be worth it if you're determined to repair your credit.
- **What is the maximum amount you can borrow?** On passbook loans, banks won't

loan you 100% of what's in your account; most will loan you between 80% and 90%. On other loans, you will face a maximum on how much you can borrow.

- **What is the repayment schedule?** Banks usually give you one to three years to repay the loan. Some banks have no minimum monthly repayment amount on passbook loans; you could pay nothing for nearly the entire loan period and then pay the entire balance in the last month. Although you can pay the loan back in only one or two payments, don't. Pay it off over at least 12 months so that monthly installment payments appear on your credit file.

H. Avoid Credit Repair Clinics

You've probably seen ads for companies that claim they can fix your credit, qualify you for a loan or get you a credit card. Their pitches are tempting, especially if your credit is bad and you desperately want to buy a new car or house.

You will want to avoid these outfits, however. Many of their practices are illegal. Some have been caught stealing the credit files or Social Security numbers of people who are under 18, have died or live in out-of-the-way places like Guam or the U.S. Virgin Islands, and substituting these for the files of people with poor credit histories.

Other credit clinics break into credit bureau computers and change or erase bad credit files. Still others suggest that you create a new identity by applying for an IRS Employer Identification number (EIN), a nine-digit number that resembles a Social Security number, and use it instead of your Social Security number. Not only is this illegal, but by using an EIN, you won't earn Social Security benefits.

These illegal methods are just the tip of the iceberg. Credit repair clinics devise new schemes as often as consumer protection agencies catch onto their previous ones.

Even assuming that a credit repair company is legitimate, don't listen to its come-ons. These companies can't do anything for you that you can't do yourself. What they will do, however, is charge you between $250 and $5,000 for their unnecessary services. Here's what credit repair clinics claim to be able to do for you:

Remove incorrect information from your credit file. You can do that yourself under the Fair Credit Reporting Act. See Chapter 4.

Remove correct, but negative, information from your credit file. Negative items in your credit file can legally stay there for seven or ten years, as long as they are correct. No one can wave a wand and make them go away. One tactic of credit repair services is to try and take advantage of the law requiring credit bureaus to verify information if the customer disputes it. Credit repair clinics do this by challenging every item in a credit file—negative, positive or neutral—with the hope of overwhelming the credit bureau into removing information without verifying it. Credit bureaus are aware of this tactic and often dismiss these challenges on the ground that they are frivolous, a right credit bureaus have under the Fair Credit Reporting Act. You are better off getting your file and selectively challenging the outdated, incorrect and ambiguous items.

Even if the credit bureau removes information that a credit bureau had the right to include in your file, it's no doubt only a temporary removal. Most correct information reappears after 30-60 days, when the creditor that first reported the information to the credit bureaus re-reports it.

Get outstanding debt balances and court judgments removed from your credit file. Credit repair clinics often advise debtors to pay outstanding debts if the creditor agrees to remove the negative information from your credit file. This is certainly a negotiation tactic you want to consider (see Chapter 3, Section C), but you don't need to pay a credit repair clinic for this advice.

Get you a major credit card. Credit repair clinics can give you a list of banks that offer

secured credit cards. While this information is helpful in rebuilding credit, it's not worth hundreds or thousands of dollars—you can get a list yourself for little or nothing. (See Appendix 1.)

Many states regulate for-profit credit repair clinics, or even prohibit them from operating. A federal law regulating for-profit credit repair clinics takes effect March 30, 1997. Some dubious credit repair clinics have tried to get around these regulations by setting themselves up as nonprofits, but they still take your money and provide poor results—or do nothing for you that you couldn't do for yourself.

If you're still tempted to use a credit repair organization (whether or not it claims to be a nonprofit), do the following:

- Ask whether or not the company is bonded. A company that is bonded has posted money in the event it goes out of business or goes bankrupt and dissatisfied consumers seek a refund. A legitimate company should be willing to give you the name of the company through which it is bonded. Call the bonding company for verification.

- Ask to see a copy of the contract before you sign. Carefully check the company's fees, claims of what it can do and your right to a refund. Avoid any company that won't give you a written agreement or a right to cancel if you change your mind.

- Call your local Better Business Bureau and your state consumer affairs office (a list is in Appendix 1) to see if either has complaints on file for the company.

- Ask for the names and phone numbers of satisfied customers. Be wary of any satisfied customers you speak to whose claims sound nearly verbatim like the claims of the company. These people are probably shills—people who pose as satisfied customers, but who never used the company's service and are simply paid to say good things about the company.

Laws Regulating For-Profit Credit Repair Clinics

Arizona   § 44-1705
Credit repair clinics must inform debtors of their rights under the Fair Credit Reporting Act, be bonded, accurately represent what they can and cannot do and let debtors cancel the contract until midnight of 3rd day after signing.

Arkansas   § 4-91-106 et seq.
Credit repair clinics must inform debtors of their rights under the Fair Credit Reporting Act, be bonded, accurately represent what they can and cannot do and let debtors cancel the contract until midnight of 5th day after signing.

California   Civil Code § 1789.15 et seq.
Credit repair clinics must inform debtors of their rights under the Fair Credit Reporting Act, be bonded, accurately represent what they can and cannot do, perform their obligations under the contract within 90 days and let debtors cancel the contract until midnight of 5th day after signing.

Colorado   § 12-14.5-101
Credit repair clinics must inform debtors of their rights under the Fair Credit Reporting Act, be bonded, accurately represent what they can and cannot do and let debtors cancel the contract until midnight of 5th day after signing.

Connecticut   § 36-435l
Credit repair clinics must inform debtors of their rights under the Fair Credit Reporting Act, be bonded and accurately represent what they can and cannot do.

Delaware   § 6-2401 et seq.
Credit repair clinics must inform debtors of their rights under the Fair Credit Reporting Act, be bonded, accurately represent what they can and cannot do and let debtors cancel the contract until midnight of 3rd day after signing.

District of Columbia   § 28-4601 et seq.
Credit repair clinics must inform debtors of their rights under the Fair Credit Reporting Act, be bonded and accurately represent what they can and cannot do.

Florida   § 817.704 et seq.
Credit repair clinics must inform debtors of their rights under the Fair Credit Reporting Act, be bonded, accurately represent what they can and cannot do and let debtors cancel the contract until midnight of 5th day after signing.

Georgia   § 16-9-59
Credit repair clinics are prohibited.

Hawaii   § 481B-12
Credit repair clinics are prohibited.

Illinois   § 815 ILCS 605/6
Credit repair clinics must inform debtors of their rights under the Fair Credit Reporting Act, be bonded, accurately represent what they can and cannot do and let debtors cancel the contract until midnight of 3rd day after signing.

Indiana   § 24-5-15-7
Credit repair clinics must inform debtors of their rights under the Fair Credit Reporting Act, be bonded, accurately represent what they can and cannot do and let debtors cancel the contract until midnight of 3rd day after signing.

Iowa   § 538A.1
Credit repair clinics must inform debtors of their rights under the Fair Credit Reporting Act, be bonded, accurately represent what they can and cannot do and let debtors cancel the contract until midnight of 3rd day after signing.

Kansas   § 50-1103
Credit repair clinics must be bonded and accurately represent what they can and cannot do.

Louisiana   § 9:3573.7
Credit repair clinics must inform debtors of their rights under the Fair Credit Reporting Act, be bonded, accurately represent what they can and cannot do and let debtors cancel the contract until midnight of 5th day after signing.

Maine   § 9-A-10-101 et seq.
Credit repair clinics must inform debtors of their rights under the Fair Credit Reporting Act, be bonded and accurately represent what they can and cannot do.

Maryland   § 14-1905 et seq.
Credit repair clinics must inform debtors of their rights under the Fair Credit Reporting Act, be bonded, accurately represent what they can and cannot do and let debtors cancel the contract until midnight of 3rd day after signing.

Massachusetts   § 93-68C et seq.
Credit repair clinics must inform debtors of their rights under the Fair Credit Reporting Act, be bonded, accurately represent what they can and cannot do and let debtors cancel the contract until midnight of 3rd day after signing.

Michigan   § 23.1195 (91) et seq.
Credit repair clinics must inform debtors of their rights under the Fair Credit Reporting Act, be bonded, accurately represent what they can and cannot do and let debtors cancel the contract until midnight of 5th day after signing.

Laws Regulating For-Profit Credit Repair Clinics

Minnesota   § 332.52 et seq.

Credit repair clinics must inform debtors of their rights under the Fair Credit Reporting Act, be bonded, accurately represent what they can and cannot do and let debtors cancel the contract until midnight of 5th day after signing.

Missouri   § 407.638

Credit repair clinics must inform debtors of their rights under the Fair Credit Reporting Act, be bonded, accurately represent what they can and cannot do and let debtors cancel the contract until midnight of 3rd day after signing.

Nebraska   § 45-807 et seq.

Credit repair clinics must inform debtors of their rights under the Fair Credit Reporting Act, be bonded, accurately represent what they can and cannot do and let debtors cancel the contract until midnight of 3rd day after signing.

Nevada   § 598.282

Credit repair clinics must inform debtors of their rights under the Fair Credit Reporting Act, be bonded, accurately represent what they can and cannot do, let debtors cancel the contract until midnight of 5th day after signing and not collect any money until all promised services are performed.

New Hampshire   § 359-D:1

Credit repair clinics must inform debtors of their rights under the Fair Credit Reporting Act, be bonded, accurately represent what they can and cannot do and let debtors cancel the contract until midnight of 5th day after signing.

New York   Gen. Bus. Law § 458-d

Credit repair clinics must inform debtors of their rights under the Fair Credit Reporting Act, be bonded, accurately represent what they can and cannot do, let debtors cancel the contract until midnight of 3rd day after signing and not collect any money until all promised services are performed.

North Carolina   § 66-220 et seq.

Credit repair clinics must inform debtors of their rights under the Fair Credit Reporting Act, be bonded, accurately represent what they can and cannot do and let debtors cancel the contract until midnight of 3rd day after signing.

Ohio   § 4712.05

Credit repair clinics must inform debtors of their rights under the Fair Credit Reporting Act, be bonded, accurately represent what they can and cannot do and let debtors cancel the contract until midnight of 3rd day after signing.

Oklahoma   § 24-136

Credit repair clinics must inform debtors of their rights under the Fair Credit Reporting Act, be bonded, accurately represent what they can and cannot do and let debtors cancel the contract until midnight of 5th day after signing.

Tennessee   § 47-18-1003

Credit repair clinics must inform debtors of their rights under the Fair Credit Reporting Act, be bonded, accurately represent what they can and cannot do and let debtors cancel the contract until midnight of 3rd day after signing.

Texas   Bus. & Comm. § 18.07

Credit repair clinics must inform debtors of their rights under the Fair Credit Reporting Act, be bonded, accurately represent what they can and cannot do and let debtors cancel the contract until midnight of 3rd day after signing.

Utah   § 13-21-6

Credit repair clinics must inform debtors of their rights under the Fair Credit Reporting Act, be bonded, accurately represent what they can and cannot do and let debtors cancel the contract until midnight of 5th day after signing.

Virginia   § 59.1-335.5

Credit repair clinics must inform debtors of their rights under the Fair Credit Reporting Act, be bonded, accurately represent what they can and cannot do, let debtors cancel the contract until midnight of 3rd day after signing and not collect any money until all promised services are performed.

Washington   § 19.134.020

Credit repair clinics must be licensed and not collect any money from debtor until all promised services are performed unless clinic has a surety bond for $10,000.

West Virginia   § 46A-6C-1 et seq.

Credit repair clinics must inform debtors of their rights under the Fair Credit Reporting Act, be bonded, accurately represent what they can and cannot do and let debtors cancel the contract until midnight of 3rd day after signing.

Wisconsin   § 422.501 et seq.

Credit repair clinics must inform debtors of their rights under the Fair Credit Reporting Act, be bonded, accurately represent what they can and cannot do and let debtors cancel the contract until midnight of 5th day after signing.

Federal (effective 3/30/97)

Credit repair clinics must inform debtors of their rights under the Fair Credit Reporting Act, accurately represent what they can and cannot do, not collect any money until all promised services are performed, provide a written contract and let debtors cancel the contract until midnight of 3rd day after signing. Any lawsuit against a credit repair clinic for violation of this Act must be brought within five years of the violation. A court may award actual damages, punitive (meant to punish) damage and attorney's fees.

I. Avoid Being the Victim of Credit Discrimination

Discrimination in granting credit is barred by the Equal Credit Opportunity Act (ECOA). (15 U.S.C. § 1691.) The ECOA prohibits a creditor from refusing to grant credit because of your race, color, religion, national origin, sex, marital status or age, or because you are on public assistance. A creditor can ask about age or public assistance, but only to determine your credit history and the likelihood of your continued income. Most allegations of credit discrimination involve women who are denied credit on the basis of their sex or marital status.

If a creditor denies you credit, changes the terms of your credit arrangement or revokes your credit, you are entitled to a written explanation. Some creditors provide this statement automatically, but most don't. If you are denied credit but are not told why, you nevertheless must be told that you can request a written explanation. If you want the written explanation, you must request it in writing (a simple letter will do) within 60 days of being denied credit. The creditor then has 30 days to respond to your request.

1. Sex Discrimination

While a creditor may ask you on an application form to designate a title (Ms., Miss, Mrs. or Mr.), the application form must make it clear that selecting a title is optional. A creditor may also ask your sex when you apply for a real estate loan; this information is collected by the federal government for statistical purposes. But a creditor cannot deny credit to a woman or offer less favorable terms if a man with the same income and property would be given credit.

Specific examples of prohibited sex discrimination include:

- rating female-specific jobs (such as waitress) lower than male-specific jobs (such as waiter) for the purpose of obtaining credit

- denying credit because an applicant's income comes from sources historically associated with women—for example, part-time jobs, alimony or child support

- requiring married women who apply for credit alone to provide information about their husbands while not requiring married men to provide information about their wives, and

- denying credit to a pregnant woman who anticipates taking a maternity leave.

2. Marital Status Discrimination

A married person must be allowed to apply for credit in her name only—a creditor cannot require an applicant's spouse to cosign an application. A creditor may, however, ask questions that would disclose marital status, such as:

- whether you pay alimony or child support
- your income sources—alimony or child support may be an answer, and
- whether any other person—such as a spouse—is jointly liable for any debts you list on a credit application.

If you live in a community property state (Arizona, California, Idaho, Louisiana, Nevada, New Mexico, Texas, Washington or Wisconsin) or you rely on property located in a community property state to establish your credit worthiness, the creditor may ask for your marital status. The creditor cannot, however, deny you credit based on marital status.

The prohibition against marital status discrimination also means that a creditor must consider the combined incomes of an unmarried couple applying for a joint obligation. (*Markham v. Colonial Mortgage Service Co.*, 605 F.2d 566 (D.C. Cir. 1979).)

If you feel that a creditor has discriminated against you, complain to the Federal Trade Commission. (See Chapter 4, Section D for addresses and phone numbers.) You also have the right to sue for actual damages, punitive damages up to $10,000, court costs and attorney fees.

3. Race Discrimination

In general, lenders are prohibited from asking a person's race on a credit application or ascertaining it from any means (such as a credit file) other than the personal observation of a loan officer. There is one important exception to this law: A mortgage lender must request a person's race for the sole purpose of monitoring home mortgage applications.

Unfortunately, the prohibition of race discrimination in credit doesn't mean that race discrimination has disappeared. In fact, lenders are accused of getting around race discrimination prohibitions by "redlining"—that is, denying credit to residents of certain—predominantly black—neighborhoods.

Congress attempted to stop redlining by enacting the Home Mortgage Disclosure Act (HMDA). (12 U.S.C. § 2801 et seq.) Under that law, mortgage lenders must maintain and disclose their lending practices for certain areas. Critics complain, however, that the data lenders must disclose is inadequate to analyze discrimination. In addition, under the HMDA, Congress stopped short of requiring lenders to extend credit to everyone who applied because Congress did not want to encourage unsound lending practices.

A second law, the Community Reinvestment Act (CRA), was enacted also to address redlining. (12 U.S.C. § 2901 et seq.) The CRA requires that bank mortgage lenders demonstrate that they serve the needs of the communities which they are chartered to serve. If the bank fails to do so, bank regulators can deny the bank the right to establish branches or other activity requiring regulatory approval.

Redlining is also barred by the Fair Housing Act of the Federal Civil Rights Act. (42 U.S.C. § 3601 et seq.) In addition, several states have laws prohibiting redlining.

If you feel that a creditor has discriminated against you because of your race or is redlining your credit application, complain to the Federal Trade Commission. (See Chapter 4, Section D for addresses and phone numbers.) Under the Equal Credit Opportunity Act, you have the right to sue for actual damages, punitive damages up to

$10,000, court costs and attorney fees. There are additional remedies under the HMDA and FHA.

4. Post-Bankruptcy Discrimination

If you're considering filing for bankruptcy or you've been through bankruptcy, you may be worried that you'll suffer discrimination.

a. Bankruptcy and Government Discrimination

All federal, state and local governmental entities are prohibited from denying, revoking, suspending or refusing to renew a license, permit, charter, franchise or other similar grant solely because you filed for bankruptcy. (11 U.S.C. § 525(a).) Judges interpreting this law have ruled that the government cannot:

- deny you a job or fire you
- deny or terminate your public benefits
- deny or evict you from public housing
- deny or refuse to renew your state liquor license
- exclude you from participating in a state home mortgage finance program
- exclude you from participating in a student loan program
- withhold your college transcript
- deny you a driver's license, or
- deny you a contract, such as a contract for a construction project.

In general, once any government-related debt has been canceled in bankruptcy, all acts against you that arise out of that debt also must end. For example, if a state university has withheld your transcript because you haven't paid back your student loan, once the loan is discharged, you must be given your transcript. If, however, the loan isn't discharged in bankruptcy, you can still be denied your transcript until you pay up.

Keep in mind that only government denials based on your bankruptcy are prohibited. You may be denied a loan, job or apartment for reasons un-related to the bankruptcy (for example, you earn too much to qualify for public housing), or for reasons related to your future credit worthiness (for instance, the government concludes you won't be able to repay a student loan).

b. Bankruptcy and Discrimination in the Private Sector

Private employers may not fire you or otherwise discriminate against you solely because you filed for bankruptcy. (11 U.S.C. § 525(b).) It is unclear whether or not the act prohibits employers from not hiring you because you went through bankruptcy.

Unfortunately, however, other forms of discrimination in the private sector aren't illegal. If you seek to rent an apartment and the landlord does a credit check and refuses to rent to you because you filed for bankruptcy, there's not much you can do other than try to show that you'll pay your rent and be a responsible tenant. If a bank refuses to give you a loan because it perceives you as a poor credit risk, you may have little recourse. ∎

Resources

Below are organizations, agencies and publications that can provide valuable help in your efforts to repair your credit.

A. Bankcard Holders of America

BHA is a nonprofit organization committed to consumer credit education and advocacy. BHA publishes a bi-monthly newsletter and several other publications, and provides lists of banks offering secured credit cards or credit cards with low interest rates and/or no annual fees. For information on membership or to obtain a publications list, contact BHA at 524 Branch Drive, Salem, VA 24153, 540-389-5445.

B. National Center for Financial Education

NCFE is a nonprofit organization "dedicated to helping people do a better job of spending, saving, investing, insuring and planning for their financial future so as not to be entirely dependent upon Social Security or Medicare." NCFE publishes a bi-monthly newsletter and several other publications, including "Money Manager for Children" and "Spending & Savings Techniques for the 1990s." NCFE's "Safe Charge Kit" includes credit card condoms (plastic covers) and credit card warning stickers. Contact NCFE at P.O. Box 34070, San Diego, CA 92163-4070, 619-232-8811.

C. Consumer Credit Counseling Service

Consumer Credit Counseling Service (CCCS) offices are nonprofit agencies funded primarily by major creditors such as department stores, credit card companies and banks, and overseen by volunteer creditors and consumer advocates. CCCS can produce a decent result for free or a low price.

To use CCCS to help you pay your debts, you must have some disposable income. A CCCS counselor contacts your creditors to let them know that you've sought CCCS assistance and need more time to pay. Based on your income and debts, the counselor, with your creditors, decides on how much you pay. You then make one or two direct payments each month to the CCCS office, which in turn pays your creditors. The CCCS office asks the creditors to return a small percentage of the money received to the CCCS office to fund its work.

A CCCS counselor can often get wage garnishments revoked and interest and late charges dropped. For example, Citicorp waives minimum payment and late charges—and may freeze interest assessments—for customers undergoing credit counseling. CCCS can also help you rebuild your credit. For instance, in some parts of the country, retailers—including Dayton-Hudson—will offer or reinstate credit for people who successfully complete a CCCS repayment program.

CCCS may charge you a small monthly fee (an average of about $9) for setting up a repayment plan. CCCS also helps people make monthly budgets, and sometimes charges a one-time fee of about $20. If you can't afford the fee, CCCS will waive it.

CCCS has more than 1,100 offices, located in every state. Look in the phone book to find the one nearest you or contact the main office at 8611 2nd Avenue, Suite 100, Silver Spring, MD 20910, 800-388-2227.

Participating in a CCCS plan is somewhat similar to filing for Chapter 13 bankruptcy. (See Chapter 1, Section C.5.) Working with CCCS has one advantage: no bankruptcy will appear on your credit record.

But CCCS also has two major disadvantages when compared to Chapter 13 bankruptcy. First, if you miss a payment, Chapter 13 protects you from creditors who would start collection actions. A CCCS plan has no such protection and any one creditor can pull the plug on your CCCS plan. Also, a CCCS plan usually requires that your debts be paid in full. In Chapter 13 bankruptcy, you're only required to pay the value of your nonexempt property, which can mean that you pay only a small fraction (as low as 0%) of your unsecured debts.

Critics of CCCS point out that CCCS offices get most of their funding from creditors. (Some offices also receive grants from private agencies such as the United Way and federal agencies including the Department of Housing and Urban Development.) Nevertheless, critics claim that CCCS counselors cannot be objective in counseling debtors to file for bankruptcy if they know the office won't receive any funds. Despite this criticism, most CCCS counselors pride themselves on giving objective and complete advice.

D. Debtors Anonymous

Debtors Anonymous is a 12-step support program which uses many of the guidelines of Alcoholics Anonymous. Debtors Anonymous groups meet all over the country. If you can't find one in your area, send a self-addressed, stamped envelope to Debtors Anonymous, General Services Board, P.O. Box 400, Grand Central Station, New York, NY 10163-0400. Or call their message machine at 212-642-8220 and leave your name and address and a request for information.

E. Nolo Press Publications

Several Nolo Press publications can provide you with information to supplement what is in this book.

Money Troubles: Legal Strategies to Cope With Your Debts, by Robin Leonard, provides extensive information on prioritizing your debts, negotiating with creditors and deciding whether or not bankruptcy is for you.

How to File for Bankruptcy, by Stephen Elias, Albin Renauer and Robin Leonard, is a detailed, thorough how-to guide for filing for Chapter 7 bankruptcy. Recommended for readers who are not sure whether they want to file for Chapter 7 or who are concerned that complicated issues may arise during their case.

Nolo's Law Form Kit: Personal Bankruptcy, by Stephen Elias, Albin Renauer, Robin Leonard and Lisa Goldoftas, contains all the forms and instructions for filing Chapter 7 bankruptcy. Recommended for readers who know they want to file for Chapter 7 and do not anticipate any complex issues coming up.

Chapter 13 Bankruptcy: Repay Your Debts, by Robin Leonard, explains Chapter 13 bankruptcy and includes the forms and instructions necessary to file a Chapter 13 bankruptcy case.

Take Control of Your Student Loans, by Robin Leonard and Shae Irving (available Spring 1997), contains extensive information on student loans, including understanding payment options, applying for a deferment or cancelation, getting out of default and determining if you can eliminate the loans in bankruptcy.

Stand Up to the IRS, by Frederick W. Daily, guides taxpayers through the ins and outs of an audit, self-representation in tax court, challenging tax bills and setting up repayment plans for tax bills they do owe. Named one of top three personal finance books by *Money* Magazine.

Everybody's Guide to Small Claims Court, by Ralph Warner, is an indispensable guide for anyone wanting to sue a credit bureau or collection agency in small claims court, or to defend a small claims court action filed by a collector.

Divorce and Money: How to Make the Best Financial Decisions During Divorce, by Violet Woodhouse and Victoria F. Collins, with M.C. Blakeman, is a thorough workbook for people making financial decisions while ending their marriage. Divorce is a time when you are at risk of damaging your credit. This book gives tips on dividing the assets and allocating the debts while protecting your precious credit rating.

F. Other Publishers

A number of publications from non-Nolo publishers have a wealth of information beyond what is in this book.

The Banker's Secret, by Marc Eisenson, shows you how to save thousands of dollars by prepaying your mortgage, student loan, car loan and other long-term debts. A credit card version helps you calculate how much interest you'll pay if you don't pay off your credit cards each month. Available from Good Advice Press, Box 78, Elizaville, NY 12523, 800-255-0899.

The Ultimate Credit Handbook, by Gerri Detweiler (Plume Books). Detweiler is the former director of Bankcard Holders of America. Her gem of a book covers everything you'd want to know about credit ratings, credit cards, completing credit applications, protecting your credit privacy and many other topics.

How to Get Out of Debt, Stay Out of Debt and Live Prosperously, by Jerrold Mundis (Bantam Books). Mundis, a recovered debtor, uses the principles of the 12-step program Debtors Anonymous to give practical and emotionally supportive tips on getting out of debt.

Surviving Debt: Counseling Families in Financial Trouble, by National Consumer Law Center. NCLC is a public interest law firm that normally publishes books to assist Legal Aid lawyers. NCLC uses its years of experience in counseling low-income debtors across the country to offer tips on all kinds of debts and income sources, including government benefits, defenses to collection lawsuits and strategies when your house is in foreclosure. Order from NCLC, 18 Tremont Street, Boston, MA 02108, 617-523-8010.

G. Online Resources

By now, most people have heard of the Internet and commercial online services. Every day more and more basic source materials are finding their way onto accessible online sites, referred to collectively as "the Net."

The Internet is a worldwide network of computers that share common rules for access to and transfer of data. There are a number of different ways to use the Internet to search for relevant material, such as Gopher (a series of nested menus), FTP (a way to

connect directly to another computer and download files) and Telenet (a way to actually use programs on remote computers to accomplish a particular task). But by far the most important tool for doing research on the Internet is something called the World Wide Web (WWW). This tool offers a point-and-click graphic interface that provides links among documents, and makes it easy to skip from one relevant resource to another. It promises to dominate the Internet for years to come.

A wide variety of legal source materials is also becoming available through large commercial online services such as CompuServe, America Online and Prodigy. These services not only have their own collections of resources, but also provide a gateway to the Internet, including the WWW.

⚠ *This section does not provide the basic instruction that some readers may need in order to understand and "get into" the services and information available on the Internet. There are several books that serve this purpose. For an exhaustive treatment of the subject, see* Law on the Net, *by James Evans (Nolo Press).* Law on the Net *is also available online through Nolo Press' site (see below).*

You can find many resources online to augment the material in this book.

http://www.nolo.com Nolo Press is forging the way in putting material online for the benefit of non-lawyer consumers. This includes sets of "FAQs" (frequently asked questions) on a wide variety of legal topics, including advice about consumer law, debts and credit. Nolo Press also includes archived articles on legal issues that have appeared in Nolo's quarterly newspaper, *The Nolo News.* From America Online, choose keyword: Nolo.

http://law.house.gov/92.htm The U.S. House of Representatives Internet Law Library provides the texts of finance, economic and consumer protection laws including the federal bankruptcy code and bankruptcy rules, banking laws, Federal Trade Commission publications and selected state consumer protection laws.

http://www.pueblo.gsa.gov/ The Consumer Information Center provides the latest in consumer news as well as many publications of interest to consumers, including the Consumer Information Catalog.

http://www.epn.com/bha Bankcard Holders of America offers information on preventing credit card fraud, protecting your privacy when using a credit card and fending off predatory merchants.

http://www.ftc.gov/ The Federal Trade Commission offers consumer protection rules, guides and publications.

http://www.irs.ustreas.gov/ The Internal Revenue Service provides tax information, forms and publications.

http://www.tiac.net/users/agin/blawfind.html This site provides an extensive list of online bankruptcy-related materials.

H. State Agencies Regulating Credit Bureaus

Often, you will want to contact your state agency that regulates credit bureaus to report illegal activity or to obtain help in getting the credit bureau to make corrections to your file. A list of these agencies is provided on the following pages.

State Agencies Regulating Credit Bureaus

Alabama
Consumer Assistance
Office of Attorney General
11 South Union Street
Montgomery, AL 36130
205-242-7334
800-392-5658
334-242 7458 (fax)

Alaska
The Consumer Protection Section was
eliminated in budget cuts in 1989; if
you write or call this office, you can ask
for a four-page letter listing various state,
federal and private consumer protection
agencies and organizations which may
be of assistance.
Office of the Attorney General
P.O. Box K—State Capitol
Juneau, AK 99811-0300
907-465-3600
907-465-2075 (fax)

Arizona
Consumer Information and Complaints
Office of Attorney General
1275 West Washington Street
Phoenix, AZ 85007
602-542-5763
800-352-8431
602-542-4085 (fax)

Arkansas
Advocacy Division of Attorney
 General's Office
200 Tower Building
323 Center Street
Little Rock, AR 72201
501-682-2007
800-482-8982
501-682-8084 (fax)

California
No state agency; you must contact the
Federal Trade Commission. See Chapter 4, Section D

Colorado
Consumer Protection Unit
Office of Attorney General
1525 Sherman Street
5th Floor
Denver, CO 80203
303-866-5189
800-332-2071
303-866-5691 (fax)

Connecticut
Department of Banking
Consumer Credit Division
260 Constitution Plaza
Hartford, CT 06106
860-240-8299
860-240-8178 (fax)

Delaware
Department of Justice
Consumer Protection Unit
820 North French Street
4th Floor
Wilmington, DE 19801
302-577-3250
302-577-2610 (fax)

District of Columbia
Department of Consumer and
 Regulatory Affairs
614 H Street, NW
Room 1120
Washington, DC 20001
202-727-7170
202-727-8073 (fax)

Florida
Division of Consumer Services
Department of Agriculture and
 Consumer Services
235 Mayo Building
Tallahassee, FL 32399
904-488-2226
800-435-7352
904-488-0863 (fax)

Georgia
Consumer Affairs Division
Office of the Attorney General
40 Capitol Square, SW
Atlanta, GA 30334-1300
404-656-3383
404-651-9148 (fax)

Hawaii
Office of Consumer Protection
Dept. of Commerce and Consumer Affairs
828 Fort Street, Room 600B
Honolulu, HI 96813
808-586-2630
808-586-2640 (fax)

Idaho
Consumer Protection Division
Office of Attorney General
700 West Jefferson Street
P.O. Box 83720
Boise, ID 83720-0010
208-334-2424
800-432-3545
208-334-2530 (fax)

Illinois
Consumer Protection Division
Office of Attorney General
500 South Second Street
Springfield, IL 62706
217-782-9011
800-252-8666
217-785-2511 (fax)

Indiana
No state agency; you must contact the
Federal Trade Commission. See Chapter 4, Section D

Iowa
Consumer Protection Division
Office of Attorney General
Hoover State Office Building
Des Moines, IA 50319
515-281-5926
515-281-4209 (fax)

State Agencies Regulating Credit Bureaus (cont'd)

Kansas
Consumer Protection Division
Office of Attorney General
301 West Tenth
Topeka, KS 66612
913-296-3751
800-432-2310
913-296-6296 (fax)

Kentucky
Consumer Protection Division
Office of Attorney General
P.O. Box 2000
Frankfort, KY 40602-2000
502-564-2200
800-432-9257
502-564-2894 (fax)

Louisiana
Consumer Protection Section
Office of Attorney General
P.O. Box 94095
Baton Rouge, LA 70804-9095
504-342-9638
504-342-7901 (fax)

Maine
Bureau of Consumer Credit Protection
State House, Station No. 35
Augusta, ME 04333-0035
207-624-8527
800-332-8529
207-624-8690 (fax)

Maryland
Consumer Protection Division
Office of Attorney General
200 St. Paul Place
Baltimore, MD 21202-2022
410-576-6550
410-576-7003 (fax)

Massachusetts
Consumer Protection Division
Dept. of Attorney General
1 Ashburton Place
Boston, MA 02111
617-727-2200
617-727-5762 (fax)

Michigan
Consumer Protection Division
Office of Attorney General
P.O. Box 30213
Lansing, MI 48909
517-335-0855
517-373-4916 (fax)

Minnesota
No state agency; you must contact the Federal Trade Commission. See Chapter 4, Section D

Mississippi
Consumer Protection Division
Office of Attorney General
P.O. Box 220
Jackson, MS 39205
601-359-4230
601-359-3441 (fax)

Missouri
Consumer Protection Division
Office of Attorney General
P.O. Box 899
Jefferson City, MO 65102
314-751-3321
800-392-8222
314-751-0774 (fax)

Montana
Consumer Affairs Unit
Dept. of Commerce
1424 Ninth Avenue
Helena, MT 59620
406-444-3553
406-444-2903 (fax)

Nebraska
No state agency; you must contact the Federal Trade Commission. See Chapter 4, Section D

Nevada
Consumer Affairs Division
State Mail Room Complex
Las Vegas, NV 89158
702-486-7355
702-486-2758 (fax)

New Hampshire
Consumer Protection Bureau
Department of Justice
33 Capitol Street
Concord, NH 03301
603-271-3641
603-271-2110 (fax)

New Jersey
No state agency; you must contact the Federal Trade Commission. See Chapter 4, Section D

New Mexico
Financial Institution Division
Office of Attorney General
Drawer 1508
Santa Fe, NM 87504
505-827-7100
505-827-5826 (fax)

New York
Consumer Protection Board
99 Washington Avenue
Albany, NY 12210
518-474-8583
518-474-2474 (fax)

North Carolina
Consumer Protection Section
Office of Attorney General
Department of Justice
P.O. Box 629
Raleigh, NC 27602
919-733-7741
919-733-7491 (fax)

North Dakota
Department of Banking and Financial Institutions
2900 North 19th Street
Bismarck, ND 58501-5305
701-224-2253
701-328-9955 (fax)

State Agencies Regulating Credit Bureaus (cont'd)

Ohio
Consumer Protection Division
Office of Attorney General
State Office Tower
30 East Broad Street
25th Floor
Columbus, OH 43215-3428
614-466-3376
800-282-0515
614-466-5087 (fax)

Oklahoma
Consumer Affairs Division
Office of Attorney General
112 State Capitol Building
Oklahoma City, OK 73105-3498
405-521-4274
405-521-6246 (fax)

Oregon
Financial Fraud
Department of Justice
1162 Court Street, NE
Salem, OR 97310
503-378-4320
503-378-3784 (fax)

Pennsylvania
Bureau of Consumer Protection
Office of Attorney General
Strawberry Square
14th Floor
Harrisburg, PA 17120
717-787-9707
800-441-2555
717-787-1190 (fax)

Rhode Island
Consumer Protection Division
Department of Attorney General
72 Pine Street
Providence, RI 02903
401-274-4400
401-277-1331 (fax)

South Carolina
Department of Consumer Affairs
P.O. Box 5757
Columbia, SC 29250
803-734-9452
800-922-1594
803-734-9365 (fax)

South Dakota
Division of Consumer Affairs
Office of Attorney General
State Capitol Building
500 East Capitol
Pierre, SD 57501
605-773-4400
605-773-4106 (fax)

Tennessee
Division of Consumer Affairs
Department of Commerce and Insurance
500 James Robertson Parkway
5th Floor
Nashville, TN 37243-0600
615-741-4737
800-342-8385
615-741-4000

Texas
Consumer Protection Division
Office of Attorney General
P.O. Box 12548
Austin, TX 78711
512-463-2070
512-463-2063 (fax)

Utah
No state agency; you must contact the Federal Trade Commission. See Chapter 4, Section D

Vermont
Consumer Assistance
Office of Attorney General
109 State Street
Montpelier, VT 05609-1001
802-828-3171
800-649-2424
802-828-2154 (fax)

Virginia
Office of Consumer Affairs
Department of Agriculture and
    Consumer Services
1100 Bank Street
Richmond, VA 23219
804-786-2042
800-552-9963
804-371-2945 (fax)

Washington
Consumer Resource Center
Office of Attorney General
P.O. Box 40100
Olympia, WA 98504-0100
360-733-6200
800-551-4636
360-664-0228 (fax)

West Virginia
Consumer Protection Division
Office of Attorney General
1900 Kanawha Blvd. E
Building 1
Charleston, WV 25305-0220
304-558-8986
800-368-8808
304-588-0140 (fax)

Wisconsin
Consumer Protection Agency
Department of Justice
123 West Washington Avenue
Room 150
Madison, WI 53707
608-266-1852
608-267-2223 (fax)

Wyoming
Consumer Affairs Division
Office of Attorney General
123 State Capitol Building
Cheyenne, WY 82002
307-777-7891
307-777-6869 (fax)

Federal and State Credit Reporting Laws
Effective until September 29, 1997

This Appendix contains many of the rules regulating credit bureaus. You'll find the federal government's rules in the Fair Credit Reporting Act (FCRA). In addition, a handful of states have enacted laws related to credit reporting and credit bureaus. Many of these laws duplicate the protections provided by the federal FCRA. But 14 states—California, Colorado, Kentucky, Maine, Michigan, Minnesota, Montana, New Hampshire, New Mexico, New York, Oklahoma, Rhode Island, Utah and Vermont—have additional laws which supplement the protections provided by the federal law. Excerpted portions of these state laws follow the federal FCRA, below.

If a credit bureau violates the federal FCRA, you can register a complaint with the Federal Trade Commission (addresses and phone numbers are in Chapter 4, Section D). You can also sue for negligent or willful noncompliance with the federal FCRA within two years of the bureau's violation. You can sue for actual damages, such as court costs, attorney's fees, lost wages, and if applicable, infliction of emotional distress. In cases of truly outrageous behavior, you can ask for punitive damages— damages meant to punish for malicious or willful conduct.

If a credit bureau violates a state law, you can register a complaint with the appropriate state agency (addresses and phone numbers are in Appendix 1, Section E). You can probably also sue for noncompliance with the state law. If you are thinking about suing, however, you'll need to find the full state law and read it carefully. (Look for the law at a local law library or a large public library.)

These lawsuits can probably be filed in small claims court without the help of an attorney. (See *Everybody's Guide to Small Claims Court*, by Ralph Warner (Nolo Press) for definitive information on suing in small claims court.) If you plan to ask for punitive damages, you'll probably need a lawyer's help to file in a regular court.

Text of the Federal Fair Credit Reporting Act

Short Title

This title may be cited as the Fair Credit Reporting Act.

15 U.S.C. § 1681. Congressional findings and statement of purpose

(a) Accuracy and fairness of credit reporting. The Congress makes the following findings:

  (1) The banking system is dependent upon fair and accurate credit reporting. Inaccurate credit reports directly impair the efficiency of the banking system, and unfair credit reporting methods undermine the public confidence which is essential to the continued functioning of the banking system.

  (2) An elaborate mechanism has been developed for investigating and evaluating the credit worthiness, credit standing, credit capacity, character, and general reputation of consumers.

  (3) Consumer reporting agencies have assumed a vital role in assembling and evaluating consumer credit and other information on consumers.

  (4) There is a need to insure that consumer reporting agencies exercise their grave responsibilities with fairness, impartiality, and a respect for the consumer's right to privacy.

(b) Reasonable procedures. It is the purpose of this subchapter to require that consumer reporting agencies adopt reasonable procedures for meeting the needs of commerce for consumer credit, personnel, insurance, and other information in a manner which is fair and equitable to the consumer, with regard to the confidentiality, accuracy, relevancy, and proper utilization of such information in accordance with the requirements of this subchapter.

15 U.S.C. § 1681a. Definitions; rules of construction

(a) Definitions and rules of construction set forth in this section are applicable for the purposes of this subchapter.

(b) The term "person" means any individual, partnership, corporation, trust, estate, cooperative, association, government or governmental subdivision or agency, or other entity.

(c) The term "consumer" means an individual.

(d) The term "consumer report" means any written, oral, or other communication of any information by a consumer reporting agency bearing on a consumer's credit worthiness, credit standing, credit capacity, character, general reputation, personal characteristics, or mode of living which is used or expected to be used or collected in whole or in part for the purpose of serving as a factor in establishing the consumer's eligibility for (1) credit or insurance to be used primarily for personal, family, or household purposes, or (2) employment purposes, or (3) other purposes authorized under section 1681b of this title. The term does not include (A) any report containing information solely as to transactions or experiences between the consumer and the person making the report; (B) any authorization or approval of a specific extension of credit directly or indirectly by the issuer of a credit card or similar device; or (C) any report in which a person who has been requested by a third party to make a specific extension of credit directly or indirectly to a consumer conveys his decision with respect to such request, if the third party advises the consumer of the name and address of the person to whom the request was made and such person makes the disclosures to the consumer required under section 1681m of this title.

(e) The term "investigative consumer report" means a consumer report or portion thereof in which information on a consumer's character, general reputation, personal characteristics, or mode of living is obtained through personal interviews with neighbors, friends, or associates of the consumer reported on or with others with whom he is acquainted or who may have knowledge concerning any such items of information. However, such information shall not include specific factual information on a consumer's credit record obtained directly from a creditor of the consumer or from a consumer reporting agency when such information was obtained directly from a creditor of the consumer or from the consumer.

(f) The term "consumer reporting agency" means any person which, for monetary fees, dues, or on a cooperative nonprofit basis, regularly engages in whole or in part in the practice of assembling or evaluating consumer credit information or other information on consumers for the purpose of furnishing consumer reports to third parties, and which uses any means or facility of interstate commerce for the purpose of preparing or furnishing consumer reports.

(g) The term "file," when used in connection with information on any consumer, means all of the information on that consumer recorded and retained by a consumer reporting agency regardless of how the information is stored.

(h) The term "employment purposes" when used in connection with a consumer report means a report used for the purpose of evaluating a consumer for employment, promotion, reassignment or retention as an employee.

(i) The term "medical information" means information or records obtained, with the consent of the individual to whom it relates, from licensed physicians or medical practitioners, hospitals, clinics, or other medical or medically related facilities.

(j) Definitions Relating to Child Support Obligations.

(1) Overdue support—The term "overdue support" has the meaning given to such term in Section 666(e) of Title 42.

(2) State or local child support enforcement agency—The term "State or local child support enforcement agency" means a State or local agency which administers a State or

local program for establishing and enforcing child support obligations.

15 U.S.C. § 1681b. Permissible purposes of consumer reports

A consumer reporting agency may furnish a consumer report under the following circumstances and no other:

(1) In response to the order of a court having jurisdiction to issue such an order, or a subpoena issued in connection with proceedings before a Federal grand jury.

(2) In accordance with the written instructions of the consumer to whom it relates.

(3) To a person which it has reason to believe—

(A) intends to use the information in connection with a credit transaction involving the consumer on whom the information is to be furnished and involving the extension of credit to, or review or collection of an account of, the consumer; or

(B) intends to use the information for employment purposes; or

(C) intends to use the information in connection with the underwriting of insurance involving the consumer; or

(D) intends to use the information in connection with a determination of the consumer's eligibility for a license or other benefit granted by a governmental instrumentality required by law to consider an applicant's financial responsibility or status; or

(E) otherwise has a legitimate business need for the information in connection with a business transaction involving the consumer.

15 U.S.C. § 1681c. Reporting of obsolete information prohibited

(a) Prohibited items. Except as authorized under subsection (b) of this section, no consumer reporting agency may make any consumer report containing any of the following items of information:

(1) Cases under title 11 or under the Bankruptcy Act that, from the date of entry of the order for relief or the date of adjudication, as the case may be, antedate the report by more than 10 years.

(2) Suits and judgments which, from date of entry, antedate the report by more than seven years or until the governing statute of limitations has expired, whichever is the longer period.

(3) Paid tax liens which, from date of payment, antedate the report by more than seven years.

(4) Accounts placed for collection or charged to profit and loss which antedate the report by more than seven years.

(5) Records of arrest, indictment, or conviction of crime which, from date of disposition, release, or parole, antedate the report by more than seven years.

(6) Any other adverse item of information which antedates the report by more than seven years.

(b) Exempted cases. The provisions of subsection (a) of this section are not applicable in the case of any consumer credit report to be used in connection with:

(1) a credit transaction involving, or which may reasonably be expected to involve, a principal amount of $50,000 or more;

(2) the underwriting of life insurance involving, or which may reasonably be expected to involve, a face amount of $50,000 or more; or

(3) the employment of any individual at an annual salary which equals, or which may reasonably be expected to equal $20,000, or more.

15 U.S.C. § 1681d. Disclosure of investigative consumer reports

(a) Disclosure of fact of preparation. A person may not procure or cause to be prepared an investigative consumer report on any consumer unless:

(1) it is clearly and accurately disclosed to the consumer that an investigative consumer report including information as to his character, general reputation, personal characteristics, and mode of living, whichever are applicable, may be made, and such disclosure (A) is made in a writing mailed, or otherwise delivered, to the consumer, not later than three days after the date on which the report was first requested, and (B) includes a statement informing the consumer of his right to request the additional disclosures provided for under subsection (b) of this section; or

(2) the report is to be used for employment purposes for which the consumer has not specifically applied.

(b) Disclosure on request of nature and scope of investigation. Any person who procures or causes to be prepared an investigative consumer report on any consumer shall, upon written request made by the consumer within a reasonable period of time after the receipt by him of the disclosure required by subsection (a)(1) of this section, shall[1] make a complete and accurate disclosure of the nature and scope of the investigation requested. This disclosure shall be made in a writing mailed, or otherwise delivered, to the consumer not later than five days after the date on which the request for such disclosure was received from the consumer or such report was first requested, whichever is the later.

(c) Limitation on liability upon showing of reasonable procedures for compliance with provisions. No person may be held liable for any violation of subsection (a) or (b) of this section if he shows by a preponderance of the evidence that at the time of the violation he maintained reasonable procedures to assure compliance with subsection (a) or (b) of this section.

15 U.S.C. § 1681e. Compliance procedures

(a) Identity and purposes of credit users. Every consumer reporting agency shall maintain reason-

able procedures designed to avoid violations of section 1681c of this title and to limit the furnishing of consumer reports to the purposes listed under section 1681b of this title. These procedures shall require that prospective users of the information identify themselves, certify the purposes for which the information is sought, and certify that the information will be used for no other purpose. Every consumer reporting agency shall make a reasonable effort to verify the identity of a new prospective user and the uses certified by such prospective user prior to furnishing such user a consumer report. No consumer reporting agency may furnish a consumer report to any person if it has reasonable grounds for believing that the consumer report will not be used for a purpose listed in section 1681b of this title.

(b) Accuracy of report. Whenever a consumer reporting agency prepares a consumer report it shall follow reasonable procedures to assure maximum possible accuracy of the information concerning the individual about whom the report relates.

15 U.S.C. § 1681f. Compliance procedures

Notwithstanding the provisions of section 1681b of this title, a consumer reporting agency may furnish identifying information respecting any consumer, limited to his name, address, former addresses, places of employment, or former places of employment, to a governmental agency.

15 U.S.C. § 1681g. Disclosures to consumers

(a) Information on file; sources; report recipients. Every consumer reporting agency shall, upon request and proper identification of any consumer, clearly and accurately disclose to the consumer:

(1) The nature and substance of all information (except medical information) in its files on the consumer at the time of the request.

(2) The sources of the information; except that the sources of information acquired solely for use in preparing an investigative con-

---

[1] As written in original. The word "shall" should not appear.

sumer report and actually used for no other purpose need not be disclosed: Provided, That in the event an action is brought under this subchapter, such sources shall be available to the plaintiff under appropriate discovery procedures in the court in which the action is brought.

(3) The recipients of any consumer report on the consumer which it has furnished:

    (A) for employment purposes within the two-year period preceding the request, and

    (B) for any other purpose within the six-month period preceding the request.

(b) Exempt information. The requirements of subsection (a) of this section respecting the disclosure of sources of information and the recipients of consumer reports do not apply to information received or consumer reports furnished prior to the effective date of this subchapter except to the extent that the matter involved is contained in the files of the consumer reporting agency on that date.

15 U.S.C. § 1681h. Conditions of disclosure to consumers

(a) Times and notice. A consumer reporting agency shall make the disclosures required under section 1681g of this title during normal business hours and on reasonable notice.

(b) Identification of consumer. The disclosures required under section 1681g of this title shall be made to the consumer:

    (1) in person if he appears in person and furnishes proper identification; or

    (2) by telephone if he has made a written request, with proper identification, for telephone disclosure and the toll charge, if any, for the telephone call is prepaid by or charged directly to the consumer.

(c) Trained personnel. Any consumer reporting agency shall provide trained personnel to explain to the consumer any information furnished to him pursuant to section 1681g of this title.

(d) Persons accompanying consumer. The consumer shall be permitted to be accompanied by one other person of his choosing, who shall furnish reasonable identification. A consumer reporting agency may require the consumer to furnish a written statement granting permission to the consumer reporting agency to discuss the consumer's file in such person's presence.

(e) Limitation of liability. Except as provided in sections 1681n and 1681o of this title, no consumer may bring any action or proceeding in the nature of defamation, invasion of privacy, or negligence with respect to the reporting of information against any consumer reporting agency, any user of information, or any person who furnishes information to a consumer reporting agency, based on information disclosed pursuant to section 1681g, 1681h, or 1681m of this title, except as to false information furnished with malice or willful intent to injure such consumer.

15 U.S.C. § 1681i. Procedure in case of disputed accuracy

(a) Dispute; reinvestigation. If the completeness or accuracy of any item of information contained in his file is disputed by a consumer, and such dispute is directly conveyed to the consumer reporting agency by the consumer, the consumer reporting agency shall within a reasonable period of time reinvestigate and record the current status of that information unless it has reasonable grounds to believe that the dispute by the consumer is frivolous or irrelevant. If after such reinvestigation such information is found to be inaccurate or can no longer be verified, the consumer reporting agency shall promptly delete such information. The presence of contradictory information in the consumer's file does not in and of itself constitute reasonable grounds for believing the dispute is frivolous or irrelevant.

(b) Statement of dispute. If the reinvestigation does not resolve the dispute, the consumer may file a brief statement setting forth the nature of the dispute. The consumer reporting agency may limit such statements to not more than one hundred words if it provides the consumer with assistance in writing a clear summary of the dispute.

(c) Notification of consumer dispute in subsequent consumer reports. Whenever a statement of a dispute is filed, unless there is reasonable grounds to believe that it is frivolous or irrelevant, the consumer reporting agency shall, in any subsequent consumer report containing the information in question, clearly note that it is disputed by the consumer and provide either the consumer's statement or a clear and accurate codification or summary thereof.

(d) Notification of deletion of disputed information. Following any deletion of information which is found to be inaccurate or whose accuracy can no longer be verified or any notation as to disputed information, the consumer reporting agency shall, at the request of the consumer, furnish notification that the item has been deleted or the statement, codification or summary pursuant to subsection (b) or (c) of this section to any person specifically designated by the consumer who has within two years prior thereto received a consumer report for employment purposes, or within six months prior thereto received a consumer report for any other purpose, which contained the deleted or disputed information. The consumer reporting agency shall clearly and conspicuously disclose to the consumer his rights to make such a request. Such disclosure shall be made at or prior to the time the information is deleted or the consumer's statement regarding the disputed information is received.

15 U.S.C. § 1681j. Charges for disclosures

A consumer reporting agency shall make all disclosures pursuant to section 1681g of this title and furnish all consumer reports pursuant to section 1681i(d) of this title without charge to the consumer if, within thirty days after receipt by such consumer of a notification pursuant to section 1681m of this title or notification from a debt collection agency

affiliated with such consumer reporting agency stating that the consumer's credit rating may be or has been adversely affected, the consumer makes a request under section 1681g or 1681i(d) of this title. Otherwise, the consumer reporting agency may impose a reasonable charge on the consumer for making disclosure to such consumer pursuant to section 1681g of this title, the charge for which shall be indicated to the consumer prior to making disclosure; and for furnishing notifications, statements, summaries, or codifications to person designated by the consumer pursuant to section 1681i(d) of this title, the charge for which shall be indicated to the consumer prior to furnishing such information and shall not exceed the charge that the consumer reporting agency would impose on each designated recipient for a consumer report except that no charge may be made for notifying such persons of the deletion of information which is found to be inaccurate or which can no longer be verified.

15 U.S.C. § 1681k. Public record information for employment purposes

A consumer reporting agency which furnishes a consumer report for employment purposes and which for that purpose compiles and reports items of information on consumers which are matters of public record and are likely to have an adverse effect upon a consumer's ability to obtain employment shall:

(1) at the time such public record information is reported to the user of such consumer report, notify the consumer of the fact that public record information is being reported by the consumer reporting agency, together with the name and address of the person to whom such information is being reported; or

(2) maintain strict procedures designed to insure that whenever public record information which is likely to have an adverse effect on a consumer's ability to obtain employment is reported it is complete and up to date. For purposes of this paragraph, items of public record relating to arrests, indictments, convictions, suits, tax liens, and outstanding

judgments shall be considered up to date if the current public record status of the item at the time of the report is reported.

15 U.S.C. § 1681l. Restrictions on investigative consumer reports

Whenever a consumer reporting agency prepares an investigative consumer report, no adverse information in the consumer report (other than information which is a matter of public record) may be included in a subsequent consumer report unless such adverse information has been verified in the process of making such subsequent consumer report, or the adverse information was received within the three-month period preceding the date the subsequent report is furnished.

15 U.S.C. § 1681m. Requirements on users of consumer reports

(a) Adverse action based on reports of consumer reporting agencies. Whenever credit or insurance for personal, family, or household purposes, or employment involving a consumer is denied or the charge for such credit or insurance is increased either wholly or partly because of information contained in a consumer report from a consumer reporting agency, the user of the consumer report shall so advise the consumer against whom such adverse action has been taken and supply the name and address of the consumer reporting agency making the report.

(b) Adverse action based on reports of persons other than consumer reporting agencies. Whenever credit for personal, family, or household purposes involving a consumer is denied or the charge for such credit is increased either wholly or partly because of information obtained from a person other than a consumer reporting agency bearing upon the consumer's credit worthiness, credit standing, credit capacity, character, general reputation, personal characteristics, or mode of living, the user of such information shall, within a reasonable period of time, upon the consumer's written request for the reasons for such adverse action received within sixty days after learning of such adverse action, disclose the nature of the information to the consumer. The user of such information shall clearly and accurately disclose to the consumer his right to make such written request at the time such adverse action is communicated to the consumer.

(c) Reasonable procedures to assure compliance. No person shall be held liable for any violation of this section if he shows by a preponderance of the evidence that at the time of the alleged violation he maintained reasonable procedures to assure compliance with the provisions of subsections (a) and (b) of this section.

15 U.S.C. § 1681n. Civil liability for willful noncompliance

Any consumer reporting agency or user of information which willfully fails to comply with any requirement imposed under this subchapter with respect to any consumer is liable to that consumer in an amount equal to the sum of:

(1) any actual damages sustained by the consumer as a result of the failure;

(2) such amount of punitive damages as the court may allow; and

(3) in the case of any successful action to enforce any liability under this section, the costs of the action together with reasonable attorney's fees as determined by the court.

15 U.S.C. § 1681o. Civil liability for negligent noncompliance

Any consumer reporting agency or user of information which is negligent in failing to comply with any requirement imposed under this subchapter with respect to any consumer is liable to that consumer in an amount equal to the sum of:

(1) any actual damages sustained by the consumer as a result of the failure;

(2) in the case of any successful action to enforce any liability under this section, the costs of the action together with reasonable attorney's fees as determined by the court.

15 U.S.C. § 1681p. Jurisdiction of courts; limitation of actions

An action to enforce any liability created under this subchapter may be brought in any appropriate United States district court without regard to the amount in controversy, or in any other court of competent jurisdiction, within two years from the date on which the liability arises, except that where a defendant has materially and willfully misrepresented any information required under this subchapter to be disclosed to an individual and the information so misrepresented is material to the establishment of the defendant's liability to that individual under this subchapter, the action may be brought at any time within two years after discovery by the individual of the misrepresentation.

15 U.S.C. § 1681q. Obtaining information under false pretenses

Any person who knowingly and willfully obtains information on a consumer from a consumer reporting agency under false pretenses shall be fined not more than $5,000 or imprisoned not more than one year, or both.

15 U.S.C. § 1681r. Unauthorized disclosures by officers or employees

Any officer or employee of a consumer reporting agency who knowingly and willfully provides information concerning an individual from the agency's files to a person not authorized to receive that information shall be fined not more than $5,000 or imprisoned not more than one year, or both.

15 U.S.C. § 1681s. Administrative enforcement

(a) Federal Trade Commission; powers. Compliance with the requirements imposed under this subchapter shall be enforced under the Federal Trade Commission Act (15 U.S.C. 41 et seq.) by the Federal Trade Commission with respect to consumer reporting agencies and all other persons subject thereto, except to the extent that enforcement of the requirements imposed under this subchapter is specifically committed to some other government agency under subsec-

tion (b) hereof. For the purpose of the exercise by the Federal Trade Commission of its functions and powers under the Federal Trade Commission Act, a violation of any requirement or prohibition imposed under this subchapter shall constitute an unfair or deceptive act or practice in commerce in violation of section 5(a) of the Federal Trade Commission Act (15 U.S.C. 45(a)) and shall be subject to enforcement by the Federal Trade Commission under section 5(b) thereof (15 U.S.C. 45(b)) with respect to any consumer reporting agency or person subject to enforcement by the Federal Trade Commission pursuant to this subsection, irrespective of whether that person is engaged in commerce or meets any other jurisdictional tests in the Federal Trade Commission Act. The Federal Trade Commission shall have such procedural, investigative, and enforcement powers, including the power to issue procedural rules in enforcing compliance with the requirements imposed under this subchapter and to require the filing of reports, the production of documents, and the appearance of witnesses as though the applicable terms and conditions of the Federal Trade Commission Act were part of this subchapter. Any person violating any of the provisions of this subchapter shall be subject to the penalties and entitled to the privileges and immunities provided in the Federal Trade Commission Act as though the applicable terms and provisions thereof were part of this subchapter.

(b) Other administrative bodies. Compliance with the requirements imposed under this subchapter with respect to consumer reporting agencies and persons who use consumer reports from such agencies shall be enforced under:

(1) section 8 of the Federal Deposit Insurance Act (12 U.S.C. 1818), in the case of:

(A) national banks, and Federal branches and Federal agencies of foreign banks, by the Office of the Comptroller of the Currency;

(B) member banks of the Federal Reserve System (other than national banks), branches and agencies of foreign banks (other than Federal branches, Federal agencies, and insured State branches of foreign banks), commercial lending companies owned or controlled by foreign banks, and organizations operating under section 25 or 25(a) of the Federal Reserve Act (12 U.S.C. 601 et seq., 611 et seq.), by the Board of Governors of the Federal Reserve System; and

(C) banks insured by the Federal Deposit Insurance Corporation (other than members of the Federal Reserve System) and insured State branches of foreign banks, by the Board of Directors of the Federal Deposit Insurance Corporation.

(2) section 8 of the Federal Deposit Insurance Act (12 U.S.C. 1818), by the Director of the Office of Thrift Supervision, in the case of a savings association the deposits of which are insured by the Federal Deposit Insurance Corporation;

(3) the Federal Credit Union Act (12 U.S.C. 1751 et seq.), by the Administrator of the National Credit Union Administration with respect to any Federal credit union;

(4) subtitle IV of title 49, by the Interstate Commerce Commission with respect to any common carrier subject to such subtitle;

(5) the Federal Aviation Act of 1958 (49 App. U.S.C. 1301 et seq.), by the Secretary of Transportation with respect to any air carrier or foreign air carrier subject to that Act; and

(6) the Packers and Stockyards Act, 1921 (7 U.S.C. 181 et seq.) (except as provided in section 406 of that Act (7 U.S.C. 226, 227)), by the Secretary of Agriculture with respect to any activities subject to that Act. The terms used in paragraph (1) that are not defined in this subchapter or otherwise defined in section 3(s) of the Federal Deposit Insurance Act (12 U.S.C. 1813(s)) shall have the meaning given to them in section 1(b) of the International Banking Act of 1978 (12 U.S.C. 3101).

(c) Enforcement under other authority. For the purpose of the exercise by any agency referred to in subsection (b) of this section of its powers under any Act referred to in that subsection, a violation of any requirement imposed under this subchapter shall be deemed to be a violation of a requirement imposed under that Act. In addition to its powers under any provision of law specifically referred to in subsection (b) of this section, each of the agencies referred to in that subsection may exercise, for the purpose of enforcing compliance with any requirement imposed under this subchapter any other authority conferred on it by law.

15 U.S.C. § 1681s-1. Information on overdue child support obligations

Notwithstanding any other provision of this subchapter, a consumer reporting agency shall include in any consumer report furnished by the agency in accordance with section 1681b of this title, any information on the failure of the consumer to pay overdue support which:

(1) is provided:

(A) to the consumer reporting agency by a State or local child support enforcement agency; or

(B) to the consumer reporting agency and verified by any local, State, or Federal Government agency; and

(2) antedates the report by 7 years or less.

15 U.S.C. § 1681t. Relation to State laws

This subchapter does not annul, alter, affect, or exempt any person subject to the provisions of this subchapter from complying with the laws of any State with respect to the collection, distribution, or use of any information on consumers, except to the extent that those laws are inconsistent with any provision of this subchapter, and then only to the extent of the inconsistency.

Excerpts from the California Consumer Credit Reporting Agencies Act

California Civil Code § 1785.13.

(a) No consumer credit reporting agency shall make any consumer credit report containing any of the following items of information:...

    (3) Unlawful detainer actions, unless the lessor was the prevailing party. For purposes of this paragraph, the lessor shall be deemed to be the party only if (A) final judgment was awarded to the lessor (i) upon entry of the tenant's default, (ii) upon the granting of the lessor's motion for summary judgment, or (iii) following trial, or (B) the action was resolved by a written settlement agreement between the parties that states that the unlawful detainer action may be reported. In any other instance in which the action is resolved by settlement agreement, the lessor shall not be deemed to be the prevailing party for purposes of this paragraph.[2]...

    (6) Records of arrest, indictment, information, misdemeanor complaint, or conviction of a crime...shall no longer be reported if at any time it is learned that in the case of a conviction a full pardon has been granted, or in the case of an arrest, indictment, information, or misdemeanor complaint a conviction did not result....

(c) Any consumer credit reporting agency that furnishes a consumer credit report containing information regarding any case involving a consumer arising under the bankruptcy provisions of Title 11 of the United States Code shall include an identification of the chapter of Title 11 of the United States Code under which the case arose if that can be ascertained from what was provided to the consumer credit reporting agency by the source of the information.

(d) A consumer credit report shall not include any adverse information concerning a consumer antedating the report by more than 10 years or that otherwise is prohibited from being included in a consumer credit report.

(e) If a consumer credit reporting agency is notified by a furnisher of credit information that an open-end credit account of the consumer has been closed by the consumer, any consumer credit report thereafter issued by the consumer credit reporting agency with respect to that consumer, and that includes information respecting that account, shall indicate the fact that the consumer has closed the account. For purposes of this subdivision, "open-end credit account" does not include any demand deposit account, such as a checking account, money market account, or share draft account.

(f) Consumer credit reporting agencies shall not include medical information in their files on consumers or furnish medical information for employment or credit purposes in a consumer credit report without the consent of the consumer.

California Civil Code § 1785.15.

(a) A...consumer has the right to request and receive all of the following:

    (1) Either a decoded written version of the file or a written copy of the file, including all information in the file at the time of the request, with an explanation of any code used.

(b) Files maintained on a consumer shall be disclosed promptly as follows:...

    (2) By mail, if the consumer makes a written request.... A disclosure pursuant to this paragraph shall be deposited in the United States mail, postage prepaid, within five business days after the consumer's written request for the disclosure is received by the consumer credit reporting agency. Consumer credit reporting agencies complying with requests for mailings under this section shall not be liable for disclosures to third parties caused by mishandling of mail after such mailings leave the consumer reporting agencies.

---

[2] This provision was held to violate the First Amendment of the U.S. Constitution; see *U.D. Registry v. California*, 34 Cal.App.4th. 107 (1995).

California Civil Code § 1785.16.

(a) ...Unless the consumer credit reporting agency determines that the dispute is frivolous or irrelevant, before the end of the five-business-day period beginning on the date the consumer credit reporting agency receives notice of dispute under this section, the agency shall notify any person who provided information in dispute at the address and in the manner specified by the person....

(c) No information may be reinserted in a consumer's file after having been deleted pursuant to this section unless the person who furnishes the information verifies that the information is accurate. If any information so deleted from a consumer's file is reinserted in the file, the consumer credit reporting agency shall promptly notify the consumer of the reinsertion in writing or, if authorized by the consumer for that purpose, by any other means available to the consumer credit reporting agency. As part of, or in addition to, this notice the consumer credit reporting agency shall, within five business days of reinserting the information, provide the consumer in writing (1) a statement that the disputed information has been reinserted, (2) a notice that the agency will provide to the consumer, within 15 days following a request, the name, address, and telephone number of any furnisher of information contacted or which contacted the consumer credit reporting agency in connection with the reinsertion, (3) the toll-free telephone number of the consumer credit reporting agency that the consumer can use to obtain this name, address, and telephone number, and (4) a notice that the consumer has the right to add a statement to his or her file disputing the accuracy or completeness of the information.

(d) A consumer credit reporting agency shall provide notice to the consumer of the results of any reinvestigation under this subdivision, within five days of completion of the reinvestigation. The notice shall include (1) a statement that the reinvestigation is completed, (2) a

consumer credit report that is based on the consumer's file as that file is revised as a result of the reinvestigation, (3) a description or indication of any changes made in the consumer credit report as a result of those revisions to the consumer's file, (4) a notice that, if requested by the consumer, a description of the procedure used to determine the accuracy and completeness of the information shall be provided to the consumer by the consumer credit reporting agency, including the name, business address, and telephone number of any furnisher of information contacted in connection with that information, (5) a notice that the consumer has the right to add a statement to the consumer's file disputing the accuracy or completeness of the information, and (6) a notice that the consumer has the right to request that the consumer credit reporting agency furnish notifications under subdivision (h). A consumer credit reporting agency shall provide the notice pursuant to this subdivision respecting the procedure used to determine the accuracy and completeness of information, not later than 15 days after receiving a request from the consumer.

(e) The presence of information in the consumer's file that contradicts the contention of the consumer shall not, in and of itself, constitute reasonable grounds for believing the dispute is frivolous or irrelevant....

(i) A consumer credit reporting agency shall maintain reasonable procedures designed to prevent the reappearance in a consumer's file and in consumer credit reports of information that has been deleted pursuant to this section and not reinserted pursuant to subdivision (c).

California Civil Code § 1785.20.5.

(a) Prior to requesting a consumer credit report for employment purposes, the user of the report shall provide written notice to the person involved. The notice shall inform the person that a report will be used and the source of the report, and shall contain a box that the person may check off to receive a copy of the credit report.

If the consumer indicates that he or she wishes to receive a copy of the report, the user shall request that a copy be provided to the person when the user requests its copy from the credit reporting agency. The report to the user and to the subject person shall be provided contemporaneously and at no charge to the subject person...

California Civil Code § 1785.25.

...

(b) A person who (1) in the ordinary course of business regularly and on a routine basis furnishes information to one or more consumer credit reporting agencies about the person's own transactions or experiences with one or more consumers and (2) determines that information on a specific transaction or experience so provided to a consumer credit reporting agency is not complete or accurate, shall promptly notify the consumer credit reporting agency of that determination and provide to the consumer credit reporting agency any corrections to that information, or any additional information, that is necessary to make the information provided by the person to the consumer credit reporting agency complete and accurate....

(d) A person who regularly furnishes information to a consumer credit reporting agency regarding a consumer who has an open-end credit account with that person, and which is closed by the consumer, shall notify the consumer credit reporting agency of the closure of that account by the consumer, in the information regularly furnished for the period in which the account is closed.

(e) A person who places a delinquent account for collection (internally or by referral to a third party), charges the delinquent account to profit or loss, or takes similar action, and subsequently furnishes information to a credit reporting agency regarding that action, shall include within the information furnished the approximate commencement date of the delinquency which gave rise to that action, unless that date

was previously reported to the credit reporting agency. Nothing in this provision shall require that a delinquency must be reported to a credit reporting agency.

(f) Upon receiving notice of a dispute noticed pursuant to subdivision (a) of Section 1785.16 with regard to the completeness or accuracy of any information provided to a consumer credit reporting agency, the person that provided the information shall (1) complete an investigation with respect to the disputed information and report to the consumer credit reporting agency the results of that investigation before the end of the 30-business-day period beginning on the date the consumer credit reporting agency receives the notice of dispute from the consumer in accordance with subdivision (a) of Section 1785.16 and (2) review relevant information submitted to it.

California Civil Code § 1785.26.

...

(b) A creditor may submit negative credit information concerning a consumer to a consumer credit reporting agency, only if the creditor notifies the consumer affected. After providing this notice, a creditor may submit additional information to a credit reporting agency respecting the same transaction or extension of credit that gave rise to the original negative credit information without providing additional notice.

(c) The notice shall be in writing and shall be delivered in person or mailed first class, postage prepaid, to the party's last known address, prior to or within 30 days after the transmission of the negative credit information.

(1) The notice may be part of any notice of default, billing statement, or other correspondence, and may be included as preprinted or standard form language in any of these from the creditor to the consumer.

(2) The notice is sufficient if it is in substantially the following form:

"As required by law, you are hereby notified that a negative credit report reflecting on your credit record may be submitted to a credit reporting agency if you fail to fulfill the terms of your credit obligations."

(3) The notice may, in the creditor's discretion, be more specific than the form given in paragraph (2). The notice may include, but shall not be limited to, particular information regarding an account or information respecting the approximate date on which the creditor submitted or intends to submit a negative credit report.

(4) The giving of notice by a creditor as provided in this subdivision does not create any requirement for the creditor to actually submit negative credit information to a consumer credit reporting agency. However, this section shall not be construed to authorize the use of notice as provided in this subdivision in violation of the federal Fair Debt Collection Practices Act (15 U.S.C., Sec. 1592 et seq.).

(d) A creditor is liable for failure to provide notice pursuant to this section, unless the creditor establishes, by a preponderance of the evidence, that at the time of that failure to give notice the creditor maintained reasonable procedures to comply with this section.

California Civil Code § 1799.101.

…

(b) Except as provided in subdivisions (d) and (e), no creditor shall provide any adverse information with respect to any cosigner, to a consumer credit reporting agency…unless, at or before the time the information is provided to the consumer credit reporting agency, written notice of the delinquency is provided to the cosigner….

(d) The notice requirements of subdivision…
(b)…[does] not apply to any cosigner whose address, as shown in the creditor's records respecting the consumer credit contract, is the same as the primary obligor.

(e) The notice requirements of subdivision…
(b)…shall be satisfied by mailing a copy of the required notice to the cosigner at the cosigner's

address, as shown in the creditor's records respecting the consumer credit contract. However, if more than one cosigner reside at the same address, as shown in the creditor's records respecting the consumer credit contract, a notice addressed to any cosigner at that address shall be deemed notice to all the cosigners residing at that address.

(f) Nothing in this section shall require any particular form or language with respect to a notice of delinquency sent to either a primary obligor or cosigner.

(g) Within a reasonable time after a creditor has reported to a credit reporting agency that a delinquency or delinquencies that have been reported to the consumer credit reporting agency and included in the cosigner's file maintained by the consumer credit reporting agency have been cured, the consumer credit reporting agency shall indicate in the file that the payment was made.

(h) Nothing in this section shall be construed to require notice of a delinquency to be provided to a cosigner in any instance not expressly specified in this section, or to provide notice to persons other than cosigners.

California Civil Code § 1799.102.

(a) A cosigner who suffers a loss as a result of a violation of Section 1799.101 may bring an action to recover actual damages or two hundred fifty dollars ($250), whichever is greater, and reasonable attorney fees.

(b) The cosigner shall, not less than 30 days prior to bringing an action pursuant to subdivision (a), notify the person alleged to have violated Section 1799. 101 of the cosigner's intention to bring an action. The notice shall include a statement of the specific evidence that proves the loss suffered by the cosigner. If within 25 days after the date of receiving the notice, the person alleged to have violated Section 1799.101 tenders to the cosigner an amount equal to the loss, or otherwise resolves the matter to the cosigner's satisfaction, the cosigner shall be barred from further recovery of that loss, including reasonable attorney fees.

Excerpts from the Colorado Credit Services Organization Act

Colorado Revised Statutes § 12-14.3-106. Procedure for disputed information

…

(2) On or before five business days after the date a consumer reporting agency receives notice of a dispute from a consumer…, the agency shall provide notice of the dispute to all persons who provided any item of information in dispute….

(5) Information deleted…may not be reinserted in the consumer's file unless the person who furnishes the information reinvestigates and states in writing or by electronic record to the consumer reporting agency that the information is complete and accurate.

(6) A consumer reporting agency shall provide written notice of the results of any reinvestigation or reinsertion made pursuant to this section within five business days of the completion of the reinvestigation or reinsertion. Such notice shall include:

(a) A statement that the reinvestigation is complete;

(b) A statement of the determination of the consumer reporting agency on the completeness or accuracy of the disputed information;

(c) A copy of the consumer's file or consumer report and a description of the results of the reinvestigation;

(d) A notice that, if requested by the consumer, a description of the procedure used to determine the accuracy and completeness of the information shall be provided to the consumer by the consumer reporting agency, including the name, business address, and, if available, the telephone number of any person contacted in connection with such information; and…

(f) A notification of the consumer's rights to dispute resolution under section 12-14.3-107, which are available after the consumer has followed all dispute procedures described in this section and has received the notice specified under this subsection (6).

Colorado Revised Statutes § 12-14.3-107. Consumer's right to file action in court or arbitrate disputes

An action to enforce any obligation of a consumer reporting agency to a consumer under this article may be brought in any court of competent jurisdiction as provided by the federal "Fair Credit Reporting Act" or submitted to binding arbitration after the consumer has followed all dispute procedures in Section 12-14.3-106 and has received the notice specified in subsection (6) of said Section in the manner set forth in the rules of the American Arbitration Association to determine whether the consumer reporting agency met its obligations under this article. No decision by an arbitrator pursuant to this section shall affect the validity of any obligations or debts owed to any party. A successful party to any such arbitration proceeding shall be compensated for the costs and attorney fees of the proceeding as determined by the court or arbitration. No consumer may submit more than one action to arbitration against any consumer reporting agency during any 120-day period. The results of an arbitration action brought against a consumer reporting agency doing business in this state shall be communicated in a timely manner with all other consumer reporting agencies doing business in this state. If, as a result of an arbitration a determination is made in favor of the consumer, any adverse information in such consumer's file or record shall be removed or stricken in a timely manner. If such adverse information is not so removed or stricken, the consumer may bring an action against the noncomplying agency pursuant to this section notwithstanding the 120-day waiting period.

Excerpts from the Kentucky Consumer Protection Act

Kentucky 367.310. Consumer reporting agency records restriction

No consumer reporting agency shall maintain any information in its files relating to any charge in a criminal case, in any court of this Commonwealth, unless the charge has resulted in a conviction.

Excerpts from the Maine Fair Credit Reporting Act

Maine Revised Statutes § 10-1320. Requirements on users of consumer reports

...

2-C.   Consumer mortgage reports. In any consumer credit transaction involving a consumer report relating to a loan to be secured by a first-mortgage on an owner-occupied dwelling, whenever a user has requested such a report and because or partly because of the information contained in the report adverse action is taken, the user shall provide a copy of the report to the consumer. This section does not apply if the consumer reporting agency provides a copy of the report to the consumer....

3-A.   Medical expenses debt; court or administrative orders. A debt collection may report overdue medical expenses for a minor child to a consumer reporting agency only in the name of the responsible party identified in a court order or administrative order if the debt collector is notified orally or in writing of the existence of the order. In addition, a report may not be made until after the debt collector has notified, or made a good faith effort to notify, the responsible party of that party's obligation to pay the overdue medical expenses. Existing information regarding overdue medical expenses for a minor child in the name of a person other than the responsible party identified in a court order or administrative order is considered inaccurate information...and is subject to correction. A debt col-

lector or consumer reporting agency may request reasonable verification of the order, including a certified copy of the order.

Excerpts from the Michigan Credit Reporting Practices Act

Michigan Statutes Annotated § 19-655(272). Prior to reporting adverse information concerning cosigner; procedure

(1) Before reporting adverse information about a cosigner to a consumer reporting agency...or providing any information regarding the cosigner's obligation to a collection agency...or taking any collection action on the obligation against the cosigner,...a person shall do both of the following:

(a) send the cosigner, by first class mail, a notice indicating that the primary debtor has become delinquent or defaulted on the obligation and that the cosigner is responsible for payment of the obligation.

(b) Allow the cosigner not less than 30 days from the date that the notice was sent to respond to the notice by doing either of the following:

(i) Paying the amount then due and owing under the obligation.

(ii) Making other arrangements satisfactory to the person to whom the obligation is owed.

(2) A person shall not report adverse information regarding a cosigner if the cosigner has responded to a notice in the manner described in subsection (1)(b).

Excerpts from the Minnesota Access to Consumer Reports Law

Minnesota Statutes Annotated § 13C.02 Disclosure of use of consumer reports for employment purposes.

Subdivision 1. Disclosure required. A person may not obtain or cause to be prepared a consumer report on a consumer for employment purposes unless the person clearly and accurately discloses to the consumer that a consumer report may be obtained or caused to be prepared. The disclosure must inform the consumer of the right to request additional information on the nature of the report under subdivision 3. In the case of an investigative consumer report, the disclosure under this subdivision must inform the consumer that the report may include information obtained through personal interviews regarding the consumer's character, general reputation, personal characteristics, or mode of living.

Subdivision 2. Form; copy. The disclosure required under Subdivision 1 must be in writing and must be provided to the consumer before the consumer report is obtained or caused to be prepared. If a written application is provided for employment purposes by an employer or prospective employer, the disclosure must be included in or accompany the application. The disclosure must include a box that the person may check off and return to receive a copy of the consumer report. If the consumer requests a copy of the report, the person requesting the report shall request the person preparing the report to provide a copy to the consumer. The report must be sent to the consumer by the person preparing the report within 24 hours of providing it to the person requesting the report. The report to the consumer must include a statement of the consumer's right to dispute and correct any errors.... A consumer may not be charged for a report provided under this section. If no report exists, the consumer reporting agency has no obligation to the consumer under this section.

Subdivision 3. Further disclosure if requested. A consumer reporting agency shall, upon written request from the consumer, make a complete and accurate disclosure of the nature and scope of the report. The disclosure under this subdivision must be in writing and must be mailed or delivered to the consumer within five days after the request for the disclosure was received or the consumer report was requested, whichever date is later.

Subdivision 4. Exception. This section does not apply to: (1) a consumer report to be used for employment purposes for which the consumer has not specifically applied; or (2) a consumer report used for an investigation of a current violation of a criminal or civil statute by a current employee or an investigation of employee conduct for which the employer may be liable, until the investigation is completed.

Excerpts from the Montana Related Credit Practices Act

Montana Code Annotated § 31-3-141. Actions available to consumer.

(1) A consumer may bring action in the nature of defamation, invasion of privacy, or negligence with respect to the reporting of information against any person who fails to comply with this part....

Excerpts from the New Hampshire Consumer Credit Reporting Act

New Hampshire Revised Statutes Annotated § 395-B:11. Procedure in case of disputed accuracy.

...

IX. No information shall be reinserted in a consumer's file after having been deleted...unless the person who furnishes the information verifies that the information is accurate. If any information so deleted from a consumer's file is reinserted in the file, the consumer reporting agency shall promptly notify the consumer of the reinsertion in writing or, if authorized by the consumer for that purpose, by any other means available to the consumer reporting agency....[T]he consumer reporting agency shall, within 5 business days of reinserting the information, provide the consumer in writing:

(a) A statement that the disputed information has been reinserted.

(b) A notice that the agency will provide the consumer, within a reasonable period of time following a request, the name, address, and telephone number of any furnisher of information contacted or which contacted the consumer reporting agency in connection with the reinsertion....

Excerpts from the New Mexico Credit Bureaus Law

New Mexico Statutes Annotated § 56-3-6. Report information; limitations.

A. A credit bureau may report the following matters for no longer than the specified periods:...

   (5) arrests and indictments pending trial, or convictions of crimes, for no longer than seven years from the date of release or parole. Such items shall no longer be reported if at any time it is learned that after a conviction a full pardon has been granted, or after an arrest or indictment a conviction did not result....

Excerpts from the New York Fair Credit Reporting Act

New York General Business Law § 380-j. Prohibited information.

(a) No consumer reporting agency shall report or maintain in the file on a consumer, information:

   (1) relative to an arrest or a criminal charge unless there has been a criminal conviction for such offense, or unless such charges are still pending,...

(b) Notwithstanding the provisions of paragraph one of subdivision (a) of this section, a consumer reporting agency may collect, evaluate, prepare, use or report information relative to a detention of an individual by a retail mercantile establishment, provided that:

   (1) the individual has executed an uncoerced admission of wrongdoing;

   (2) with respect to a detention made on or after the effective date of this article the retail mercantile establishment has, prior to transmitting to a consumer reporting agency information concerning such detention, delivered to the individual a written notice containing:

      (i) a statement that the information may be furnished to a consumer reporting agency, and that such information may be reported to a retail mercantile establishment for employment purposes,

      (ii) a statement that the individual may request disclosure by the consumer reporting agency of information in the agency's file on such individual, and that the completeness or accuracy of such information may be disputed by the individual, and

      (iii) the name and address of such consumer reporting agency; and

   (3) the user of such information certifies to the consumer reporting agency that such information will be used only in connection with employment purposes.

(c) In the event that a criminal charge is filed subsequent to the detention described in subdivision (b) of this section, the disposition of such charge shall be recorded by the consumer reporting agency in the file on such individual upon the request of such individual and upon his furnishing proof of such disposition....

(f)

   (1) Except as authorized under paragraph two of this subdivision, no consumer reporting agency may make any consumer report con-

taining any of the following items of information....

    (vi) information regarding drug or alcoholic addiction where the last reported incident relating to such addiction antedates the consumer report or investigative consumer report by more than seven years;

    (vii) information relating to past confinement in a mental institution where the date of last confinement antedates the report by more than seven years....

(2) The provisions of this subdivision shall not apply to:...

    (iii) the employment of any individual at an annual salary which equals, or which may reasonably be expected to equal twenty-five thousand dollars, or more.

(g) No consumer reporting agency shall collect, evaluate, report, or maintain in the file on a consumer any results, opinions, analyses, transcripts or information of any nature concerning, related to, or derived from a polygraph examination, an examination by any device or instrument of any type used to test or question individuals for the purpose of detecting deception, verifying truthfulness, or measuring deceptive tendencies, or the questioning or interviewing of an individual by the examiner prior to or after such an examination.

Excerpts from the Oklahoma Credit Ratings Act

Oklahoma Statutes Annotated § 24-81. Persons furnishing ratings to request statement of assets and liabilities.

Any person, firm or corporation engaged in or purporting to furnish retail merchants the financial or credit rating of any person who is the actual or prospective customer of such retail merchant shall, before furnishing such rating, submit, either in person or by mailing to his last known post office address to the person whose rating is about to be reported, a request asking for a statement of the assets and liabilities of such person.

Excerpts from the Rhode Island Deceptive Trade Practices Act

General Laws of Rhode Island § 6-3.2-21. Credit reports - Notice to individual - Requirements of users of credit reports.

(a) No person or business shall request a credit report in connection with a consumer's application for credit, employment or insurance unless a consumer is first informed that a credit report may be requested in connection with such application.

Excerpts from the Utah Consumer Credit Code

Utah Code § 70C-7-107. Notice of negative credit report required.

...

(2) A creditor may submit a negative credit report to a credit reporting agency, only if the creditor notifies the party whose credit record is the subject of the negative report. After providing this notice, a creditor may submit additional information to a credit reporting agency respecting the same transaction or extension of credit that gave rise to the original negative credit report without providing any additional notice.

(3)

    (a) Notice shall be in writing and shall be delivered in person or mailed first class, postage prepaid, to the party's last-known address prior to or within 30 days after the transmission of the report.

    (b) The notice may be part of any notice of default, billing statement or other correspondence from the creditor to the party.

    (c) The notice is sufficient if it takes substantially the following form: "As required by Utah law, you are hereby notified that a negative credit report reflecting on your credit record may be submitted to a credit reporting agency if you fail to fulfill the terms of your credit obligations."...

(4)...

    (b) If a creditor willfully violates this section, the court may award punitive damages in an amount not in excess of two times the amount of the actual damages awarded.

Excerpts from the Vermont Consumer Fraud Act

Vermont Statutes Annotated Title 9 § 2480e. Consumer Consent

(a) A person shall not obtain the credit report of a consumer unless:...

(2) the person has secured the consent of the consumer, and the report is used for the purpose consented to by the consumer.

Vermont Statutes Annotated Title 9 § 2480g. Exemptions

(a) The provisions of this subchapter shall not apply to education loans made, guaranteed or serviced by the Vermont student assistance corporation....

(b) The provisions of section 2480e of this title shall not apply to the office of child support services when investigating a child support case....

(c) The provisions of section 2480e of this title shall not apply to credit transactions entered into prior to January 1, 1993. ■

Federal and State Credit Reporting Laws
Effective September 30, 1997

This Appendix contains many of the rules regulating credit bureaus. You'll find the federal government's rules in the Fair Credit Reporting Act (FCRA). In addition, a handful of states have enacted laws related to credit reporting and credit bureaus. Many of these laws duplicate the protections provided by the federal FCRA. But 14 states—California, Colorado, Kentucky, Maine, Michigan, Minnesota, Montana, New Hampshire, New Mexico, New York, Oklahoma, Rhode Island, Utah and Vermont—have additional laws which supplement the protections provided by the federal law. Excerpted portions of these state laws follow the federal FCRA, below.

If a credit bureau violates the federal FCRA, you can register a complaint with the Federal Trade Commission (addresses and phone numbers are in Chapter 4, Section D). You can also sue for negligent or willful noncompliance with the federal FCRA within two years of the bureau's violation. You can sue for actual damages, such as court costs, attorney's fees, lost wages, and if applicable, infliction of emotional distress. In cases of truly outrageous behavior, you can ask for punitive damages— damages meant to punish for malicious or willful conduct.

If a credit bureau violates a state law, you can register a complaint with the appropriate state agency (addresses and phone numbers are in Appendix 1, Section E). You can probably also sue for noncompliance with the state law. If you are thinking about suing, however, you'll need to find the full state law and read it carefully. (Look for the law at a local law library or a large public library.)

These lawsuits can probably be filed in small claims court without the help of an attorney. (See *Everybody's Guide to Small Claims Court*, by Ralph Warner (Nolo Press) for definitive information on suing in small claims court.) If you plan to ask for punitive damages, you'll probably need a lawyer's help to file in a regular court.

Text of the Federal Fair Credit Reporting Act

Short Title

This title may be cited as the Fair Credit Reporting Act.

15 U.S.C. § 1681. Congressional findings and statement of purpose

(a) Accuracy and fairness of credit reporting. The Congress makes the following findings:

(1) The banking system is dependent upon fair and accurate credit reporting. Inaccurate credit reports directly impair the efficiency of the banking system, and unfair credit reporting methods undermine the public confidence which is essential to the continued functioning of the banking system.

(2) An elaborate mechanism has been developed for investigating and evaluating the credit worthiness, credit standing, credit capacity, character, and general reputation of consumers.

(3) Consumer reporting agencies have assumed a vital role in assembling and evaluating consumer credit and other information on consumers.

(4) There is a need to insure that consumer reporting agencies exercise their grave responsibilities with fairness, impartiality, and a respect for the consumer's right to privacy.

(b) Reasonable procedures. It is the purpose of this subchapter to require that consumer reporting agencies adopt reasonable procedures for meeting the needs of commerce for consumer credit, personnel, insurance, and other information in a manner which is fair and equitable to the consumer, with regard to the confidentiality, accuracy, relevancy, and proper utilization of such information in accordance with the requirements of this subchapter.

15 U.S.C. § 1681a. Definitions; rules of construction

(a) Definitions and rules of construction set forth in this section are applicable for the purposes of this subchapter.

(b) The term "person" means any individual, partnership, corporation, trust, estate, cooperative, association, government or governmental subdivision or agency, or other entity.

(c) The term "consumer" means an individual.

(d) Consumer report.

   (1) In general. The term "consumer report" means any written, oral, or other communication of any information by a consumer reporting agency bearing on a consumer's credit worthiness, credit standing, credit capacity, character, general reputation, personal characteristics, or mode of living which is used or expected to be used or collected in whole or in part for the purpose of serving as a factor in establishing the consumer's eligibility for:

   (A) credit or insurance to be used primarily for personal, family, or household purposes;

   (B) employment purposes; or

   (C) any other purpose authorized under section 1681b.

   (2) Exclusions. The term 'consumer report' does not include:

   (A) any:

      (i) report containing information solely as to transactions or experiences between the consumer and the person making the report;

      (ii) communication of that information among persons related by common ownership or affiliated by corporate control; or

      (iii) any communication of other information among persons related by common ownership or affiliated by corporate control, if it is clearly and conspicuously disclosed to the consumer that the information may be communicated among such persons and the consumer is given the opportunity, before the time that the information is initially communicated, to direct that such information not be communicated among such persons;

   (B) any authorization or approval of a specific extension of credit directly or indirectly by the issuer of a credit card or similar device;

   (C) any report in which a person who has been requested by a third party to make a specific extension of credit directly or indirectly to a consumer conveys his or her decision with respect to such request, if the third party advises the consumer of the name and address of the person to whom the request was made, and such person makes the disclosures to the consumer required under section 1681m; or

   (D) a communication described in subsection (o).

(e) The term "investigative consumer report" means a consumer report or portion thereof in which information on a consumer's character, general reputation, personal characteristics, or mode of living is obtained through personal interviews with neighbors, friends, or associates of the consumer reported on or with others with whom he is acquainted or who may have knowledge concerning any such items of information. However, such information shall not include specific factual information on a consumer's credit record obtained directly from a creditor of the consumer or from a consumer reporting agency when such information was obtained directly from a creditor of the consumer or from the consumer.

(f) The term "consumer reporting agency" means any person which, for monetary fees, dues, or on a cooperative nonprofit basis, regularly engages in whole or in part in the practice of assembling or evaluating consumer credit information or other information on consumers for the purpose of furnishing consumer reports to third parties, and which uses any means or facility of interstate commerce for the purpose of preparing or furnishing consumer reports.

(g) The term "file," when used in connection with information on any consumer, means all of the information on that consumer recorded and retained by a consumer reporting agency regardless of how the information is stored.

(h) The term "employment purposes" when used in connection with a consumer report means a report used for the purpose of evaluating a consumer for employment, promotion, reassignment or retention as an employee.

(i) The term "medical information" means information or records obtained, with the consent of the individual to whom it relates, from licensed physicians or medical practitioners, hospitals, clinics, or other medical or medically related facilities.

(j) Definitions relating to child support obligations.

(1) Overdue support. The term "overdue support" has the meaning given to such term in Section 666(e) of Title 42.

(2) State or local child support enforcement agency. The term "State or local child support enforcement agency" means a State or local agency which administers a State or local program for establishing and enforcing child support obligations.

(k) Adverse action.

(1) Actions included. The term "adverse action":

(A) has the same meaning as in section 701(d)(6) of the Equal Credit Opportunity Act; and

(B) means:

(i) a denial or cancellation of, an increase in any charge for, or a reduction or other adverse or unfavorable change in the terms of coverage or amount of, any insurance, existing or applied for, in connection with the underwriting of insurance;

(ii) a denial of employment or any other decision for employment purposes that adversely affects any current or prospective employee;

(iii) a denial or cancellation of, an increase in any charge for, or any other adverse or unfavorable change in the terms of, any license or benefit described in section 1681b(a)(3)(D); and

(iv) an action taken or determination that is:

(I) made in connection with an application that was made by, or a transaction that was initiated by, any consumer, or in connection with a review of an account under section 1681(a)(3)(F)(ii); and

(II) adverse to the interests of the consumer.

(2) Applicable findings, decisions, commentary, and orders. For purposes of any determination of whether an action is an adverse action under paragraph (1)(A), all appropriate final findings, decisions, commentary, and orders issued under section 701(d)(6) of the Equal Credit Opportunity Act by the Board of Governors of the Federal Reserve System or any court shall apply.

(l) Firm offer of credit or insurance. The term "firm offer of credit or insurance" means any offer of credit or insurance to a consumer that will be honored if the consumer is determined, based on information in a consumer report on the consumer, to meet the specific criteria used to select the consumer for the offer, except that the offer may be further conditioned on one or more of the following:

(1) The consumer being determined, based on information in the consumer's application for the credit or insurance, to meet specific criteria bearing on credit worthiness or insurability, as applicable, that are established:

(A) before selection of the consumer for the offer; and

(B) for the purpose of determining whether to extend credit or insurance pursuant to the offer.

(2) Verification:

(A) that the consumer continues to meet the specific criteria used to select the consumer for the offer, by using information in a consumer report on the consumer, information in the consumer's application for the credit or insurance, or other information bearing on the credit worthiness or insurability of the consumer; or

(B) of the information in the consumer's application for the credit or insurance, to determine that the consumer meets the specific criteria bearing on credit worthiness or insurability.

(3) The consumer furnishing any collateral that is a requirement for the extension of the credit or insurance that was:

(A) established before selection of the consumer for the offer of credit or insurance; and

(B) disclosed to the consumer in the offer of credit or insurance.

(m) Credit or insurance transaction that is not initiated by the consumer. The term "credit or insurance transaction that is not initiated by the consumer" does not include the use of a consumer report by a person with which the consumer has an account or insurance policy, for purposes of:

(1) reviewing the account or insurance policy; or

(2) collecting the account.

(n) State. The term "State" means any State, the Commonwealth of Puerto Rico, the District of Columbia, and any territory or possession of the United States.

(o) Excluded communications. A communication is described in this subsection if it is a communication:

(1) that, but for subsection (d)(2)(E), would be an investigative consumer report;

(2) that is made to a prospective employer for the purpose of:

(A) procuring an employee for the employer; or

(B) procuring an opportunity for a natural person to work for the employer;

(3) that is made by a person who regularly performs such procurement;

(4) that is not used by any person for any purpose other than a purpose described in subparagraph (A) or (B) of paragraph (2); or

(5) with respect to which:

(A) the consumer who is the subject of the communication:

(i) consents orally or in writing to the nature and scope of the communication, before the collection of any information for the purpose of making the communication;

(ii) consents orally or in writing to the making of the communication to a prospective employer, before the making of the communication; and

(iii) in the case of consent under clause (i) or (ii) given orally, is provided written confirmation of that consent by the person making the communication, not later than three business days after the receipt of the consent by that person;

(B) the person who makes the communication does not, for the purpose of making the communication, make any inquiry that if made by a prospective employer of the consumer who is the subject of the communication would violate any applicable Federal or State equal employment opportunity law or regulation; and

(C) the person who makes the communication:

(i) discloses in writing to the consumer who is the subject of the communication, not later than five business days after receiving any request from the consumer for such disclosure, the nature and substance of all information in the consumer's file at the time of the request, except that the sources of any information that is acquired solely for use in making the communication and is actually used for no other purpose, need not be disclosed other than under appropriate discovery procedures in any court of competent jurisdiction in which an action is brought; and

    (ii) notifies the consumer who is the subject of the communication, in writing, of the consumer's right to request the information described in clause (i).

(p) Consumer reporting agency that compiles and maintains files on consumers on a nationwide basis. The term "consumer reporting agency that compiles and maintains files on consumers on a nationwide basis" means a consumer reporting agency that regularly engages in the practice of assembling or evaluating, and maintaining, for the purpose of furnishing consumer reports to third parties bearing on a consumer's credit worthiness, credit standing, or credit capacity, each of the following regarding consumers residing nationwide:

(1) Public record information.

(2) Credit account information from persons who furnish that information regularly and in the ordinary course of business.

15 U.S.C. § 1681b. Permissible purposes of consumer reports

(a) In general. Subject to subsection (c), any consumer reporting agency may furnish a consumer report under the following circumstances and no other:

(1) In response to the order of a court having jurisdiction to issue such an order, or a subpoena issued in connection with proceedings before a Federal grand jury.

(2) In accordance with the written instructions of the consumer to whom it relates.

(3) To a person which it has reason to believe:

    (A) intends to use the information in connection with a credit transaction involving the consumer on whom the information is to be furnished and involving the extension of credit to, or review or collection of an account of, the consumer; or

    (B) intends to use the information for employment purposes; or

    (C) intends to use the information in connection with the underwriting of insurance involving the consumer; or

    (D) intends to use the information in connection with a determination of the consumer's eligibility for a license or other benefit granted by a governmental instrumentality required by law to consider an applicant's financial responsibility or status; or

    (E) intends to use the information, as a potential investor or servicer, or current insurer, in connection with a valuation of, or an assessment of the credit or prepayment risks associated with, an existing credit obligation; or

    (F) otherwise has a legitimate business need for the information:

        (i) in connection with a business transaction that is initiated by the consumer; or

        (ii) to review an account to determine whether the consumer continues to meet the terms of the account.

(b) Conditions for furnishing and using consumer reports for employment purposes.

(1) Certification from user. A consumer reporting agency may furnish a consumer report for employment purposes only if:

    (A) the person who obtains such report from the agency certifies to the agency that:

        (i) the person has complied with paragraph (2) with respect to the consumer report, and the person will comply with paragraph (3) with respect to the consumer report if paragraph (3) becomes applicable; and

    (ii) information from the consumer report will not be used in violation of any applicable Federal or State equal employment opportunity law or regulation; and

  (B) the consumer reporting agency provides with the report a summary of the consumer's rights under this title, as prescribed by the Federal Trade Commission under section 1681g(c)(3).

(2) Disclosure to consumer. A person may not procure a consumer report, or cause a consumer report to be procured, for employment purposes with respect to any consumer, unless:

  (A) a clear and conspicuous disclosure has been made in writing to the consumer at any time before the report is procured or caused to be procured, in a document that consists solely of the disclosure, that a consumer report may be obtained for employment purposes; and

  (B) the consumer has authorized in writing the procurement of the report by that person.

(3) Conditions on use for adverse actions. In using a consumer report for employment purposes, before taking any adverse action based in whole or in part on the report, the person intending to take such adverse action shall provide to the consumer to whom the report relates:

  (A) a copy of the report; and

  (B) a description in writing of the rights of the consumer under this title, as prescribed by the Federal Trade Commission under section 1681g(c)(3).

(c) Furnishing reports in connection with credit or insurance transactions that are not initiated by the consumer.

(1) In general. A consumer reporting agency may furnish a consumer report relating to any consumer pursuant to subparagraph (A) or (C) of subsection (a)(3) in connection with any credit or insurance transaction that is not initiated by the consumer only if:

  (A) the consumer authorizes the agency to provide such report to such person; or

  (B)

    (i) the transaction consists of a firm offer of credit or insurance;

    (ii) the consumer reporting agency has complied with subsection (e); and

    (iii) there is not in effect an election by the consumer, made in accordance with subsection (e), to have the consumer's name and address excluded from lists of names provided by the agency pursuant to this paragraph.

(2) Limits on information received under paragraph (1)(b). A person may receive pursuant to paragraph (1)(B) only:

  (A) the name and address of a consumer;

  (B) an identifier that is not unique to the consumer and that is used by the person solely for the purpose of verifying the identity of the consumer; and

  (C) other information pertaining to a consumer that does not identify the relationship or experience of the consumer with respect to a particular creditor or other entity.

(3) Information regarding inquiries. Except as provided in section 1681g(a)(5), a consumer reporting agency shall not furnish to any person a record of inquiries in connection with a credit or insurance transaction that is not initiated by a consumer.

(d) Reserved.

(e) Election of consumer to be excluded from lists.

(1) In general. A consumer may elect to have the consumer's name and address excluded from any list provided by a consumer reporting agency under subsection (c)(1)(B) in

connection with a credit or insurance transaction that is not initiated by the consumer by notifying the agency in accordance with paragraph (2) that the consumer does not consent to any use of a consumer report relating to the consumer in connection with any credit or insurance transaction that is not initiated by the consumer.

(2) Manner of notification. A consumer shall notify a consumer reporting agency under paragraph (1):

    (A) through the notification system maintained by the agency under paragraph (5); or

    (B) by submitting to the agency a signed notice of election form issued by the agency for purposes of this subparagraph.

(3) Response of agency after notification through system. Upon receipt of notification of the election of a consumer under paragraph (1) through the notification system maintained by the agency under paragraph (5), a consumer reporting agency shall:

    (A) inform the consumer that the election is effective only for the 2-year period following the election if the consumer does not submit to the agency a signed notice of election form issued by the agency for purposes of paragraph (2)(B); and

    (B) provide to the consumer a notice of election form, if requested by the consumer, not later than five business days after receipt of the notification of the election through the system established under paragraph (5), in the case of a request made at the time the consumer provides notification through the system.

(4) Effectiveness of election. An election of a consumer under paragraph (1):

    (A) shall be effective with respect to a consumer reporting agency beginning five business days after the date on which the consumer notifies the agency in accordance with paragraph (2);

    (B) shall be effective with respect to a consumer reporting agency:

        (i) subject to subparagraph (C), during the two-year period beginning five business days after the date on which the consumer notifies the agency of the election, in the case of an election for which a consumer notifies the agency only in accordance with paragraph (2)(A); or

        (ii) until the consumer notifies the agency under subparagraph (C), in the case of an election for which a consumer notifies the agency in accordance with paragraph (2)(B);

    (C) shall not be effective after the date on which the consumer notifies the agency, through the notification system established by the agency under paragraph (5), that the election is no longer effective; and

    (D) shall be effective with respect to each affiliate of the agency.

(5) Notification system.

    (A) In general. Each consumer reporting agency that, under subsection (c)(1)(B), furnishes a consumer report in connection with a credit or insurance transaction that is not initiated by a consumer shall:

        (i) establish and maintain a notification system, including a toll-free telephone number, which permits any consumer whose consumer report is maintained by the agency to notify the agency, with appropriate identification, of the consumer's election to have the consumer's name and address excluded from any such list of names and addresses provided by the agency for such a transaction; and

        (ii) publish by not later than 365 days after the date of enactment of the Consumer Credit Reporting Reform

Act of 1996, and not less than annually thereafter, in a publication of general circulation in the area served by the agency:

   (I)   a notification that information in consumer files maintained by the agency may be used in connection with such transactions; and

   (II) the address and toll-free telephone number for consumers to use to notify the agency of the consumer's election under clause (i).

   (B) Establishment and maintenance as compliance. Establishment and maintenance of a notification system (including a toll-free telephone number) and publication by a consumer reporting agency on the agency's own behalf and on behalf of any of its affiliates in accordance with this paragraph is deemed to be compliance with this paragraph by each of those affiliates.

(6) Notification system by agencies that operate nationwide. Each consumer reporting agency that compiles and maintains files on consumers on a nationwide basis shall establish and maintain a notification system for purposes of paragraph (5) jointly with other such consumer reporting agencies.

(f) Certain use or obtaining of information prohibited. A person shall not use or obtain a consumer report for any purpose unless:

   (1) the consumer report is obtained for a purpose for which the consumer report is authorized to be furnished under this section; and

   (2) the purpose is certified in accordance with section 1681e by a prospective user of the report through a general or specific certification.

(g) Furnishing reports containing medical information. A consumer reporting agency shall not furnish for employment purposes, or in connection with a credit or insurance transaction or a direct marketing transaction, a consumer report that contains medical information about a consumer, unless the consumer consents to the furnishing of the report.

15 U.S.C. § 1681c. Reporting requirements relating to information contained in consumer reports

(a) Information excluded from consumer reports. Except as authorized under subsection (b) of this section, no consumer reporting agency may make any consumer report containing any of the following items of information:

   (1) Cases under title 11 or under the Bankruptcy Act that, from the date of entry of the order for relief or the date of adjudication, as the case may be, antedate the report by more than ten years.

   (2) Suits and judgments which, from date of entry, antedate the report by more than seven years or until the governing statute of limitations has expired, whichever is the longer period.

   (3) Paid tax liens which, from date of payment, antedate the report by more than seven years.

   (4) Accounts placed for collection or charged to profit and loss which antedate the report by more than seven years.

   (5) Records of arrest, indictment, or conviction of crime which, from date of disposition, release, or parole, antedate the report by more than seven years.

   (6) Any other adverse item of information which antedates the report by more than seven years.

(b) Exempted cases. The provisions of subsection (a) of this section are not applicable in the case of any consumer credit report to be used in connection with:

   (1) a credit transaction involving, or which may reasonably be expected to involve, a principal amount of $150,000 or more;

(2) the underwriting of life insurance involving, or which may reasonably be expected to involve, a face amount of $150,000 or more; or

(3) the employment of any individual at an annual salary which equals, or which may reasonably be expected to equal, $75,000 or more.

(c) Running of reporting period.

(1) In general. The seven-year period referred to in paragraphs (4) and (6) of subsection (a) shall begin, with respect to any delinquent account that is placed for collection (internally or by referral to a third party, whichever is earlier), charged to profit and loss, or subjected to any similar action, upon the expiration of the 180-day period beginning on the date of the commencement of the delinquency which immediately preceded the collection activity, charge to profit and loss, or similar action.

(2) Effective date. Paragraph (1) shall apply only to items of information added to the file of a consumer on or after the date that is 455 days after the date of enactment of the Consumer Credit Reporting Reform Act of 1996.

(d) Information required to be disclosed. Any consumer reporting agency that furnishes a consumer report that contains information regarding any case involving the consumer that arises under title 11, United States Code, shall include in the report an identification of the chapter of such title 11 under which such case arises if provided by the source of the information. If any case arising or filed under title 11, United States Code, is withdrawn by the consumer before a final judgment, the consumer reporting agency shall include in the report that such case or filing was withdrawn upon receipt of documentation certifying such withdrawal.

(e) Indication of closure of account by consumer. If a consumer reporting agency is notified pursuant to section 1681t(a)(4) that a credit account of a consumer was voluntarily closed by the consumer, the agency shall indicate that fact in any consumer report that includes information related to the account.

(f) Indication of dispute by consumer. If a consumer reporting agency is notified pursuant to section 1681t(a)(3) that information regarding a consumer who was furnished to the agency is disputed by the consumer, the agency shall indicate that fact in each consumer report that includes the disputed information.

15 U.S.C. § 1681d. Disclosure of investigative consumer reports

(a) Disclosure of fact of preparation. A person may not procure or cause to be prepared an investigative consumer report on any consumer unless:

(1) it is clearly and accurately disclosed to the consumer that an investigative consumer report including information as to his character, general reputation, personal characteristics, and mode of living, whichever are applicable, may be made, and such disclosure (A) is made in a writing mailed, or otherwise delivered, to the consumer, not later than three days after the date on which the report was first requested, and (B) includes a statement informing the consumer of his right to request the additional disclosures provided for under subsection (b) of this section and the written summary of the rights of the consumer prepared pursuant to section 1681g; and

(2) the person certifies or has certified to the consumer reporting agency that:

(A) the person has made the disclosures to the consumer required by paragraph (1); and

(B) the person will comply with subsection (b).

(b) Disclosure on request of nature and scope of investigation. Any person who procures or causes to be prepared an investigative consumer report on any consumer shall, upon written request made by the consumer within a reasonable period of time after the receipt by him of the disclosure required by subsection (a)(1) of this section, make a complete and accurate disclosure of the nature and scope of the investigation requested. This disclosure shall be made in a writing mailed, or otherwise delivered, to the consumer not later than five days after the date on which the request for such disclosure was received from the consumer or such report was first requested, whichever is the later.

(c) Limitation on liability upon showing of reasonable procedures for compliance with provisions. No person may be held liable for any violation of subsection (a) or (b) of this section if he shows by a preponderance of the evidence that at the time of the violation he maintained reasonable procedures to assure compliance with subsection (a) or (b) of this section.

(d) Prohibitions.

(1) Certification. A consumer reporting agency shall not prepare or furnish an investigative consumer report unless the agency has received a certification under subsection (a)(2) from the person who requested the report.

(2) Inquiries. A consumer reporting agency shall not make an inquiry for the purpose of preparing an investigative consumer report on a consumer for employment purposes if the making of the inquiry by an employer or prospective employer of the consumer would violate any applicable Federal or State equal employment opportunity law or regulation.

(3) Certain public record information. Except as otherwise provided in section 613, a consumer reporting agency shall not furnish an investigative consumer report that includes information that is a matter of public record and that relates to an arrest, indictment, conviction, civil judicial action, tax lien, or outstanding judgment, unless the agency has verified the accuracy of the information during the 30-day period ending on the date on which the report is furnished.

(4) Certain adverse information. A consumer reporting agency shall not prepare or furnish an investigative consumer report on a

consumer that contains information that is adverse to the interest of the consumer and that is obtained through a personal interview with a neighbor, friend, or associate of the consumer or with another person with whom the consumer is acquainted or who has knowledge of such item of information, unless:

(A) the agency has followed reasonable procedures to obtain confirmation of the information, from an additional source that has independent and direct knowledge of the information; or

(B) the person interviewed is the best possible source of the information.

15 U.S.C. § 1681e. Compliance procedures

(a) Identity and purposes of credit users. Every consumer reporting agency shall maintain reasonable procedures designed to avoid violations of section 1681c of this title and to limit the furnishing of consumer reports to the purposes listed under section 1681b of this title. These procedures shall require that prospective users of the information identify themselves, certify the purposes for which the information is sought, and certify that the information will be used for no other purpose. Every consumer reporting agency shall make a reasonable effort to verify the identity of a new prospective user and the uses certified by such prospective user prior to furnishing such user a consumer report. No consumer reporting agency may furnish a consumer report to any person if it has reasonable grounds for believing that the consumer report will not be used for a purpose listed in section 1681b of this title.

(b) Accuracy of report. Whenever a consumer reporting agency prepares a consumer report it shall follow reasonable procedures to assure maximum possible accuracy of the information concerning the individual about whom the report relates.

(c) Disclosure of consumer reports by users allowed. A consumer reporting agency may not prohibit a user of a consumer report furnished by the agency on a consumer from disclosing the contents of the report to the consumer, if adverse action against the consumer has been taken by the user based in whole or in part on the report.

(d) Notice to users and furnishers of information.

  (1) Notice requirement. A consumer reporting agency shall provide to any person:

    (A) who regularly and in the ordinary course of business furnishes information to the agency with respect to any consumer; or

    (B) to whom a consumer report is provided by the agency;

    a notice of such person's responsibilities under this title.

  (2) Content of notice. The Federal Trade Commission shall prescribe the content of notices under paragraph (1), and a consumer reporting agency shall be in compliance with this subsection if it provides a notice under paragraph (1) that is substantially similar to the Federal Trade Commission prescription under this paragraph.

(e) Procurement of consumer report for resale.

  (1) Disclosure. A person may not procure a consumer report for purposes of reselling the report (or any information in the report) unless the person discloses to the consumer reporting agency that originally furnishes the report:

    (A) the identity of the end-user of the report (or information); and

    (B) each permissible purpose under section 1681b for which the report is furnished to the end-user of the report (or information).

  (2) Responsibilities of procurers for resale. A person who procures a consumer report for purposes of reselling the report (or any information in the report) shall:

    (A) establish and comply with reasonable procedures designed to ensure that the report (or information) is resold by the person only for a purpose for which the report may be furnished under section 1681b, including by requiring that each person to which the report (or information) is resold and that resells or provides the report (or information) to any other person:

      (i) identifies each end user of the resold report (or information);

      (ii) certifies each purpose for which the report (or information) will be used; and

      (iii) certifies that the report (or information) will be used for no other purpose; and

    (B) before reselling the report, make reasonable efforts to verify the identifications and certifications made under subparagraph (A).

15 U.S.C. § 1681f. Compliance procedures

Notwithstanding the provisions of section 1681b of this title, a consumer reporting agency may furnish identifying information respecting any consumer, limited to his name, address, former addresses, places of employment, or former places of employment, to a governmental agency.

15 U.S.C. § 1681g. Disclosures to consumers

(a) Information on file; sources; report recipients. Every consumer reporting agency shall, upon request, and subject to section 1681(a)(1), clearly and accurately disclose to the consumer:

  (1) All information in the consumer's file at the time of the request, except that nothing in this paragraph shall be construed to require a consumer reporting agency to disclose to a consumer any information concerning credit scores or any other risk scores or predictors relating to the consumer.

  (2) The sources of the information; except that the sources of information acquired solely for use in preparing an investigative consumer report and actually used for no other purpose need not be disclosed: Provided, That in the event an action is brought under

this subchapter, such sources shall be available to the plaintiff under appropriate discovery procedures in the court in which the action is brought.

(3)

    (A) Identification of each person (including each end-user identified under section 1681e(e)(1)) that procured a consumer report:

        (i) for employment purposes, during the two-year period preceding the date on which the request is made; or

        (ii) for any other purpose, during the one-year period preceding the date on which the request is made.

    (B) An identification of a person under subparagraph (A) shall include:

        (i) the name of the person or, if applicable, the trade name (written in full) under which such person conducts business; and

        (ii) upon request of the consumer, the address and telephone number of the person.

(5) [1]A record of all inquiries received by the agency during the one-year period preceding the request that identified the consumer in connection with a credit or insurance transaction that was not initiated by the consumer.

(b) Exempt information. The requirements of subsection (a) of this section respecting the disclosure of sources of information and the recipients of consumer reports do not apply to information received or consumer reports furnished prior to the effective date of this subchapter except to the extent that the matter involved is contained in the files of the consumer reporting agency on that date.

(c) Summary of rights required to be included with disclosure.

---

[1] As numbered in original. (4) is missing.

(1) Summary of rights. A consumer reporting agency shall provide to a consumer, with each written disclosure by the agency to the consumer under this section:

    (A) a written summary of all of the rights that the consumer has under this title; and

    (B) in the case of a consumer reporting agency that compiles and maintains files on consumers on a nationwide basis, a toll-free telephone number established by the agency, at which personnel are accessible to consumers during normal business hours.

(2) Specific items required to be included. The summary of rights required under paragraph (1) shall include:

    (A) a brief description of this title and all rights of consumers under this title;

    (B) an explanation of how the consumer may exercise the rights of the consumer under this title;

    (C) a list of all Federal agencies responsible for enforcing any provision of this title and the address and any appropriate phone number of each such agency, in a form that will assist the consumer in selecting the appropriate agency;

    (D) a statement that the consumer may have additional rights under State law and that the consumer may wish to contact a State or local consumer protection agency or a State attorney general to learn of those rights; and

    (E) a statement that a consumer reporting agency is not required to remove accurate derogatory information from a consumer's file, unless the information is outdated under section 1681c or cannot be verified.

(3) Form of summary of rights. For purposes of this subsection and any disclosure by a consumer reporting agency required under this title with respect to consumers' rights, the Federal Trade Commission (after consul-

tation with each Federal agency referred to in section 1681s(b)) shall prescribe the form and content of any such disclosure of the rights of consumers required under this title. A consumer reporting agency shall be in compliance with this subsection if it provides disclosures under paragraph (1) that are substantially similar to the Federal Trade Commission prescription under this paragraph.

(4) Effectiveness. No disclosures shall be required under this subsection until the date on which the Federal Trade Commission prescribes the form and content of such disclosures under paragraph (3).

15 U.S.C. § 1681h. Conditions and form of disclosure to consumers

(a) In general.

(1) Proper identification. A consumer reporting agency shall require, as a condition of making the disclosures required under section 1681g, that the consumer furnish proper identification.

(2) Disclosure in writing. Except as provided in subsection (b), the disclosures required to be made under section 1681g shall be provided under that section in writing.

(b) Other forms of disclosure.

(1) In general. If authorized by a consumer, a consumer reporting agency may make the disclosures required under 1681g:

(A) other than in writing; and

(B) in such form as may be:

(i) specified by the consumer in accordance with paragraph (2); and

(ii) available from the agency.

(2) Form. A consumer may specify pursuant to paragraph (1) that disclosures under section 1681g shall be made:

(A) in person, upon the appearance of the consumer at the place of business of the consumer reporting agency where disclosures are regularly provided, during normal business hours, and on reasonable notice;

(B) by telephone, if the consumer has made a written request for disclosure by telephone;

(C) by electronic means, if available from the agency; or

(D) by any other reasonable means that is available from the agency.

(c) Trained personnel. Any consumer reporting agency shall provide trained personnel to explain to the consumer any information furnished to him pursuant to section 1681g of this title.

(d) Persons accompanying consumer. The consumer shall be permitted to be accompanied by one other person of his choosing, who shall furnish reasonable identification. A consumer reporting agency may require the consumer to furnish a written statement granting permission to the consumer reporting agency to discuss the consumer's file in such person's presence.

(e) Limitation of liability. Except as provided in sections 1681n and 1681o of this title, no consumer may bring any action or proceeding in the nature of defamation, invasion of privacy, or negligence with respect to the reporting of information against any consumer reporting agency, any user of information, or any person who furnishes information to a consumer reporting agency, based on information disclosed pursuant to section 1681g, 1681h, or 1681m of this title or based on information disclosed by a user of a consumer report to or for a consumer against whom the user has taken adverse action, based whole or in part on the report, except as to false information furnished with malice or willful intent to injure such consumer.

15 U.S.C. § 1681i. Procedure in case of disputed accuracy

(a) Reinvestigations of disputed information.

(1) Reinvestigation required.

(A) In general. If the completeness or accuracy of any item of information contained in a consumer's file at a consumer reporting agency is disputed by the consumer and the consumer notifies the agency directly of such dispute, the agency shall reinvestigate free of charge and record the current status of the disputed information, or delete the item from the file in accordance with paragraph (5), before the end of the 30-day period beginning on the date on which the agency receives the notice of the dispute from the consumer.

(B) Extension of period to reinvestigate. Except as provided in subparagraph (C), the 30-day period described in subparagraph (A) may be extended for not more than 15 additional days if the consumer reporting agency receives information from the consumer during that 30-day period that is relevant to the reinvestigation.

(C) Limitations on extension of period to reinvestigate. Subparagraph (B) shall not apply to any reinvestigation in which, during the 30-day period described in subparagraph (A), the information that is the subject of the reinvestigation is found to be inaccurate or incomplete or the consumer reporting agency determines that the information cannot be verified.

(2) Prompt notice of dispute to furnisher of information.

(A) In general. Before the expiration of the five-business-day period beginning on the date on which a consumer reporting agency receives notice of a dispute from any consumer in accordance with paragraph (1), the agency shall provide notification of the dispute to any person who provided any item of information in dispute, at the address and in the manner established with the person. The notice shall include all relevant information regarding the dispute that the agency has received from the consumer.

(B) Provision of other information from consumer. The consumer reporting agency shall promptly provide to the person who provided the information in dispute all relevant information regarding the dispute that is received by the agency from the consumer after the period referred to in subparagraph (A) and before the end of the period referred to in paragraph (1)(A).

(3) Determination that dispute is frivolous or irrelevant.

(A) In general. Notwithstanding paragraph (1), a consumer reporting agency may terminate a reinvestigation of information disputed by a consumer under that paragraph if the agency reasonably determines that the dispute by the consumer is frivolous or irrelevant, including by reason of a failure by a consumer to provide sufficient information to investigate the disputed information.

(B) Notice of determination. Upon making any determination in accordance with subparagraph (A) that a dispute is frivolous or irrelevant, a consumer reporting agency shall notify the consumer of such determination not later than 5 business days after making such determination, by mail or, if authorized by the consumer for that purpose, by any other means available to the agency.

(C) Contents of notice. A notice under subparagraph (B) shall include:

(i) the reasons for the determination under subparagraph (A); and

(ii) identification of any information required to investigate the disputed information, which may consist of a standardized form describing the general nature of such information.

(4) Consideration of consumer information. In conducting any reinvestigation under paragraph (1) with respect to disputed information in the file of any consumer, the con-

sumer reporting agency shall review and consider all relevant information submitted by the consumer in the period described in paragraph (1)(A) with respect to such disputed information.

(5) Treatment of inaccurate or unverifiable information.

(A) In general. If, after any reinvestigation under paragraph (1) of any information disputed by a consumer, an item of the information is found to be inaccurate or incomplete or cannot be verified, the consumer reporting agency shall promptly delete that item of information from the consumer's file or modify that item of information, as appropriate, based on the results of the reinvestigation.

(B) Requirements relating to reinsertion of previously deleted material.

(i) Certification of accuracy of information. If any information is deleted from a consumer's file pursuant to subparagraph (A), the information may not be reinserted in the file by the consumer reporting agency unless the person who furnishes the information certifies that the information is complete and accurate.

(ii) Notice to consumer. If any information that has been deleted from a consumer's file pursuant to subparagraph (A) is reinserted in the file, the consumer reporting agency shall notify the consumer of the reinsertion in writing not later than five business days after the reinsertion or, if authorized by the consumer for that purpose, by any other means available to the agency.

(iii) Additional information. As part of, or in addition to, the notice under clause (ii), a consumer reporting agency shall provide to a consumer in writing not later than five busi-

ness days after the date of the reinsertion:

(I) a statement that the disputed information has been reinserted;

(II) the business name and address of any furnisher of information contacted and the telephone number of such furnisher, if reasonably available, or of any furnisher of information that contacted the consumer reporting agency, in connection with the reinsertion of such information; and

(III) a notice that the consumer has the right to add a statement to the consumer's file disputing the accuracy or completeness of the disputed information.

(C) Procedures to prevent reappearance. A consumer reporting agency shall maintain reasonable procedures designed to prevent the reappearance in a consumer's file, and in consumer reports on the consumer, of information that is deleted pursuant to this paragraph (other than information that is reinserted in accordance with subparagraph (B)(i)).

(D) Automated reinvestigation system. Any consumer reporting agency that compiles and maintains files on consumers on a nationwide basis shall implement an automated system through which furnishers of information to that consumer reporting agency may report the results of a reinvestigation that finds incomplete or inaccurate information in a consumer's file to other such consumer reporting agencies.

(6) Notice of results of reinvestigation.

(A) In general. A consumer reporting agency shall provide written notice to a consumer of the results of a reinvestigation under this subsection not later than five business days after the completion of the reinvestigation, by mail or, if authorized by the consumer for that purpose, by other means available to the agency.

(B) Contents. As part of, or in addition to, the notice under subparagraph (A), a consumer reporting agency shall provide to a consumer in writing before the expiration of the five-day period referred to in subparagraph (A):

(i) a statement that the reinvestigation is completed;

(ii) a consumer report that is based upon the consumer's file as that file is revised as a result of the reinvestigation;

(iii) a notice that, if requested by the consumer, a description of the procedure used to determine the accuracy and completeness of the information shall be provided to the consumer by the agency, including the business name and address of any furnisher of information contacted in connection with such information and the telephone number of such furnisher, if reasonably available;

(iv) a notice that the consumer has the right to add a statement to the consumer's file disputing the accuracy or completeness of the information; and

(v) a notice that the consumer has the right to request under subsection (d) that the consumer reporting agency furnish notifications under that subsection.

(7) Description of reinvestigation procedure. A consumer reporting agency shall provide to a consumer a description referred to in paragraph (6)(B)(iv) by not later than 15 days after receiving a request from the consumer for that description.

(8) Expedited dispute resolution. If a dispute regarding an item of information in a consumer's file at a consumer reporting agency is resolved in accordance with paragraph (5)(A) by the deletion of the disputed information by not later than three business days after the date on which the agency receives notice of the dispute from the consumer in accordance with paragraph (1)(A), then the agency shall not be required to comply with paragraphs (2), (6), and (7) with respect to that dispute if the agency:

(A) provides prompt notice of the deletion to the consumer by telephone;

(B) includes in that notice, or in a written notice that accompanies a confirmation and consumer report provided in accordance with subparagraph (C), a statement of the consumer's right to request under subsection (d) that the agency furnish notifications under that subsection; and

(C) provides written confirmation of the deletion and a copy of a consumer report on the consumer that is based on the consumer's file after the deletion, not later than five business days after making the deletion.

(b) Statement of dispute. If the reinvestigation does not resolve the dispute, the consumer may file a brief statement setting forth the nature of the dispute. The consumer reporting agency may limit such statements to not more than one hundred words if it provides the consumer with assistance in writing a clear summary of the dispute.

(c) Notification of consumer dispute in subsequent consumer reports. Whenever a statement of a dispute is filed, unless there is reasonable grounds to believe that it is frivolous or irrelevant, the consumer reporting agency shall, in any subsequent consumer report containing the information in question, clearly note that it is disputed by the consumer and provide either the consumer's statement or a clear and accurate codification or summary thereof.

(d) Notification of deletion of disputed information. Following any deletion of information which is found to be inaccurate or whose accuracy can no longer be verified or any notation as to disputed information, the consumer reporting agency shall, at the request of the consumer, furnish notification that the item has been deleted or the statement, codification or summary pursuant to subsection (b) or (c) of this section to any person specifically designated by the consumer who has within two years prior thereto received a consumer report for employment purposes, or within six months prior thereto received a consumer report for any other purpose, which contained the deleted or disputed information.

15 U.S.C. § 1681j. Charges for disclosures

(a) Reasonable charges allowed for certain disclosures.

   (1) In general. Except as provided in subsections (b), (c), and (d), a consumer reporting agency may impose a reasonable charge on a consumer:

      (A) for making a disclosure to the consumer pursuant to section 1681g, which charge:

         (i) shall not exceed $8; and

         (ii) shall be indicated to the consumer before making the disclosure; and

      (B) for furnishing, pursuant to section 1681i(d), following a reinvestigation under section 1681i(a), a statement, codification, or summary to a person designated by the consumer under that section after the 30-day period beginning on the date of notification of the consumer under paragraph (6) or (8) of section 611(a) with respect to the reinvestigation, which charge:

         (i) shall not exceed the charge that the agency would impose on each designated recipient for a consumer report; and

         (ii) shall be indicated to the consumer before furnishing such information.

   (2) Modification of amount. The Federal Trade Commission shall increase the amount referred to in paragraph (1)(A)(i) on January 1 of each year, based proportionally on changes in the Consumer Price Index, with fractional changes rounded to the nearest fifty cents.

(b) Free disclosure after adverse notice to consumer. Each consumer reporting agency that maintains a file on a consumer shall make all disclosures pursuant to section 1681g without charge to the consumer if, not later than 60 days after receipt by such consumer of a notification pursuant to section 1681m, or of a notification from a debt collection agency affiliated with that consumer reporting agency stating that the consumer's credit rating may be or has been adversely affected, the consumer makes a request under section 1681g.

(c) Free disclosure under certain other circumstances. Upon the request of the consumer, a consumer reporting agency shall make all disclosures pursuant to section 1681g once during any 12-month period without charge to that consumer if the consumer certifies in writing that the consumer:

   (1) is unemployed and intends to apply for employment in the 60-day period beginning on the date on which the certification is made;

   (2) is a recipient of public welfare assistance; or

   (3) has reason to believe that the file on the consumer at the agency contains inaccurate information due to fraud.

(d) Other charges prohibited. A consumer reporting agency shall not impose any charge on a consumer for providing any notification required by this title or making any disclosure required by this title, except as authorized by subsection (a).

15 U.S.C. § 1681k. Public record information for employment purposes

A consumer reporting agency which furnishes a consumer report for employment purposes and which for that purpose compiles and reports items of information on consumers which are matters of public record and are likely to have an adverse effect upon a consumer's ability to obtain employment shall:

    (1) at the time such public record information is reported to the user of such consumer report, notify the consumer of the fact that public record information is being reported by the consumer reporting agency, together with the name and address of the person to whom such information is being reported; or

    (2) maintain strict procedures designed to insure that whenever public record information which is likely to have an adverse effect on a consumer's ability to obtain employment is reported it is complete and up to date. For purposes of this paragraph, items of public record relating to arrests, indictments, convictions, suits, tax liens, and outstanding judgments shall be considered up to date if the current public record status of the item at the time of the report is reported.

15 U.S.C. § 1681l. Restrictions on investigative consumer reports

Whenever a consumer reporting agency prepares an investigative consumer report, no adverse information in the consumer report (other than information which is a matter of public record) may be included in a subsequent consumer report unless such adverse information has been verified in the process of making such subsequent consumer report, or the adverse information was received within the three-month period preceding the date the subsequent report is furnished.

15 U.S.C. § 1681m. Requirements on users of consumer reports

(a) Duties of users taking adverse actions on the basis of information contained in consumer reports. If any person takes any adverse action with respect to any consumer that is based in whole or in part on any information contained in a consumer report, the person shall:

    (1) provide oral, written, or electronic notice of the adverse action to the consumer;

    (2) provide to the consumer orally, in writing, or electronically:

        (A) the name, address, and telephone number of the consumer reporting agency (including a toll-free telephone number established by the agency if the agency compiles and maintains files on consumers on a nationwide basis) that furnished the report to the person; and

        (B) a statement that the consumer reporting agency did not make the decision to take the adverse action and is unable to provide the consumer the specific reasons why the adverse action was taken; and

    (3) provide to the consumer an oral, written, or electronic notice of the consumer's right:

        (A) to obtain, under section 1681j, a free copy of a consumer report on the consumer from the consumer reporting agency referred to in paragraph (2), which notice shall include an indication of the 60-day period under that section for obtaining such a copy; and

        (B) to dispute, under section 1681i, with a consumer reporting agency the accuracy or completeness of any information in a consumer report furnished by the agency.

(b) Adverse action based on reports of persons other than consumer reporting agencies.

    (1) In general. Whenever credit for personal, family, or household purposes involving a consumer is denied or the charge for such credit is increased either wholly or partly because of information obtained from a person other than a consumer reporting agency bearing upon the consumer's credit worthiness, credit standing, credit capacity, character, general reputation, personal characteristics, or mode of living, the user of such information shall, within a reasonable period of time, upon the consumer's written request

for the reasons for such adverse action received within sixty days after learning of such adverse action, disclose the nature of the information to the consumer. The user of such information shall clearly and accurately disclose to the consumer his right to make such written request at the time such adverse action is communicated to the consumer.

(2) Duties of person taking certain actions based on information provided by affiliate.

    (A) Duties, generally. If a person takes an action described in subparagraph (B) with respect to a consumer, based in whole or in part on information described in subparagraph (C), the person shall:

        (i) notify the consumer of the action, including a statement that the consumer may obtain the information in accordance with clause (ii); and

        (ii) upon a written request from the consumer received within 60 days after transmittal of the notice required by clause (i), disclose to the consumer the nature of the information upon which the action is based by not later than 30 days after receipt of the request.

    (B) Action described. An action referred to in subparagraph (A) is an adverse action described in section 1681a(k)(1)(A), taken in connection with a transaction initiated by the consumer, or any adverse action described in clause (i) or (ii) of section 1681a(k)(1)(B).

    (C) Information described. Information referred to in subparagraph (A):

        (i) except as provided in clause (ii), is information that:

            (I) is furnished to the person taking the action by a person related by common ownership or affiliated by common corporate control to the person taking the action; and

            (II) bears on the credit worthiness, credit standing, credit capacity, character, general reputation, personal characteristics, or mode of living of the consumer; and

        (ii) does not include:

            (I) information solely as to transactions or experiences between the consumer and the person furnishing the information; or

            (II) information in a consumer report.

(c) Reasonable procedures to assure compliance. No person shall be held liable for any violation of this section if he shows by a preponderance of the evidence that at the time of the alleged violation he maintained reasonable procedures to assure compliance with the provisions of this section.

(d) Duties of users making written credit or insurance solicitations on the basis of information contained in consumer files.

    (1) In general. Any person who uses a consumer report on any consumer in connection with any credit or insurance transaction that is not initiated by the consumer, that is provided to that person under section 1681b(c)(1)(B), shall provide with each written solicitation made to the consumer regarding the transaction a clear and conspicuous statement that:

        (A) information contained in the consumer's consumer report was used in connection with the transaction;

        (B) the consumer received the offer of credit or insurance because the consumer satisfied the criteria for credit worthiness or insurability under which the consumer was selected for the offer;

        (C) if applicable, the credit or insurance may not be extended if, after the consumer responds to the offer, the consumer does not meet the criteria used to select the consumer for the offer or any applicable criteria bearing on credit worthiness or insurability or does not furnish any required collateral;

(D) the consumer has a right to prohibit information contained in the consumer's file with any consumer reporting agency from being used in connection with any credit or insurance transaction that is not initiated by the consumer; and

(E) the consumer may exercise the right referred to in subparagraph (D) by notifying a notification system established under section 1681b(e).

(2) Disclosure of address and telephone number. A statement under paragraph (1) shall include the address and toll-free telephone number of the appropriate notification system established under section 1681b(e).

(3) Maintaining criteria on file. A person who makes an offer of credit or insurance to a consumer under a credit or insurance transaction described in paragraph (1) shall maintain on file the criteria used to select the consumer to receive the offer, all criteria bearing on credit worthiness or insurability, as applicable, that are the basis for determining whether or not to extend credit or insurance pursuant to the offer, and any requirement for the furnishing of collateral as a condition of the extension of credit or insurance, until the expiration of the three-year period beginning on the date on which the offer is made to the consumer.

(4) Authority of federal agencies regarding unfair or deceptive acts or practices not affected. This section is not intended to affect the authority of any Federal or State agency to enforce a prohibition against unfair or deceptive acts or practices, including the making of false or misleading statements in connection with a credit or insurance transaction that is not initiated by the consumer.

15 U.S.C. § 1681n. Civil liability for willful noncompliance

(a) In general. Any person who willfully fails to comply with any requirement imposed under this subchapter with respect to any consumer is liable to that consumer in an amount equal to the sum of:

(1)

(A) any actual damages sustained by the consumer as a result of the failure or damages of not less than $100 and not more than $1,000; or

(B) in the case of liability of a natural person for obtaining a consumer report under false pretenses or knowingly without a permissible purpose, actual damages sustained by the consumer as a result of the failure or $1,000, whichever is greater;

(2) such amount of punitive damages as the court may allow; and

(3) in the case of any successful action to enforce any liability under this section, the costs of the action together with reasonable attorney's fees as determined by the court.

(b) Civil liability for knowing noncompliance. Any person who obtains a consumer report from a consumer reporting agency under false pretenses or knowingly without a permissible purpose shall be liable to the consumer reporting agency for actual damages sustained by the consumer reporting agency or $1,000, whichever is greater.

(c) Attorney's fees. Upon a finding by the court that an unsuccessful pleading, motion, or other paper filed in connection with an action under this section was filed in bad faith or for purposes of harassment, the court shall award to the prevailing party attorney's fees reasonable in relation to the work expended in responding to the pleading, motion, or other paper.

15 U.S.C. § 1681o. Civil liability for negligent noncompliance

(a) In general. Any person who is negligent in failing to comply with any requirement imposed under this subchapter with respect to any consumer is liable to that consumer in an amount equal to the sum of:

(1) any actual damages sustained by the consumer as a result of the failure;

(2) in the case of any successful action to enforce any liability under this section, the costs of the action together with reasonable attorney's fees as determined by the court.

(b) Attorney's fees. On a finding by the court that an unsuccessful pleading, motion, or other paper filed in connection with an action under this section was filed in bad faith or for purposes of harassment, the court shall award to the prevailing party attorney's fees reasonable in relation to the work expended in responding to the pleading, motion, or other paper.

15 U.S.C. § 1681p. Jurisdiction of courts; limitation of actions

An action to enforce any liability created under this subchapter may be brought in any appropriate United States district court without regard to the amount in controversy, or in any other court of competent jurisdiction, within two years from the date on which the liability arises, except that where a defendant has materially and willfully misrepresented any information required under this subchapter to be disclosed to an individual and the information so misrepresented is material to the establishment of the defendant's liability to that individual under this subchapter, the action may be brought at any time within two years after discovery by the individual of the misrepresentation.

15 U.S.C. § 1681q. Obtaining information under false pretenses

Any person who knowingly and willfully obtains information on a consumer from a consumer reporting agency under false pretenses shall be fined

under Title 18, United States Code, imprisoned for not more than two years, or both.

15 U.S.C. § 1681r. Unauthorized disclosures by officers or employees

Any officer or employee of a consumer reporting agency who knowingly and willfully provides information concerning an individual from the agency's files to a person not authorized to receive that information shall be fined under Title 18, United States Code, imprisoned for not more than two years, or both.

15 U.S.C. § 1681s. Administrative enforcement

(a)

(1) Enforcement by Federal Trade Commission. Compliance with the requirements imposed under this subchapter shall be enforced under the Federal Trade Commission Act (15 U.S.C. 41 et seq.) by the Federal Trade Commission with respect to consumer reporting agencies and all other persons subject thereto, except to the extent that enforcement of the requirements imposed under this subchapter is specifically committed to some other government agency under subsection (b) hereof. For the purpose of the exercise by the Federal Trade Commission of its functions and powers under the Federal Trade Commission Act, a violation of any requirement or prohibition imposed under this subchapter shall constitute an unfair or deceptive act or practice in commerce in violation of section 5(a) of the Federal Trade Commission Act (15 U.S.C. 45(a)) and shall be subject to enforcement by the Federal Trade Commission under section 5(b) thereof (15 U.S.C. 45(b)) with respect to any consumer reporting agency or person subject to enforcement by the Federal Trade Commission pursuant to this subsection, irrespective of whether that person is engaged in commerce or meets any other jurisdictional tests in the Federal Trade Commission Act. The Federal Trade Commission shall have

such procedural, investigative, and enforcement powers, including the power to issue procedural rules in enforcing compliance with the requirements imposed under this subchapter and to require the filing of reports, the production of documents, and the appearance of witnesses as though the applicable terms and conditions of the Federal Trade Commission Act were part of this subchapter. Any person violating any of the provisions of this subchapter shall be subject to the penalties and entitled to the privileges and immunities provided in the Federal Trade Commission Act as though the applicable terms and provisions thereof were part of this subchapter.

(2)

(A) In the event of a knowing violation, which constitutes a pattern or practice of violations of this title, the Commission may commence a civil action to recover a civil penalty in a district court of the United States against any person that violates this title. In such action, such person shall be liable for a civil penalty of not more than $2,500 per violation.

(B) In determining the amount of a civil penalty under subparagraph (A), the court shall take into account the degree of culpability, any history of prior such conduct, ability to pay, effect on ability to continue to do business, and such other matters as justice may require.

(3) Notwithstanding paragraph (2), a court may not impose any civil penalty on a person for a violation of section 1681u(a)(1) unless the person has been enjoined from committing the violation, or ordered not to commit the violation, in an action or proceeding brought by or on behalf of the Federal Trade Commission, and has violated the injunction or order, and the court may not impose any civil penalty for any violation occurring before the date of the violation of the injunction or order.

(4) Neither the Commission nor any other agency referred to in subsection (b) may prescribe trade regulation rules or other regulations with respect to this title.

(b) Enforcement by other agencies. Compliance with the requirements imposed under this title with respect to consumer reporting agencies, persons who use consumer reports from such agencies, persons who furnish information to such agencies, and users of information that are subject to subsection (d) or (e) of section 1681m shall be enforced under:

(1) section 8 of the Federal Deposit Insurance Act (12 U.S.C. 1818), in the case of:

(A) national banks, and Federal branches and Federal agencies of foreign banks, by the Office of the Comptroller of the Currency;

(B) member banks of the Federal Reserve System (other than national banks), branches and agencies of foreign banks (other than Federal branches, Federal agencies, and insured State branches of foreign banks), commercial lending companies owned or controlled by foreign banks, and organizations operating under section 25 or 25(a) of the Federal Reserve Act (12 U.S.C. 601 et seq., 611 et seq.), by the Board of Governors of the Federal Reserve System; and

(C) banks insured by the Federal Deposit Insurance Corporation (other than members of the Federal Reserve System) and insured State branches of foreign banks, by the Board of Directors of the Federal Deposit Insurance Corporation.

(2) section 8 of the Federal Deposit Insurance Act (12 U.S.C. 1818), by the Director of the Office of Thrift Supervision, in the case of a savings association the deposits of which are insured by the Federal Deposit Insurance Corporation;

(3) the Federal Credit Union Act (12 U.S.C. 1751 et seq.), by the Administrator of the National

Credit Union Administration with respect to any Federal credit union;

(4) subtitle IV of title 49, by the Interstate Commerce Commission with respect to any common carrier subject to such subtitle;

(5) the Federal Aviation Act of 1958 (49 App. U.S.C. 1301 et seq.), by the Secretary of Transportation with respect to any air carrier or foreign air carrier subject to that Act; and

(6) the Packers and Stockyards Act, 1921 (7 U.S.C. 181 et seq.) (except as provided in section 406 of that Act (7 U.S.C. 226, 227)), by the Secretary of Agriculture with respect to any activities subject to that Act. The terms used in paragraph (1) that are not defined in this subchapter or otherwise defined in section 3(s) of the Federal Deposit Insurance Act (12 U.S.C. 1813(s)) shall have the meaning given to them in section 1(b) of the International Banking Act of 1978 (12 U.S.C. 3101).

(c) State action for violations.

(1) Authority of states. In addition to such other remedies as are provided under State law, if the chief law enforcement officer of a State, or an official or agency designated by a State, has reason to believe that any person has violated or is violating this title, the State:

(A) may bring an action to enjoin such violation in any appropriate United States district court or in any other court of competent jurisdiction;

(B) subject to paragraph (5), may bring an action on behalf of the residents of the State to recover:

(i) damages for which the person is liable to such residents under sections 1681n and 1681o as a result of the violation;

(ii) in the case of a violation of section 1681t(a), damages for which the person would, but for section 1681t(c), be liable to such residents as a result of the violation; or

(iii) damages of not more than $1,000 for each willful or negligent violation; and

(C) in the case of any successful action under subparagraph (A) or (B), shall be awarded the costs of the action and reasonable attorney fees as determined by the court.

(2) Rights of federal regulators. The State shall serve prior written notice of any action under paragraph (1) upon the Federal Trade Commission or the appropriate Federal regulator determined under subsection (b) and provide the Commission or appropriate Federal regulator with a copy of its complaint, except in any case in which such prior notice is not feasible, in which case the State shall serve suchnotice immediately upon instituting such action. The Federal Trade Commission or appropriate Federal regulator shall have the right:

(A) to intervene in the action;

(B) upon so intervening, to be heard on all matters arising therein;

(C) to remove the action to the appropriate United States district court; and

(D) to file petitions for appeal.

(3) Investigatory powers. For purposes of bringing any action under this subsection, nothing in this subsection shall prevent the chief law enforcement officer, or an official or agency designated by a State, from exercising the powers conferred on the chief law enforcement officer or such official by the laws of such State to conduct investigations or to administer oaths or affirmations or to compel the attendance of witnesses or the production of documentary and other evidence.

(4) Limitation on state action while federal action pending. If the Federal Trade Commission or the appropriate Federal regulator has instituted a civil action or an administrative action under section 8 of the Federal Deposit Insurance Act for a violation of this title, no State may, during the pendency of

such action, bring an action under this section against any defendant named in the complaint of the Commission or the appropriate Federal regulator for any violation of this title that is alleged in that complaint.

(5) Limitations on state actions for violation of section 1681t(a)(1).

(A) Violation of injunction required. A State may not bring an action against a person under paragraph (1)(B) for a violation of section 1681t(a)(1), unless:

(i) the person has been enjoined from committing the violation, in an action brought by the State under paragraph (1)(A); and

(ii) the person has violated the injunction.

(B) Limitation on damages recoverable. In an action against a person under paragraph (1)(B) for a violation of section 1681t(a)(1), a State may not recover any damages incurred before the date of the violation of an injunction on which the action is based.

(d) Enforcement under other authority. For the purpose of the exercise by any agency referred to in subsection (b) of this section of its powers under any Act referred to in that subsection, a violation of any requirement imposed under this subchapter shall be deemed to be a violation of a requirement imposed under that Act. In addition to its powers under any provision of law specifically referred to in subsection (b) of this section, each of the agencies referred to in that subsection may exercise, for the purpose of enforcing compliance with any requirement imposed under this subchapter any other authority conferred on it by law. Notwithstanding the preceding, no agency referred to in subsection (b) may conduct an examination of a bank, savings association, or credit union regarding compliance with the provisions of this title, except in response to a complaint (or if the agency otherwise has knowledge) that the bank, savings association, or credit union has violated a provi-

sion of this title, in which case the agency may conduct an examination as necessary to investigate the complaint. If an agency determines during an investigation in response to a complaint that a violation of this title has occurred, the agency may, during its next 2 regularly scheduled examinations of the bank, savings association, or credit union, examine for compliance with this title.

(e) Interpretive authority. The Board of Governors of the Federal Reserve System may issue interpretations of any provision of this title as such provision may apply to any persons identified under paragraph (1), (2), and (3) of subsection (b), or to the holding companies and affiliates of such persons, in consultation with Federal agencies identified in paragraphs (1), (2), and (3) of subsection (b).

15 U.S.C. § 1681s-1. Information on overdue child support obligations

Notwithstanding any other provision of this subchapter, a consumer reporting agency shall include in any consumer report furnished by the agency in accordance with section 1681b of this title, any information on the failure of the consumer to pay overdue support which:

(1) is provided:

(A) to the consumer reporting agency by a State or local child support enforcement agency; or

(B) to the consumer reporting agency and verified by any local, State, or Federal Government agency; and

(2) antedates the report by 7 years or less.

15 U.S.C. § 1681t. Responsibilities of persons who furnish information to consumer reporting agencies

(a) Duty of furnishers of information to provide accurate information.

(1) Prohibition.

(A) Reporting information with actual knowledge of errors. A person shall not furnish any information relating to a consumer to any consumer reporting agency if the person knows or consciously avoids knowing that the information is inaccurate.

(B) Reporting information after notice and confirmation of errors. A person shall not furnish information relating to a consumer to any consumer reporting agency if:

    (i) the person has been notified by the consumer, at the address specified by the person for such notices, that specific information is inaccurate; and

    (ii) the information is, in fact, inaccurate.

(C) No address requirement. A person who clearly and conspicuously specifies to the consumer an address for notices referred to in subparagraph (B) shall not be subject to subparagraph (A); however, nothing in subparagraph (B) shall require a person to specify such an address.

(2) Duty to correct and update information. A person who:

(A) regularly and in the ordinary course of business furnishes information to one or more consumer reporting agencies about the person's transactions or experiences with any consumer; and

(B) has furnished to a consumer reporting agency information that the person determines is not complete or accurate,

shall promptly notify the consumer reporting agency of that determination and provide to the agency any corrections to that information, or any additional information, that is necessary to make the information provided by the person to the agency complete and accurate, and shall not thereafter furnish to the agency any of the information that remains not complete or accurate.

(3) Duty to provide notice of dispute. If the completeness or accuracy of any information furnished by any person to any consumer reporting agency is disputed to such person by a consumer, the person may not furnish the information to any consumer reporting agency without notice that such information is disputed by the consumer.

(4) Duty to provide notice of closed accounts. A person who regularly and in the ordinary course of business furnishes information to a consumer reporting agency regarding a consumer who has a credit account with that person shall notify the agency of the voluntary closure of the account by the consumer, in information regularly furnished for the period in which the account is closed.

(5) Duty to provide notice of delinquency of accounts. A person who furnishes information to a consumer reporting agency regarding a delinquent account being placed for collection, charged to profit or loss, or subjected to any similar action shall, not later than 90 days after furnishing the information, notify the agency of the month and year of the commencement of the delinquency that immediately preceded the action.

(b) Duties of furnishers of information upon notice of dispute.

(1) In general. After receiving notice pursuant to section 1681i(a)(2) of a dispute with regard to the completeness or accuracy of any information provided by a person to a consumer reporting agency, the person shall:

(A) conduct an investigation with respect to the disputed information;

(B) review all relevant information provided by the consumer reporting agency pursuant to section 1681i(a)(2);

(C) report the results of the investigation to the consumer reporting agency; and

(D) if the investigation finds that the information is incomplete or inaccurate, report those results to all other consumer reporting agencies to which the person furnished the information and that compile and maintain files on consumers on a nationwide basis.

(2) Deadline. A person shall complete all investigations, reviews, and reports required under paragraph (1) regarding information provided by the person to a consumer reporting agency, before the expiration of the period under section 1681i(a)(1) within which the consumer reporting agency is required to complete actions required by that section regarding that information.

(c) Limitation on liability. Sections 1681n and 1681o do not apply to any failure to comply with subsection (a), except as provided in section 1681s(c)(1)(B).

(d) Limitation on enforcement. Subsection (a) shall be enforced exclusively under section 1681s by the Federal agencies and officials and the State officials identified in that section.

15 U.S.C. § 1681u. Relation to State laws

(a) In general. Except as provided in subsections (b) and (c), this title does not annul, alter, affect, or exempt any person subject to the provisions of this subchapter from complying with the laws of any State with respect to the collection, distribution, or use of any information on consumers, except to the extent that those laws are inconsistent with any provision of this subchapter, and then only to the extent of the inconsistency.

(b) General exceptions. No requirement or prohibition may be imposed under the laws of any State:

(1) with respect to any subject matter regulated under:

(A) subsection (c) or (e) of section 1681b, relating to the prescreening of consumer reports;

(B) section 1681i, relating to the time by which a consumer reporting agency must take any action, including the provision of notification to a consumer or other person, in any procedure related to the disputed accuracy of information in a consumer's file, except that this sub-

paragraph shall not apply to any State law in effect on the date of enactment of the Consumer Credit Reporting Reform Act of 1996;

(C) subsections (a) and (b) of section 1681m, relating to the duties of a person who takes any adverse action with respect to a consumer;

(D) section 1681m(d), relating to the duties of persons who use a consumer report of a consumer in connection with any credit or insurance transaction that is not initiated by the consumer and that consists of a firm offer of credit or insurance;

(E) section 1681c, relating to information contained in consumer reports, except that this subparagraph shall not apply to any State law in effect on the date of enactment of the Consumer Credit Reporting Reform Act of 1996; or

(F) section 1681t, relating to the responsibilities of persons who furnish information to consumer reporting agencies, except that this paragraph shall not apply:

(i) with respect to section 54A(a) of chapter 93 of the Massachusetts Annotated Laws (as in effect on the date of enactment of the Consumer Credit Reporting Reform Act of 1996); or

(ii) with respect to section 1785.25(a) of the California Civil Code (as in effect on the date of enactment of the Consumer Credit Reporting Reform Act of 1996);

(2) with respect to the exchange of information among persons affiliated by common ownership or common corporate control, except that this paragraph shall not apply with respect to subsection (a) or (c)(1) of section 2480e of title 9, Vermont Statutes Annotated (as in effect on the date of enactment of the Consumer Credit Reporting Reform Act of 1996); or

(3) with respect to the form and content of any disclosure required to be made under section 1681g(c).

(c) Definition of firm offer of credit or insurance. Notwithstanding any definition of the term "firm offer of credit or insurance" (or any equivalent term) under the laws of any State, the definition of that term contained in section 1681a(l) shall be construed to apply in the enforcement and interpretation of the laws of any State governing consumer reports.

(d) Limitations. Subsections (b) and (c):

(1) do not affect any settlement, agreement, or consent judgment between any State Attorney General and any consumer reporting agency in effect on the date of enactment of the Consumer Credit Reporting Reform Act of 1996; and

(2) do not apply to any provision of State law (including any provision of a State constitution) that:

(A) is enacted after January 1, 2004;

(B) states explicitly that the provision is intended to supplement this title; and

(C) gives greater protection to consumers than is provided under this title.

Excerpts from the California Consumer Credit Reporting Agencies Act

California Civil Code § 1785.13.

(a) No consumer credit reporting agency shall make any consumer credit report containing any of the following items of information:...

(3) Unlawful detainer actions, unless the lessor was the prevailing party. For purposes of this paragraph, the lessor shall be deemed to be the party only if (A) final judgment was awarded to the lessor (i) upon entry of the tenant's default, (ii) upon the granting of the lessor's motion for summary judgment, or (iii) following trial, or (B) the action was resolved by a written settlement agreement between the parties that states that the unlawful detainer action may be reported. In any other instance in which the action is resolved by settlement agreement, the lessor shall not be deemed to be the prevailing party for purposes of this paragraph.[2]...

(6) Records of arrest, indictment, information, misdemeanor complaint, or conviction of a crime...shall no longer be reported if at any time it is learned that in the case of a conviction a full pardon has been granted, or in the case of an arrest, indictment, information, or misdemeanor complaint a conviction did not result....

(d) A consumer credit report shall not include any adverse information concerning a consumer antedating the report by more than 10 years or that otherwise is prohibited from being included in a consumer credit report.

California Civil Code § 1785.15.

(a) A...consumer has the right to request and receive all of the following:

(1) Either a decoded written version of the file or a written copy of the file, including all information in the file at the time of the request, with an explanation of any code used.

(b) Files maintained on a consumer shall be disclosed promptly as follows:...

(2) By mail, if the consumer makes a written request.... A disclosure pursuant to this paragraph shall be deposited in the United States mail, postage prepaid, within five business days after the consumer's written request for the disclosure is received by the consumer credit reporting agency. Consumer credit reporting agencies complying with requests for mailings under this section shall not be liable for disclosures to third parties caused by mishandling of mail after such mailings leave the consumer reporting agencies.

---

[2] This provision was held to violate the First Amendment of the U.S. Constitution; see *U.D. Registry v. California*, 34 Cal.App.4th. 107 (1995).

California Civil Code § 1785.26.

...

(b) A creditor may submit negative credit information concerning a consumer to a consumer credit reporting agency, only if the creditor notifies the consumer affected. After providing this notice, a creditor may submit additional information to a credit reporting agency respecting the same transaction or extension of credit that gave rise to the original negative credit information without providing additional notice.

(c) The notice shall be in writing and shall be delivered in person or mailed first class, postage prepaid, to the party's last known address, prior to or within 30 days after the transmission of the negative credit information.

(1) The notice may be part of any notice of default, billing statement, or other correspondence, and may be included as preprinted or standard form language in any of these from the creditor to the consumer.

(2) The notice is sufficient if it is in substantially the following form:
"As required by law, you are hereby notified that a negative credit report reflecting on your credit record may be submitted to a credit reporting agency if you fail to fulfill the terms of your credit obligations."

(3) The notice may, in the creditor's discretion, be more specific than the form given in paragraph (2). The notice may include, but shall not be limited to, particular information regarding an account or information respecting the approximate date on which the creditor submitted or intends to submit a negative credit report.

(4) The giving of notice by a creditor as provided in this subdivision does not create any requirement for the creditor to actually submit negative credit information to a consumer credit reporting agency. However, this section shall not be construed to authorize the use of notice as provided in this subdivision in violation of the federal Fair Debt Collection Practices Act (15 U.S.C., Sec. 1592 et seq.).

(d) A creditor is liable for failure to provide notice pursuant to this section, unless the creditor establishes, by a preponderance of the evidence, that at the time of that failure to give notice the creditor maintained reasonable procedures to comply with this section.

California Civil Code § 1799.101.

...

(b) Except as provided in subdivisions (d) and (e), no creditor shall provide any adverse information with respect to any cosigner, to a consumer credit reporting agency...unless, at or before the time the information is provided to the consumer credit reporting agency, written notice of the delinquency is provided to the cosigner....

(d) The notice requirements of subdivision...(b)... [does] not apply to any cosigner whose address, as shown in the creditor's records respecting the consumer credit contract, is the same as the primary obligor.

(e) The notice requirements of subdivision...(b)...shall be satisfied by mailing a copy of the required notice to the cosigner at the cosigner's address, as shown in the creditor's records respecting the consumer credit contract. However, if more than one cosigner reside at the same address, as shown in the creditor's records respecting the consumer credit contract, a notice addressed to any cosigner at that address shall be deemed notice to all the cosigners residing at that address.

(f) Nothing in this section shall require any particular form or language with respect to a notice of delinquency sent to either a primary obligor or cosigner.

(g) Within a reasonable time after a creditor has reported to a credit reporting agency that a delinquency or delinquencies that have been reported to the consumer credit reporting agency and included in the cosigner's file maintained by the consumer credit reporting agency have been cured, the consumer credit reporting agency shall indicate in the file that the payment was made.

(h) Nothing in this section shall be construed to require notice of a delinquency to be provided to a cosigner in any instance not expressly specified in this section, or to provide notice to persons other than cosigners.

California Civil Code § 1799.102.

(a) A cosigner who suffers a loss as a result of a violation of Section 1799.101 may bring an action to recover actual damages or two hundred fifty dollars ($250), whichever is greater, and reasonable attorney fees.

(b) The cosigner shall, not less than 30 days prior to bringing an action pursuant to subdivision (a), notify the person alleged to have violated Section 1799.101 of the cosigner's intention to bring an action. The notice shall include a statement of the specific evidence that proves the loss suffered by the cosigner. If within 25 days after the date of receiving the notice, the person alleged to have violated Section 1799.101 tenders to the cosigner an amount equal to the loss, or otherwise resolves the matter to the cosigner's satisfaction, the cosigner shall be barred from further recovery of that loss, including reasonable attorney fees.

Excerpts from the Colorado Credit Services Organization Act

Colorado Revised Statutes § 12-14.3-107. Consumer's right to file action in court or arbitrate disputes

An action to enforce any obligation of a consumer reporting agency to a consumer under this article may be brought in any court of competent jurisdiction as provided by the federal "Fair Credit Reporting Act" or submitted to binding arbitration after the consumer has followed all dispute procedures in Section 12-14.3-106 and has received the notice specified in subsection (6) of said Section in the manner set forth in the rules of the American Arbitration Association to determine whether the consumer reporting agency met its obligations under this article. No decision by an arbitrator pursuant to this section shall affect the validity of any obligations or debts owed to any party. A successful party to any such arbitration proceeding shall be compensated for the costs and attorney fees of the proceeding as determined by the court or arbitration. No consumer may submit more than one action to arbitration against any consumer reporting agency during any 120-day period. The results of an arbitration action brought against a consumer reporting agency doing business in this state shall be communicated in a timely manner with all other consumer reporting agencies doing business in this state. If, as a result of an arbitration a determination is made in favor of the consumer, any adverse information in such consumer's file or record shall be removed or stricken in a timely manner. If such adverse information is not so removed or stricken, the consumer may bring an action against the noncomplying agency pursuant to this section notwithstanding the 120-day waiting period.

Excerpts from the Kentucky Consumer Protection Act

Kentucky 367.310. Consumer reporting agency records restriction

No consumer reporting agency shall maintain any information in its files relating to any charge in a criminal case, in any court of this Commonwealth, unless the charge has resulted in a conviction.

Excerpts from the Maine Fair Credit Reporting Act

Maine Revised Statutes § 10-1320. Requirements on users of consumer reports

…

2-C. Consumer mortgage reports. In any consumer credit transaction involving a consumer report relating to a loan to be secured by a first-mortgage on an owner-occupied dwelling, whenever a user has requested such a report and because or partly because of the information contained in the report adverse action is taken, the user shall provide a copy of the report to the consumer. This section does not apply if the consumer reporting agency provides a copy of the report to the consumer....

3-A. Medical expenses debt; court or administrative orders. A debt collection may report overdue medical expenses for a minor child to a consumer reporting agency only in the name of the responsible party identified in a court order or administrative order if the debt collector is notified orally or in writing of the existence of the order. In addition, a report may not be made until after the debt collector has notified, or made a good faith effort to notify, the responsible party of that party's obligation to pay the overdue medical expenses. Existing information regarding overdue medical expenses for a minor child in the name of a person other than the responsible party identified in a court order or administrative order is considered inaccurate information...and is subject to correction. A debt collector or consumer reporting agency may request reasonable verification of the order, including a certified copy of the order.

Excerpts from the Michigan Credit Reporting Practices Act

Michigan Statutes Annotated § 19-655(272). Prior to reporting adverse information concerning cosigner; procedure

(1) Before reporting adverse information about a cosigner to a consumer reporting agency...or providing any information regarding the cosigner's obligation to a collection agency...or taking any collection action on the obligation against the cosigner, ...a person shall do both of the following:

(a) send the cosigner, by first class mail, a notice indicating that the primary debtor has

become delinquent or defaulted on the obligation and that the cosigner is responsible for payment of the obligation.

(b) Allow the cosigner not less than 30 days from the date that the notice was sent to respond to the notice by doing either of the following:

(i) Paying the amount then due and owing under the obligation.

(ii) Making other arrangements satisfactory to the person to whom the obligation is owed.

(2) A person shall not report adverse information regarding a cosigner if the cosigner has responded to a notice in the manner described in subsection (1)(b).

Excerpts from the Montana Related Credit Practices Act

Montana Code Annotated § 31-3-141. Actions available to consumer.

(1) A consumer may bring action in the nature of defamation, invasion of privacy, or negligence with respect to the reporting of information against any person who fails to comply with this part....

Excerpts from the New Mexico Credit Bureaus Law

New Mexico Statutes Annotated § 56-3-6. Report information; limitations.

A. A credit bureau may report the following matters for no longer than the specified periods:...

(5) arrests and indictments pending trial, or convictions of crimes, for no longer than seven years from the date of release or parole. Such items shall no longer be reported if at any time it is learned that after a conviction a full pardon has been granted, or after an arrest or indictment a conviction did not result....

Excerpts from the New York Fair Credit Reporting Act

New York General Business Law § 380-j. Prohibited information.

(a) No consumer reporting agency shall report or maintain in the file on a consumer, information:

   (1) relative to an arrest or a criminal charge unless there has been a criminal conviction for such offense, or unless such charges are still pending,...

(b) Notwithstanding the provisions of paragraph one of subdivision (a) of this section, a consumer reporting agency may collect, evaluate, prepare, use or report information relative to a detention of an individual by a retail mercantile establishment, provided that:

   (1) the individual has executed an uncoerced admission of wrongdoing;

   (2) with respect to a detention made on or after the effective date of this article the retail mercantile establishment has, prior to transmitting to a consumer reporting agency information concerning such detention, delivered to the individual a written notice containing:

   (i) a statement that the information may be furnished to a consumer reporting agency, and that such information may be reported to a retail mercantile establishment for employment purposes,

   (ii) a statement that the individual may request disclosure by the consumer reporting agency of information in the agency's file on such individual, and that the completeness or accuracy of such information may be disputed by the individual, and

   (iii) the name and address of such consumer reporting agency; and

   (3) the user of such information certifies to the consumer reporting agency that such information will be used only in connection with employment purposes.

(c) In the event that a criminal charge is filed subsequent to the detention described in subdivision (b) of this section, the disposition of such charge shall be recorded by the consumer reporting agency in the file on such individual upon the request of such individual and upon his furnishing proof of such disposition....

(f)

   (1) Except as authorized under paragraph two of this subdivision, no consumer reporting agency may make any consumer report containing any of the following items of information.

   (vi) information regarding drug or alcoholic addiction where the last reported incident relating to such addiction antedates the consumer report or investigative consumer report by more than seven years;

   (vii) information relating to past confinement in a mental institution where the date of last confinement antedates the report by more than seven years....

   (2) The provisions of this subdivision shall not apply to:...

   (iii) the employment of any individual at an annual salary which equals, or which may reasonably be expected to equal twenty-five thousand dollars, or more.

(g) No consumer reporting agency shall collect, evaluate, report, or maintain in the file on a consumer any results, opinions, analyses, transcripts or information of any nature concerning, related to, or derived from a polygraph examination, an examination by any device or instrument of any type used to test or question individuals for the purpose of detecting deception, verifying truthfulness, or measuring deceptive tendencies, or the questioning or interviewing of an individual by the examiner prior to or after such an examination.

Excerpts from the Oklahoma Credit Ratings Act

Oklahoma Statutes Annotated § 24-81. Persons furnishing ratings to request statement of assets and liabilities.

Any person, firm or corporation engaged in or purporting to furnish retail merchants the financial or credit rating of any person who is the actual or prospective customer of such retail merchant shall, before furnishing such rating, submit, either in person or by mailing to his last know post office address to the person whose rating is about to be reported, a request asking for a statement of the assets and liabilities of such person.

Excerpts from the Rhode Island Deceptive Trade Practices Act

General Laws of Rhode Island § 6-3.2-21. Credit reports - Notice to individual - Requirements of users of credit reports.

(a) No person or business shall request a credit report in connection with a consumer's application for credit, employment or insurance unless a consumer is first informed that a credit report may be requested in connection with such application.

Excerpts from the Utah Consumer Credit Code

Utah Code § 70C-7-107. Notice of negative credit report required.

...

(2) A creditor may submit a negative credit report to a credit reporting agency, only if the creditor notifies the party whose credit record is the subject of the negative report. After providing this notice, a creditor may submit additional information to a credit reporting agency respecting the same transaction or extension of credit that gave rise to the original negative credit report without providing any additional notice.

(3)
  (a) Notice shall be in writing and shall be delivered in person or mailed first class, postage prepaid, to the party's last-known address prior to or within 30 days after the transmission of the report.
  (b) The notice may be part of any notice of default, billing statement or other correspondence from the creditor to the party.
  (c) The notice is sufficient if it takes substantially the following form: "As required by Utah law, you are hereby notified that a negative credit report reflecting on your credit record may be submitted to a credit reporting agency if you fail to fulfill the terms of your credit obligations."...

(4)
  (b) If a creditor willfully violates this section, the court may award punitive damages in an amount not in excess of two times the amount of the actual damages awarded.

Excerpts from the Vermont Consumer Fraud Act

Vermont Statutes Annotated Title 9 § 2480e. Consumer Consent

(a) A person shall not obtain the credit report of a consumer unless:...
  (2) the person has secured the consent of the consumer, and the report is used for the purpose consented to by the consumer.

Vermont Statutes Annotated Title 9 § 2480g. Exemptions

(a) The provisions of this subchapter shall not apply to education loans made, guaranteed or serviced by the Vermont student assistance corporation....

(b) The provisions of section 2480e of this title shall not apply to the office of child support services when investigating a child support case....

(c) The provisions of section 2480e of this title shall
    not apply to credit transactions entered into
    prior to January 1, 1993.

                                        ■

Forms and Letters

F-21: Complain of Collection Agency Harassment

F-22: Request Credit File

F-23: Request Reinvestigation

F-24: Request Follow-Up After Reinvestigation

F-25: Request Removal of Incorrect Information by Creditor

F-26: Creditor Verification

F-27: Request Addition of Account Histories

F-28: Request Addition of Information Showing Stability

F-29: Request Credit in Own Name

F-30: Request Merged Credit Reports

Outstanding Debts

Outstanding Debts	Monthly Payment	Amount Behind
Rent or mortgage (include second mortgage, home equity loans)		
Utilities and telephone		
Transportation expenses		
car loans		
maintenance payments		
auto insurance		
Child care worker		
Alimony or child support		
Education expenses		
student loans		
tuition expenses		
Personal and other loans		
bank loans		
loan consolidator		
Lawyers' or accountants' bills		

Outstanding Debts (cont'd)

Outstanding Debts	Monthly Payment	Amount Behind
Medical (doctors' and hospital) bills		
Insurance		
homeowner's or renter's		
disability		
medical or dental		
life		
Credit and charge cards		
Department store charges		
Back taxes		
Federal		
State		
Other (such as property)		
Other unpaid bills		
TOTALS	$	$

Daily Expenditures for Week of _____

Sunday's Expenditures	Cost	Monday's Expenditures	Cost	Tuesday's Expenditures	Cost	Wednesday's Expenditures	Cost
Daily Total:		Daily Total:		Daily Total:		Daily Total:	

Thursday's Expenditures	Cost	Friday's Expenditures	Cost	Saturday's Expenditures	Cost	Other Expenditures	Cost
Daily Total:		Daily Total:		Daily Total:		Weekly Total:	

Monthly Income From All Sources

1 Source of Income	2 Amount of each payment	3 Period covered by each payment	4 Amount per month

A. Wages or Salary

   Job 1:

   _____

Gross pay, including overtime: $ _____   _____

Subtract:

   Federal taxes   _____

   State taxes   _____

   Social Security (FICA)   _____

   Union dues   _____

   Insurance payments   _____

   Child support wage withholding   _____

   Other mandatory deductions (specify):

   _____   _____

Subtotal $ _____   _____   _____

   Job 2:

   _____

Gross pay, including overtime: $ _____   _____

Subtract:

   Federal taxes   _____

   State taxes   _____

   Social Security (FICA)   _____

   Union dues   _____

   Insurance payments   _____

   Child support wage withholding   _____

   Other mandatory deductions (specify):

   _____   _____

Subtotal $ _____   _____   _____

   Job 3:

   _____

Gross pay, including overtime: $ _____   _____

Subtract:

   Federal taxes   _____

   State taxes   _____

   Social Security (FICA)   _____

   Union dues   _____

   Insurance payments   _____

   Child support wage withholding   _____

   Other mandatory deductions (specify):

   _____   _____

Subtotal $ _____   _____   _____

Monthly Income From All Sources (cont'd)

1 Source of Income	2 Amount of each payment	3 Period covered by each payment	4 Amount per month

B. Self-Employment Income

Job 1:   Gross pay, including overtime: $ _____   _____

_____   Subtract:

      Federal taxes   _____

      State taxes   _____

      Self-employment taxes   _____

      Other mandatory deductions (specify):

      _____   _____

| **Subtotal** | $ _____ | _____ | _____ |

Job 2:   Gross pay, including overtime: $ _____   _____

_____   Subtract:

      Federal taxes   _____

      State taxes   _____

      Self-employment taxes   _____

      Other mandatory deductions (specify): _____

      _____   _____

| **Subtotal** | $ _____ | _____ | _____ |

C. Other Sources

Bonuses	_____	_____	_____
Dividends and interest	_____	_____	_____
Rent, lease or license income	_____	_____	_____
Royalties	_____	_____	_____
Note or trust income	_____	_____	_____
Alimony or child support you receive	_____	_____	_____
Pension or retirement income	_____	_____	_____
Social Security	_____	_____	_____
Other public assistance	_____	_____	_____
Other (specify):	_____	_____	_____
	_____	_____	_____
	_____	_____	_____
	_____	_____	_____
	_____	_____	_____

| **Total monthly income** | | | $ _____ |

_____

_____

_____

Attn: Customer Service

Date:_____

Name(s) on account:_____

Account number:_____

To Whom It May Concern:

I am writing to dispute the following charge that appears on my billing statement dated _____
_____, 19_____.

Merchant's name:_____

Amount in dispute:_____

I am disputing this amount for the following reason(s):

_____

_____

_____

_____

_____

_____

As required by law, I have tried in good faith to resolve this dispute with the merchant. Furthermore, I wish to point out that this purchase was for more than $50 and was made [cross out one:] in the state in which I live/within 100 miles of my home.

Please verify this dispute with the merchant and remove this item, and all late and interest charges attributed to this item, from my billing statement.

Sincerely,

_____
[your signature]

Name:_____

Address:_____

_____

Home phone:_____

_____

_____

_____

Attn: Customer Service

Date: _____

Name(s) on account: _____

Account number: _____

To Whom It May Concern:

I am writing to point out an error that appears on my billing statement dated _____,
19_____.

Merchant's name: _____

Amount in error: _____

The problem is as follows:

_____

_____

_____

_____

_____

_____

_____

_____

_____

I understand that the law requires you to acknowledge receipt of this letter within 30 days unless you correct this billing error before then. Furthermore, I understand that within two billing cycles (but in no event more than 90 days), you must correct the error or explain why you believe the amount to be correct.

Sincerely,

_____
[your signature]

Name: _____

Address: _____

_____

Home phone: _____

_____

_____

_____

Attn: Customer Service

Date:_____

Name(s) on account:_____

Account number:_____

To Whom It May Concern:

On _____, 19_____, I received a copy of my credit report from
_____. It lists my payments to you as delinquent.

My past financial problems are behind me and I am now in a position to pay off this debt. I can pay a
lump sum amount of $_____ or I can pay installments in the amount of $_____
per month for _____ months if you will agree to either of the following:

☐ If I make a lump sum payment, you agree to remove the negative information from my credit file associated with the debt.

☐ If I agree to pay off the debt in installments, you agree to re-age my account—that is, make the current
month the first repayment month and show no late payments as long as I make the agreed upon
monthly payments.

If my offer is acceptable to you, please initial one of the above lines, sign the acceptance below and
return this letter to me in the enclosed envelope.

Sincerely,

_____
[your signature]

Name:_____

Address:_____

_____

Home phone:_____

Agreed to and accepted to on this _____ day of _____, 19_____.

By:_____

Name (print):_____

Title:_____

_____

_____

_____

Attn: Customer Service

Date: _____

Name(s) on account: _____

Account number: _____

Date loan/account opened: _____

Total amount due: _____

Monthly payment amount: _____

To Whom It May Concern:

At the present, I cannot pay the monthly amount required under the agreement for the following reason(s):

_____

_____

_____

_____

_____

_____

I can pay $_____ per month right now and expect to resume making the full monthly payment when the following occurs:

_____

_____

_____

Please accept the reduced payments until then. If necessary, add the unpaid amount to the end of the loan or account period and extend it by a few months.

Thank you for your understanding and help. Please call or write within 20 days to let me know if this is acceptable.

Sincerely,

_____
[your signature]

Name: _____

Address: _____

_____

Home phone: _____

_____

_____

_____

Attn: Customer Service

Date:_____

Name(s) on account:_____

Account number:_____

Date loan/account opened:_____

Total amount due:_____

Monthly payment amount:_____

To Whom It May Concern:

At the present, I cannot pay the monthly amount required under the agreement for the following reason(s):

_____

_____

_____

_____

_____

_____

_____

_____

_____

I can pay you only $_____ per month for the indefinite future. Please accept the reduced payments. I promise to inform you immediately if my financial condition improves and I am able to resume making normal payments.

Thank you for your understanding and help. Please call or write within 20 days to let me know if this is acceptable.

Sincerely,

_____
[your signature]

Name:_____

Address:_____

_____

Home phone:_____

_____

_____

_____

Attn: Customer Service

Date:_____

Name(s) on account:_____

Account number:_____

Date loan/account opened:_____

Total amount due:_____

Monthly payment amount:_____

To Whom It May Concern:

At the present, I cannot pay the monthly amount required under the agreement for the following reason(s):

_____

_____

_____

_____

_____

_____

For now, I cannot make any payments. I expect to resume making the full monthly payment when the following occurs:

_____

_____

_____

_____

If necessary, add the unpaid amount to the end of the loan or account period and extend it by a few months. Thank you for your understanding and help. Please call or write within 20 days if this is unacceptable.

Sincerely,

_____
[your signature]

Name:_____

Address:_____

_____

Home phone:_____

_____

_____

_____

Attn: Customer Service

Date:_____

Name(s) on account:_____

Account number:_____

Date loan/account opened:_____

Total amount due:_____

Monthly payment amount:_____

To Whom It May Concern:

At the present, I cannot pay the monthly amount required under the agreement for the following reason(s):

_____

_____

_____

_____

_____

_____

_____

_____

_____

_____

Due to my desperate financial situation, I cannot make any payments for the indefinite future. I promise to inform you immediately if my financial condition improves and I am able to resume making normal payments.

Thank you for your understanding and help. Please call or write within 20 days if this is unacceptable.

Sincerely,

_____
[your signature]

Name:_____

Address:_____

_____

Home phone:_____

_____

_____

_____

Attn: Customer Service

Date:_____

Name(s) on account:_____

Account number:_____

Date loan/account opened:_____

Total amount due:_____

Monthly payment amount:_____

To Whom It May Concern:

At the present, I cannot pay the monthly amount required under the agreement for the following reason(s):

_____

_____

_____

_____

_____

_____

_____

_____

_____

_____

I would like the terms of the loan rewritten in order to reduce the amount of the monthly payments.

Thank you for your understanding and help. Please call me as soon as possible in order that we may discuss new loan terms.

Sincerely,

_____
[your signature]

Name:_____

Address:_____

_____

Home phone:_____

Attn: Customer Service

Date:_____

Name(s) on account:_____

Account number:_____

Date loan/account opened:_____

Total amount due:_____

Monthly payment amount:_____

Collateral:_____

To Whom It May Concern:

I cannot pay the monthly amount required under my agreement with you. I invite you to come pick up the collateral, or to let me know where I can return it to you, if you can assure me in writing that the entire debt will be canceled when the property is returned—that is, that I will not be liable for any deficiency judgment.

Thank you for your attention to this matter. Please send me a confirmation within 20 days if this is acceptable.

Sincerely,

_____
[your signature]

Name:_____

Address:_____

_____

Home phone:_____

_____

_____

_____

Attn: Customer Service

Date: _____

Name(s) on account: _____

Account number: _____

To Whom It May Concern:

Enclosed is a check for $_____ to cover the balance of the account. Cashing this check constitutes payment in full.

Sincerely,

_____
                [your signature]

Name: _____

Address: _____

_____

Home phone: _____

_____

_____

_____

Attn: Customer Service

Date:_____

Name(s) on account:_____

Account number:_____

To Whom It May Concern:

Regarding the above-referenced account, I dispute the amount you claim that I owe you for the following reason(s):

_____

_____

_____

_____

_____

_____

_____

_____

_____

_____

I believe that I owe you no more than $_____. It is obvious that there is a good faith dispute over the amount of this bill.

To satisfy this debt, I will send you a check for $_____ with a restrictive endorsement; if you cash that check, it will constitute an accord and satisfaction. In other words, you will receive from me a check that states "cashing this check constitutes payment in full." If you cash that check, it will take care of what I owe you.

Sincerely,

_____
[your signature]

Name:_____

Address:_____

_____

Home phone:_____

_____

_____

_____

Attn: Collections Department

Date:_____

Name(s) on account:_____

Account number:_____

To Whom It May Concern:

Between 15 days and 90 days have passed since I sent you a letter dated _____,
19_____ stating my intention to send you a check with a restrictive endorsement.

Enclosed is a check for $_____ to cover the balance of my account. This check is tendered
in accordance with my earlier letter. If you cash this check, you agree that my debt is satisfied in full.

Sincerely,

_____
[your signature]

Name:_____

Address:_____

_____

Home phone:_____

Enclosed: Check stating on front: "This check is tendered in accordance with my letter of
_____, 19_____. Cashing this check constitutes payment in full."

_____

_____

_____

Attn: Collections Department

Date:_____

Name(s) on account:_____

Account number:_____

To Whom It May Concern:

This letter is to advise you that I am not able to make payments on my account due to the following conditions:

_____

_____

_____

_____

_____

_____

I cannot work sufficient hours to meet my current expenses. My only sources of income are:

_____

_____

I am familiar with the law and know that I am "judgment proof." If I file for bankruptcy, I will claim all my property as exempt, and if you sue me and obtain a judgment, you could not collect any of my property to satisfy the judgment.

Please cease all collection activities you have taken or are considering taking. While I will provide you with reasonable financial or medical information, I must avoid stress. This includes high-pressure collection activity and lawsuits.

If my current situation improves and I am able to resume payments, I will notify you at once.

Thank you for your understanding and help.

Sincerely,

_____
                [your signature]

Name:_____

Address:_____

_____

Home phone:_____

_____

_____

_____

Attn: Collections Department

Date:_____

Name(s) on account:_____

Account number:_____

To Whom It May Concern:

Please cease all collection activities you have taken or are considering taking against me. I am planning to file a petition in bankruptcy court in the coming months.

Sincerely,

_____
                    [your signature]

Name:_____

Address:_____

_____

Home phone:_____

_____

_____

_____

Date: _____

Name(s) on account: _____

Account number: _____

Creditor: _____

To _____ :

I have been contacted several times by you regarding my past due account with the credit grantor referenced above. I do not, however, wish to discuss this matter with you. I would like to talk directly with the collections department with the credit grantor.

Please contact the collections department of the credit grantor and indicate my desire to be in touch with them.

Thank you for your help.

Sincerely,

_____
[your signature]

Name: _____

Address: _____

_____

Home phone: _____

cc: Credit grantor, _____

_____

_____

_____

Date: _____

To _____ :

I am writing to dispute the following bill you are attempting to collect.

Name(s) on account: _____

Account number: _____

Creditor: _____

Amount in dispute: _____

I am disputing this bill for the following reason(s):

_____

_____

_____

_____

_____

_____

_____

_____

Please return this bill to the creditor immediately and remove any "sent to collection agency" notation that may be in my credit file.

Thank you for your attention to this matter.

Sincerely,

_____
[your signature]

Name: _____

Address: _____

_____

Home phone: _____

cc: Credit grantor, _____

_____

_____

_____

Date:_____

Name(s) on account:_____

Account number:_____

Creditor:_____

To _____ :

Since approximately _____, 19_____, I have received several phone calls and letters from you concerning my overdue account with the above-named creditor.

Accordingly, under 15 U.S.C. § 1692c, this is my formal notice to you to cease all further communications with me except for the reasons specifically set forth in the federal law.

Sincerely,

_____
                    [your signature]

Name:_____

Address:_____

_____

Home phone:_____

_____

_____

_____

Date: _____

Name(s) on account: _____

Account number: _____

Date loan/debt incurred: _____

Original loan/debt amount: _____

Amount past due: _____

Re: Collection agency: _____

To Whom It May Concern:

I have been unable to pay the full amount of the loan/debt noted above for the following reason(s):

_____

_____

_____

Although I have an outstanding debt, I have the right to be treated by a collection agency with dignity and respect. The collection agency you hired (and noted above), however, has engaged in the following practices which violate the federal Fair Debt Collection Practices Act:

_____

_____

_____

I am willing to forego the legal remedies I have available, including a lawsuit in small claims court seeking punitive damages against you and the agency, in exchange for your written promise to permanently cease all efforts to collect this debt and remove all negative entries regarding this debt from my credit file. I expect to hear from you immediately.

Sincerely,

_____
[your signature]

Name: _____

Address: _____

_____

Home phone: _____

cc: Federal Trade Commission
    State Collection Agency Licensing Board
    Collection Agency: _____

_____

_____

_____

Date:_____

To Whom It May Concern:

Please send me a copy of my credit report.

Full name:_____

Date of birth:_____

Social Security number:_____

Spouse's name:_____

Telephone number:_____

Current address:_____

_____

Previous address:_____

_____

(Check one:)

☐ I was denied credit on _____ by _____
_____. Enclosed is a copy of the rejection letter.

☐ I am requesting my annual complimentary Experian credit report. Enclosed is a copy of a document identifying me by my name and address.

☐ I have not been denied credit within the preceding 60 days. Enclosed is a copy of a document identifying me by my name and address and a check for $_____.

☐ *[After September 30, 1997]* I hereby certify that I am unemployed and intend to apply for a job within the next 60 days.

☐ *[After September 30, 1997]* I hereby certify that I receive public assistance/welfare.

☐ *[After September 30, 1997]* I hereby certify that I believe there is erroneous information in my file due to fraud.

Thank you for your attention to this matter.

Sincerely,

_____
[your signature]

F-22

_____

_____

_____

Attn: Customer Service

Date:_____

Name(s) on account:_____

Account number:_____

To Whom It May Concern:

On _____, 19_____, I received a copy of my credit report from you.
It included erroneous information reported by _____.
I just received a letter from that creditor indicating that in fact, the information in my credit report is not
accurate and should not be in my credit file. I have enclosed a copy of the letter.

OR

On _____, 19_____, I met with _____
_____ from the above-named creditor. This person agreed
with me that the information in my credit report is not accurate and should not be in my credit file. You can
reach this person at (_____) _____.

This negative mark is damaging my credit. Please remove the information at once and issue me and anyone who has requested a copy of my credit report with the previous six months (one year after September
30, 1997) or within the previous two years if requested for employment purposes a new credit report.

Sincerely,

_____
[your signature]

Name:_____

Address:_____

_____

Home phone:_____

Social Security number:_____

_____

_____

_____

Date: _____

Re (name): _____

Current address: _____

_____

Telephone number: _____

Date of birth: _____

Social Security number: _____

Spouse's name: _____

To Whom It May Concern:

I received a copy of my credit report from your company on _____ and found accounts missing. Please add the following account histories to my credit file. I have enclosed photocopies of my most recent account statement and photocopies of canceled checks showing my payment history.

Creditor's Name	Creditor's Billing Address	Account Number	Date Opened	Credit Limit or Amount of Loan	Outstanding Balance

Once you have processed this request, please send me an updated credit report. If there is a fee of any kind, please let me know the amount so that I can send you a check. If you are unable to add these accounts to my credit report, please send me an explanation.

Thank you for your prompt attention to this matter.

Sincerely,

_____
[your signature]

_____

_____

_____

Date:_____

Re (name): _____

Current address: _____

_____

Telephone number: _____

Date of birth: _____

Social Security number:_____

Spouse's name: _____

To Whom It May Concern:

I received a copy of my credit report from your company on _____ and found that important information was missing. Please add the following information to my credit file. I have enclosed photocopies of verifying documentation.

_____

_____

_____

_____

_____

_____

_____

_____

_____

_____

Once you have processed this request, please send me an updated credit report. If there is a fee of any kind, please let me know the amount so that I can send you a check. If you are unable to add this information to my credit report, please send me an explanation.

Thank you for your prompt attention to this matter.

Sincerely,

_____

[your signature]

_____

_____

_____

Date: _____

Re (name): _____

Current address: _____

_____

Telephone number: _____

Date of birth: _____

Social Security number: _____

Spouse's name: _____

To Whom It May Concern:

Please issue a credit report in my name only and remove the following account histories from my credit file. My spouse is solely responsible for these accounts. I have enclosed photocopies of account statements and loan agreements showing that I am not liable for these accounts.

Creditor's Name	Creditor's Billing Address	Account Number

Once you have processed this request, please send me an updated credit report. If you are unwilling to remove these accounts from my credit report, please send me an explanation.

Thank you for your prompt attention to this matter.

Sincerely,

_____
[your signature]

_____

_____

_____

Date: _____

Re (name): _____

Current address: _____

_____

Telephone number: _____

Date of birth: _____

Social Security number: _____

Spouse's name: _____

Spouse's date of birth: _____

Spouse's Security number: _____

To Whom It May Concern:

Please merge the account information contained in my spouse's and my credit reports. Once you have processed this request, please send us updated credit reports, one in my name and one in my spouse's name.

Thank you for your prompt attention to this matter.

Sincerely,

_____
[your signature]

Index

CATALOG
...more from Nolo Press

	EDITION	PRICE	CODE
BUSINESS			
Business Plans to Game Plans	1st	$29.95	GAME
The California Nonprofit Corporation Handbook	7th	$29.95	NON
The California Professional Corporation Handbook	5th	$34.95	PROF
The Employer's Legal Handbook	1st	$29.95	EMPL
Form Your Own Limited Liability Company	1st	$24.95	LIAB
Helping Employees Achieve Retirement Security	1st	$16.95	HEAR
▣ Hiring Indepedent Contractors: The Employer's Legal Guide	1st	$29.95	HICI
How to Finance a Growing Business	4th	$24.95	GROW
▣ How to Form a CA Nonprofit Corp.—w/Corp. Records Binder & PC Disk	1st	$49.95	CNP
▣ How to Form a Nonprofit Corp., Book w/Disk (PC)—National Edition	3rd	$39.95	NNP
▣ How to Form Your Own Calif. Corp.—w/Corp. Records Binder & Disk—PC	1st	$39.95	CACI
How to Form Your Own California Corporation	8th	$29.95	CCOR
▣ How to Form Your Own Florida Corporation, (Book w/Disk—PC)	3rd	$39.95	FLCO
▣ How to Form Your Own New York Corporation, (Book w/Disk—PC)	3rd	$39.95	NYCO
▣ How to Form Your Own Texas Corporation, (Book w/Disk—PC)	4th	$39.95	TCOR
How to Handle Your Workers' Compensation Claim (California Edition)	1st	$29.95	WORK
How to Market a Product for Under $500	1st	$29.95	UN500
How to Mediate Your Dispute	1st	$18.95	MEDI
How to Write a Business Plan	4th	$21.95	SBS
How to Write a Business Plan	4th	$21.95	SBS
The Independent Paralegal's Handbook	4th	$29.95	PARA
Insuring the Bottom Line	1st	$29.95	BOTT
The Legal Guide for Starting & Running a Small Business	2nd	$24.95	RUNS

▣ Book with disk

	EDITION	PRICE	CODE
Make Up Your Mind: Entrepreneurs Talk About Decision Making	1st	$19.95	MIND
Managing Generation X: How to Bring Out the Best in Young Talent	1st	$19.95	MANX
Marketing Without Advertising	1st	$14.00	MWAD
Mastering Diversity: Managing for Success Under ADA and Other Anti-Discrimination Laws	1st	$29.95	MAST
▣ OSHA in the Real World: (Book w/Disk—PC)	1st	$29.95	OSHA
Pay For Results	1st	$29.95	PAY
The Partnership Book: How to Write a Partnership Agreement	4th	$24.95	PART
Rightful Termination	1st	$29.95	RITE
Sexual Harassment on the Job	2nd	$18.95	HARS
▣ Taking Care of Your Corporation, Vol. 1, (Book w/Disk—PC)	1st	$26.95	CORK
▣ Taking Care of Your Corporation, Vol. 2, (Book w/Disk—PC)	1st	$39.95	CORK2
Tax Savvy for Small Business	1st	$26.95	SAVVY
Trademark: How to Name Your Business & Product	2nd	$29.95	TRD
Workers' Comp for Employers	2nd	$29.95	CNTRL
Your Rights in the Workplace	3rd	$19.95	YRW

CONSUMER

	EDITION	PRICE	CODE
Fed Up With the Legal System: What's Wrong & How to Fix It	2nd	$9.95	LEG
Glossary of Insurance Terms	6th	$14.95	GLINT
How to Insure Your Car	1st	$12.95	INCAR
How to Insure Your Home	1st	$12.95	INTRO
How to Insure Your Life	1st	$12.95	INLIF
How to Win Your Personal Injury Claim	2nd	$24.95	PICL
Nolo's Everyday Law Book	1st	$21.95	EVL
Nolo's Pocket Guide to California Law	4th	$10.95	CLAW
The Over 50 Insurance Survival Guide	1st	$16.95	OVER50
Trouble-Free Travel...And What to Do When Things Go Wrong	1st	$14.95	TRAV
True Odds: How Risk Affects Your Everyday Life	1st	$19.95	TROD
What Do You Mean It's Not Covered?	1st	$19.95	COVER

ESTATE PLANNING & PROBATE

	EDITION	PRICE	CODE
8 Ways to Avoid Probate	1st	$15.95	PRO8
How to Probate an Estate (California Edition)	8th	$34.95	PAE
Make Your Own Living Trust	2nd	$21.95	LITR
Nolo's Simple Will Book	2nd	$17.95	SWIL
Plan Your Estate	3rd	$24.95	NEST
The Quick and Legal Will Book	1st	$15.95	QUIC
Nolo's Law Form Kit: Wills	1st	$14.95	KWL

▣ Book with disk

	EDITION	PRICE	CODE

FAMILY MATTERS

	EDITION	PRICE	CODE
A Legal Guide for Lesbian and Gay Couples	9th	$24.95	LG
California Marriage Law	12th	$19.95	MARR
Child Custody: Building Partnership Agreements That Work	2nd	$24.95	CUST
Divorce & Money: How to Make the Best Financial Decisions During Divorce	3rd	$26.95	DIMO
Get A Life: You Don't Need a Million to Retire	1st	$18.95	LIFE
The Guardianship Book (California Edition)	2nd	$24.95	GB
How to Adopt Your Stepchild in California	4th	$22.95	ADOP
How to Do Your Own Divorce in California	21st	$24.95	CDIV
How to Do Your Own Divorce in Texas	6th	$19.95	TDIV
How to Raise or Lower Child Support in California	3rd	$18.95	CHLD
The Living Together Kit	7th	$24.95	LTK
Nolo's Law Form Kit: Hiring Childcare & Household Help	1st	$14.95	KCHD
Nolo's Pocket Guide to Family Law	4th	$14.95	FLD
Practical Divorce Solutions	1st	$14.95	PDS
Smart Ways to Save Money During and After Divorce	1st	$14.95	SAVMO

GOING TO COURT

	EDITION	PRICE	CODE
Collect Your Court Judgment (California Edition)	2nd	$19.95	JUDG
The Criminal Records Book (California Edition)	5th	$21.95	CRIM
How to Sue For Up to 25,000...and Win!	2nd	$29.95	MUNI
Everybody's Guide to Small Claims Court in California	12th	$18.95	CSCC
Everybody's Guide to Small Claims Court (National Edition)	6th	$18.95	NSCC
Fight Your Ticket ... and Win! (California Edition)	6th	$19.95	FYT
How to Change Your Name (California Edition)	6th	$24.95	NAME
Mad at Your Lawyer	1st	$21.95	MAD
Represent Yourself in Court: How to Prepare & Try a Winning Case	1st	$29.95	RYC
Taming the Lawyers	1st	$19.95	TAME

HOMEOWNERS, LANDLORDS & TENANTS

	EDITION	PRICE	CODE
The Deeds Book (California Edition)	3rd	$16.95	DEED
Dog Law	2nd	$12.95	DOG
🖫 Every Landlord's Legal Guide (National Edition)	1st	$34.95	ELLI
For Sale by Owner (California Edition)	2nd	$24.95	FSBO
Homestead Your House (California Edition)	8th	$9.95	HOME
How to Buy a House in California	4th	$24.95	BHCA
The Landlord's Law Book, Vol. 1: Rights & Responsibilities (California Edition)	5th	$34.95	LBRT
The Landlord's Law Book, Vol. 2: Evictions (California Edition)	5th	$34.95	LBEV

🖫 Book with disk

CALL 800-992-6656 OR USE THE ORDER FORM IN THE BACK OF THE BOOK

	EDITION	PRICE	CODE

Leases & Rental Agreements (National Edition) .... 1st $18.95 LEAR
Neighbor Law: Fences, Trees, Boundaries & Noise .... 2nd $16.95 NEI
Safe Homes, Safe Neighborhoods: Stopping Crime Where You Live .... 1st $14.95 SAFE
Tenants' Rights (California Edition) .... 12th $18.95 CTEN

HUMOR

29 Reasons Not to Go to Law School 1st $9.95 29R
Poetic Justice .... 1st $9.95 PJ

IMMIGRATION

How to Become a United States Citizen .... 5th $14.95 CIT
How to Get a Green Card: Legal Ways to Stay in the U.S.A. .... 2nd $24.95 GRN
U.S. Immigration Made Easy .... 5th $39.95 IMEZ

MONEY MATTERS

Building Your Nest Egg With Your 401(k) .... 1st $16.95 EGG
Chapter 13 Bankruptcy: Repay Your Debts 2nd $29.95 CH13
Credit Repair .... 1st $15.95 CREP
How to File for Bankruptcy .... 6th $26.95 HFB
Money Troubles: Legal Strategies to Cope With Your Debts .... 4th $19.95 MT
Nolo's Law Form Kit: Personal Bankruptcy .... 1st $14.95 KBNK
Nolo's Law Form Kit: Rebuild Your Credit .... 1st $14.95 KCRD
Simple Contracts for Personal Use .... 2nd $16.95 CONT
Stand Up to the IRS .... 3rd $24.95 SIRS
The Under 40 Financial Planning Guide 1st $19.95 UN40

PATENTS AND COPYRIGHTS

The Copyright Handbook: How to Protect and Use Written Works .... 3rd $24.95 COHA
Copyright Your Software .... 1st $39.95 CYS
Patent, Copyright & Trademark: A Desk Reference to Intellectual Property Law .... 1st $24.95 PCTM
Patent It Yourself .... 5th $44.95 PAT
⊡ Software Development: A Legal Guide (Book with disk—PC) .... 1st $44.95 SFT
The Inventor's Notebook .... 2nd $19.95 INOT

RESEARCH & REFERENCE

Law on the Net .... 1st $39.95 LAWN
Legal Research: How to Find & Understand the Law .... 4th $19.95 LRES
Legal Research Made Easy (Video) .... 1st $89.95 LRME

⊡ Book with disk

CALL 800-992-6656 OR USE THE ORDER FORM IN THE BACK OF THE BOOK

	EDITION	PRICE	CODE

SENIORS

	EDITION	PRICE	CODE
Beat the Nursing Home Trap: A Consumer's Guide	2nd	$18.95	ELD
Social Security, Medicare & Pensions	6th	$19.95	SOA
The Conservatorship Book (California Edition)	2nd	$29.95	CNSV

SOFTWARE

	EDITION	PRICE	CODE
California Incorporator 2.0—DOS	2.0	$47.97	INCI2
Living Trust Maker 2.0—Macintosh	2.0	$47.97	LTM2
Living Trust Maker 2.0—Windows	2.0	$47.97	LTWI2
Small Business Legal Pro—Macintosh	2.0	$25.97	SBM2
Small Business Legal Pro—Windows	2.0	$25.97	SBW2
Small Business Legal Pro Deluxe CD—Windows/Macintosh CD-ROM	2.0	$35.97	SBCD
Nolo's Partnership Maker 1.0—DOS	1.0	$47.97	PAGI1
Personal RecordKeeper 4.0—Macintosh	4.0	$29.97	RKM4
Personal RecordKeeper 4.0—Windows	4.0	$29.97	RKP4
Patent It Yourself 1.0—Windows	1.0	$149.97	PYW1
WillMaker 6.0—Macintosh	6.0	$29.97	WM6
WillMaker 6.0—Windows	6.0	$29.97	WIW6

◪ Book with disk

CALL 800-992-6656 OR USE THE ORDER FORM IN THE BACK OF THE BOOK

ORDER FORM

Code	Quantity	Title	Unit price	Total

	Subtotal	
	California residents add Sales Tax	
Basic Shipping (*$5.50 for 1 item; $6.50 for 2-3 items, $7.50 for 4 or more*)		
	UPS RUSH delivery $7.50–any size order*	
	TOTAL	

Name

Address

(UPS to street address, Priority Mail to P.O. boxes)   * Delivered in 3 business days from receipt of order. S.F. Bay Area use regular shipping.

FOR FASTER SERVICE, USE YOUR CREDIT CARD AND OUR TOLL-FREE NUMBERS

Order 24 hours a day	1-800-992-6656
Fax your order	1-800-645-0895
e-mail	cs@nolo.com
General Information	1-510-549-1976
Customer Service	1-800-728-3555, Mon.-Fri. 9am-5pm, PST

METHOD OF PAYMENT

☐ Check enclosed

☐ VISA   ☐ MasterCard   ☐ Discover Card   ☐ American Express

Account #   Expiration Date

Authorizing Signature

Daytime Phone

PRICES SUBJECT TO CHANGE.

VISIT OUR OUTLET STORES!

You'll find our complete line of books and software, all at a discount.

BERKELEY
950 Parker Street
Berkeley, CA 94710
1-510-704-2248

SAN JOSE
111 N. Market Street, #115
San Jose, CA 95113
1-408-271-7240

VISIT US ONLINE!

on AOL — keyword: NOLO   **on the INTERNET** — www.nolo.com

N O L O   P R E S S   9 5 0   P A R K E R   S T . ,   B E R K E L E Y ,   C A   9 4 7 1 0

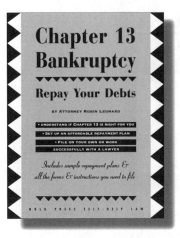
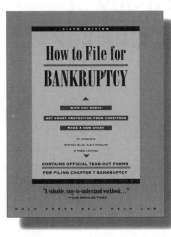

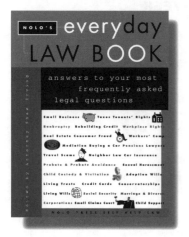